MW00640258

Advance Praise for *The Weird Sister Collection*

"*The Weird Sister Collection* is a hilarious, delicious, and earnest dive into the intersection of feminism and culture. Reminiscent of not just zine-style writing but era-defining collections like *To Be Real* and *Making Face, Making Soul*, this experimental collection of writing is a must-have for anyone asking questions about identity, belonging, and the current and future state of not just feminism but all the intersectional 'isms' that can either hold our imaginations captive or free us."

—SAMHITA MUKHOPADHYAY,
former executive editor of *Teen Vogue*

"Feminist thought is alive and well in *The Weird Sister Collection*. Whether it drives you to start a zine or tear down a statue of a Confederate general, one thing's for sure: after you read this book, you won't want to just sit there and suffer anymore."

—RAX KING, author of *Tacky: Love Letters*
to the Worst Culture We Have to Offer

"*The Weird Sister Collection* captures with audacious wit and unapologetic earnestness the zeitgeist of the eponymous blogging community that published at the intersection of the feminist and the literary. To read this book is to know that I am not alone in reading passionately in feminist community outside of the academy and traditional literary establishment. I am grateful for the space that *Weird Sister* made online and am immensely thankful now to have this collection with so many fierce writers in one place, re-creating the delightfully weird online village that continues to inspire so many."

—SUSANA M. MORRIS, coeditor of
The Crunk Feminist Collection

THE
Weird Sister
COLLECTION

WRITING AT THE INTERSECTIONS OF
FEMINISM, LITERATURE, AND POP CULTURE

EDITED BY MARISA CRAWFORD
FOREWORD BY MICHELLE TEA

THE FEMINIST PRESS
AT THE CITY UNIVERSITY OF NEW YORK
NEW YORK CITY

Published in 2024 by the Feminist Press
at the City University of New York
The Graduate Center
365 Fifth Avenue, Suite 5406
New York, NY 10016

feministpress.org

First Feminist Press edition 2024

 This book was made possible thanks to a grant from the New York State Council on the Arts with the support of Governor Kathy Hochul and the New York State Legislature.

 This book was published with financial support from the Jerome Foundation.

 This book is supported in part by public funds from the New York City Department of Cultural Affairs in partnership with the City Council.

First printing February 2024

Cover design by Mary Anne Carter
Hand-lettered title text by Matt L. Roar
Text design by Drew Stevens

Library of Congress Cataloging-in-Publication Data
Names: Crawford, Marisa, editor. | Tea, Michelle, writer of foreword.
Title: The Weird Sister collection : writing at the intersections of
   feminism, literature, and pop culture / edited by Marisa Crawford ;
   foreword by Michelle Tea.
Description: First Feminist Press edition. | New York City : The Feminist
   Press at the City University of New York, 2024.
Identifiers: LCCN 2023046787 (print) | LCCN 2023046788 (ebook) | ISBN
   9781558613003 (paperback) | ISBN 9781558613010 (ebook)
Subjects: LCSH: Feminism in literature. | Feminism and the arts. | Feminist
   theory. | LCGFT: Literary criticism. | Essays.
Classification: LCC PN56.F46 W45 2024 (print) | LCC PN56.F46 (ebook) |
   DDC 809/.933522—dc23/eng/20231019
LC record available at https://lccn.loc.gov/2023046787
LC ebook record available at https://lccn.loc.gov/2023046788

PRINTED IN THE UNITED STATES OF AMERICA

Contents

Talking Back to the Canon

Calling On Our Feminist Elders

Living and Shaping Literary Legacies

Double, Double Pop Culture Trouble

Performance, Identity, and Public Space

Weird Sisters in Conversation

Foreword: Weird 4 Weird

Michelle Tea

MY SECOND TATTOO was made with a sewing needle, a length of thread, and a bottle cap splashed with India ink. The cap had come off a forty of malt liquor, which everybody drank as it was economical— more potent than a normal jug of beer, and so cheap, just two-fifty. Call it *malt liqueur* if you're feeling campy. We were having a tattoo party at GingerandPatriciaandChristina's house, and none of us would want to leave once we got there. We settled in for the night with our booze and our smokes and the supplies we needed to do a craft project on our bodies.

I wondered, prudently, what to get. The whole pokey tattoo thing was a crapshoot; who knew if whoever poked mine into my skin would do a good job. Maybe it would be a shaky mess; maybe the ink would fall out (both happened). It seemed something simple and small, on a tucked-away part of my body, was the best bet. A small, black motif, a symbol? I recalled a book I used to own, having accidentally stolen / never returned it to the Boston Public Library (sorry). I'd lugged it around the country with me for a while, despite its heft, and somehow lost it along the way, again despite its heft. *The Woman's Dictionary of Symbols and Sacred Objects* by Barbara G. Walker is five hundred and seventy-six pages of symbols I wanted to mark my body up with. Discovering it had felt like stumbling onto an ancient document that had been wrapped and stuffed in a cave; it felt holy and secret. Page after page of marks and emblems, glyphs and icons that spoke to a history of spiritual, often spooky, women's culture. It was the early nineties, a time without internet, and I was just waking up to the world's bullshit, mostly on my own, in Boston, Massachusetts. I was feeding myself a constant diet of books that supported my new consciousness, whatever I could find. They were mostly the writings of previous generations, and I appreciated them, I read them all and

felt a connection with this idea of feminism, women being important and standing together, going back decades. With the *Dictionary*,
it went back eons. Every time I went to return it, I realized I wasn't
quite done with it. I guess I never was.

Ginger, a snaggletoothed Southern butch both cynical and silly,
had wound the thread around the needle and was dunking it in the
bottle cap, saturating it in ink. I knew what I wanted. It was small,
hopefully simple, and it was *me*. *Weird Sister*, a downward-pointing
triangle surrounded by circles on each of its three sides. I remembered
it meant general weirdness, being weird in a specifically *female* way—
witchy, but also transgressing certain expectations, allying yourself
outside those expectations. I liked it better than the women's symbol,
which also meant Venus and love and was too—if I may—*commercial*
of a feminist symbol for me. Not *weird* enough. It felt coven-y, Ginger
gripping my foot and stabbing the mark onto the plane between my
heel and ankle. It hurt, and was too creepy a sensation—stabbing your
friend!—for Ginger to go at it as hard as she'd have needed to for it to
really stick. But it's still there, faint and shadowy outlines of a moment
trapped under my skin. I wanted to be branded forever a weird one,
and now, freed from Boston, really starting my life in San Francisco,
I'd found my people, was learning new ways of feminism from them
every day; they were my new books, and this tattoo marked my belonging to a spectral and embodied cadre of similar weird, seeking sisters.

I GOT SO excited when I learned about *Weird Sister*, the blog, because—
Weird Sister! Here it was again. Something that had felt so private
and obscure to me had also been found and claimed by others. *Weird
Sister* seemed to be an internet-age mash-up of all sorts of knowledge
I had been (forever am) so hungry for, my feminist history, feminists'
places in the past, and the feminism we're all making *right now* with
the stuff of our lives. And books were central, as they always will be,
for weird sisters are frequently nerdy bookworms. So it makes sense
that, as everything is in constant motion, forward and backward, *Weird
Sister* should now move from the new technology into the old—so
that we can feel the heft of thought in our bags as we walk through
the world, have it on our lap on the train, let our eager engagement
with it show in the thumbprints and smears of jelly, the dog-eared
corners and frayed cover. A well-worn book is what it is destined to
be. A type of reference tome, not unlike *The Women's Dictionary of
Symbols and Sacred Objects*, to be sought by those who seek it and

to pop up unexpected in the shelves of weird sisters seeking themselves, making them think that the Goddexx has left it right there for them to marvel at.

I learned *so much* from *The Weird Sister Collection*. Editor Marisa Crawford's "The White Male Canon in Nineties Pop Songs" is one of the best things I've ever read, soothing my latent shame at *not knowing any of this shit*—not the canon (didn't go to college), not the songs (was already gay in the nineties and listened exclusively to Sleater-Kinney). On the one hand, who cares about the *white male canon*, but on the other, a lot of us are forced to. I'm not one of them, but also, I want to know what everyone is talking about. I would have gladly gone to school and studied this crap if Marisa Crawford had been the teacher, insightful and snarky and clever.

All of the writers anthologized here are our teachers and translators, merging their lives with the wider life—culture, I guess—and the feminist lives that came before, all of it brimming with story right now. It makes you feel so sane and hopeful to watch Sam Cohen contextualize the family Trump through the writing of Kate Zambreno. Or Vanessa Willoughby parse publishing's racism through reviews of Sister Souljah's *The Coldest Winter Ever*. Or Megan Milks explore queer literary ancestry through the work of Barbara Grier. It was amazing to remember and re-think the thoughts of kari edwards via Trace Peterson. To learn of the wonderful existence of 1920s anarchist party poet Lola Ridge through Terese Svoboda. On and on it goes, a veritable catalog of all the writers I want to know about, written by all the writers I want to be friends with. Morgan Parker on the glow of Afrofuturism, broadcast from the heart of our current racist death culture. Jennif(f)er Tamayo's epic manifesto "On Being Unreasonable," a design for living for femme poets and poets of color. Emily Brandt looking back on *Twin Peaks*. Cathy de la Cruz on the chaos of going viral. An interview with Myriam Gurba exploring her singular, iconic creepiness; an interview with Mecca Jamilah Sullivan about June Jordan. Are you in heaven? Yes, you are in heaven.

I can imagine that it could, on the surface, seem incongruous: a collection that brings Filipinx spaghetti, Lord Byron, *The Dinner Party*, Raven-Symoné, abortion, *Fifty Shades of Grey*, Lisa Frank, Guns N' Roses, "sad girl" aesthetics, Lean Cuisine, and Destiny's Child together for the cause of feminist literature. And yet. If you know, you know: weird sisters thrill to these intellectual crossroads—cross-hatchings of identities and cultures, the high and the low, the aspirational undertakings and the guilty pleasures. The joy of thinking is palpable in these pieces that pull together disparate personal references and obsessions and merge them—seamless—with the cultures that loom above us, oppressive but giving us *so much to think about*. Weird sisters are compulsive *thinkers*, and maybe talkers, and certainly, by virtue of this, community makers, whether they want to be or not. In *The Weird Sister Collection*, subcultures become dominant; the places where the action is, where the big ideas are percolating, the truer lives lived. In creating *Weird Sister*, Marisa Crawford carved out a necessary space for the literary musings, bitching and ranting, fun-poking and dreaming that we always badly need. This book is a gift, a place to think weird and radical thoughts among a community of feminist freaks.

—Michelle Tea
September 2023

Introduction

Marisa Crawford

I DIDN'T DEIGN to call myself a feminist until I was nineteen years old, in my second year of college. Before then, I just wanted to be a writer. Reading Judy Blume and the Baby-Sitters Club books obsessively as a kid, I decided I wanted to be an "author" when I grew up, and started writing my own poems and young adult novels in fourth grade (a baby poet at heart, I could never get past chapter two). "Feminist" was a word I rarely heard growing up. If I did, it was mentioned with suspicion at best and disdain at worst. My first encounter with feminism as not purely negative came at fourteen, when my friend's dad took us to a feminist vegetarian bookstore and restaurant in Bridge-port, Connecticut, called Bloodroot (it's still there; please go). There, customers brought their own used dishes up to the counter in an apparent rejection of female subserviency that set off a little spark in my brain about the roles of women in the world around me, even if we sort of made fun of it after we left. I bought a bumper sticker that said "Vegetarians Taste Better," uncertain if the sexual under-tone was intended. I also bought a book of poems called *Used to the Dark* by Vicky Edmonds, a totally obscure small-press work, but the sole example I had at the time of what might be called feminist poetry. Of course, I wouldn't have used that shameful word, "feminist," to describe Edmonds's book—maybe "writing by a woman about the dark parts of how it feels to be a woman," like so much of my favorite music was? Weird, outspoken women artists like Tori Amos and Ani DiFranco and Courtney Love, who all my boyfriends and boy friends made fun of.

In college when I finally started calling myself a feminist—after meeting cool feminist friends who were nothing like the humor-less stereotypes I had been warned about, and who told me I needed to throw out my bleached tampons and listen to Le Tigre and take women's studies classes—I wanted desperately to make up for lost time, realizing that my whole life had been missing this essential perspective. So I read any and all feminist media I could get my hands on: I borrowed Inga Muscio's book *Cunt* from a friend and read it along with every issue of *Bitch* magazine. I declared a minor in women's studies and took classes where I learned about intersectionality, agency, privilege.

In my creative writing classes, we never talked about those things; in my first workshop that same year, the MFA student instructor was so infectious in his excitement about literature that I didn't even notice the syllabus he handed out had zero women writers on it until another female student in the class pointed it out—I was too busy becoming obsessed with Frank O'Hara's *Lunch Poems*. Slowly I learned about feminism on a parallel path just next to the one where I was learning about how to be a writer. But I couldn't quite figure out how these two spaces could coexist, let alone collide, and how on earth to go about building my own life within that collision.

YEARS LATER, I started the blog *Weird Sister* in 2014 because these two worlds—the feminist world that was incisive and inclusive, and the literary world that was performative, tongue-in-cheek, and experimental—still felt far too separate to me, even as I entered my thirties. In college, I'd started to see glimpses of the intersections between them: in women's lit courses where we read Jamaica Kincaid, Toni Morrison, Maxine Hong Kingston, June Jordan, Gloria Anzaldúa. I went to see Eileen Myles read for extra class credit. I found Arielle Greenberg's Small Press Traffic talk "On the Gurlesque" on the internet one night. Each piece of the feminist literary puzzle I learned about blew my mind all over again, and it occurred to me that there was not just one right way but many, many ways to be a feminist writer.

All these rich lineages of literary work and activism were out there, but where were the spaces outside of academia for people to come together to think and talk about them? From the mid-2000s into the 2010s, the blogosphere was where people talked about things. After college, I discovered the blog *Feministing* and made it my computer's homepage so I wouldn't forget to read it every day. That blog—along with other feminist blogs of that era like *Crunk Feminist Collective*, *Everyday Feminism*, *Black Girl Dangerous*, *Tiger Beatdown*, *Racialicious*, and the Women's Media Center blog—offered supersmart, inclusive takes on politics and pop culture in an accessible, conversational tone that helped me and so many other young people better understand the world. But they didn't often include literary content—how could they, strapped as they were with the task of breaking down the entire world for young feminists, and payment-free at that? When these spaces did cover books, they were more commercial publications, not the niche-within-a-niche world of experimental poetry where I had found my home as a writer.

At the same time—but in a separate sphere—lit blogs were where my particular literary world found community and dialogue on the internet. On blogs like *HTMLGiant*, *Coldfront*, *The Rumpus*, and *We Who Are About To Die*, poets and experimental writers wrote and read about the small poetry presses and underground literary culture that rarely got covered in larger venues. I remember reading some posts that addressed feminist issues by writers like Roxane Gay and Melissa Broder, then still aspiring writers themselves, but more often I read a lot of posts by cis white men that were interesting, insightful, and funny but lacked the political analysis I was looking for about how poetry related to gender and race and the other aspects of identity and power that mattered most when it came to living in the world.

These indie lit blogs were mostly edited by men and featured long rosters of mostly male contributors, mirroring the gender disparities of more mainstream literary publishing outlets and gatekeepers of the time. Of course there were, thankfully, some exceptions. Pussipo (later renamed HemPo), a collective of 160 feminist poets, started the blog *Delirious Hem* in 2006, which featured feminist poetics forums, roundtables with feminist small presses, feminist poets writing about everything from rape culture to movies, fashion, and fitness ("It's a blog, it's a poetics journal, it's a platform. From time to time, a post will appear," reads the description on the now archived Blogspot website). In 2009 I was forwarded a mass email from poet and professor Cate Marvin called "Women's Writing Now!" which began "Dear Female Writer." The email—which explained that Marvin's panel proposal on Contemporary Women's Poetry had been rejected by the annual writing conference AWP, while the conference regularly accepted proposals on topics unrelated to women (Birds in Poetry, for example, stands out in the mind from my own years of attending)—was a rallying call for the creation of a whole new organization dedicated exclusively to women's writing. As a result, Marvin, along with Erin Belieu and Ann Townsend, soon founded VIDA: Women in Literary Arts, and in 2010 the organization began, among other vital literary projects, their annual VIDA Count to draw attention to gender disparities in publishing. With the Count, VIDA was not just critiquing inequities in literary culture but also holding institutions and gatekeepers accountable to do better in a very clear, measurable way.

But as Christopher Soto writes in his piece "The Limits of Representation" (page 113), equity in numbers, while hugely important, is only one measure of progress. I still longed for an intentional, energetic, creative, and community-building space to fill in even just some of the lack of feminist literary commentary online, to bridge a bit of the gap between these two distinct worlds I inhabited, and to disrupt the white male lit-blog industrial complex with an explicitly feminist Blog of One's Own. Boosted by the encouragement of a girl gang of feminist poet friends (special shout-out to Becca Klaver for helping me get the blog off the ground), I bought a web domain, went into a temporary and never-to-be-replicated fugue state wherein I designed a website, and asked a roster of the smartest, coolest feminist writers I knew to join me in launching *Weird Sister*.

I WANTED *WEIRD SISTER* to be a space for talking about the feminist poems and books that inspired us, the contemporary literature that was doing interesting work around gender and other aspects of identity, the sexist shit that happened in the literary world but that nobody talked about publicly, how the established canon we all learned in school upheld what bell hooks calls the white supremacist capitalist patriarchy, the exciting readings and events going on, and the pop culture we consumed alongside it all with glasses of wine or Dr. Pepper—because we were not, after all, monoliths who existed only within the literary world. Like Becca Klaver writes in her piece about Bernadette Mayer's poetics of "radical inclusiveness" (page 74), it felt feminist and unapologetic to show ourselves as full people who were not just poets and literary critics but also nostalgists and reality TV watchers and record collectors and parents and teachers and people working to survive in the world.

With *Weird Sister*, I wanted to create an online platform that was filled with serious ideas, but didn't feel stuffy and exclusionary like poetry criticism so often can. Emulating the chatty, conversational tone of my favorite feminist blogs, *Weird Sister* aimed to be open and unpretentious. Vernacular language and oft-ridiculed traditionally feminine speech patterns like saying "like" too much were welcomed and encouraged. And, as on the best lit blogs, conventional criticism, creative forms, and personal elements could all, like, blend together. It was a space to celebrate and encourage dialogue between seemingly divergent aspects of culture, both "highbrow" (poetry, film, visual art, politics) and "lowbrow" (pop music, nostalgia, TV, celebrity gossip), and to take to task those supposed cultural distinctions with a glitter-nail-polished middle finger held high.

When it came to the blog's name, I wanted to invoke the ineffable, the interplanetary; the glittery liminal spaces that art comes from. The "Weird Sisters" are the three witches in Shakespeare's *Macbeth*, double-double-ing and leading the play's hero to his demise. They're prophets, goddesses, bearded hags stirring a glowing cauldron. A weird sister is also an outcast, a goth girl, a nerd, a poet. Her existence is a disruption to the status quo. In my own family, I always felt like the weird one—sandwiched between my two sisters, the art-y and sensitive one traced in heavy black eyeliner. Seeing other "weird" girls and women and femmes in pop culture growing up made me feel seen and inspired.

Weird Sister emerged as a space where we and others like us could see ourselves reflected back, and where we could hang out together and talk and write and multiply; a weird sister to both the more journalistic feminist blogs and the less feminist lit blogs that came before us. A platform and community of feminist poets and creative writers, many of whom were trying out writing critically for the first time in a collaborative blog space, all of whom have gone on to do so many incredible things in the literary world.

I DIDN'T REALIZE it at the time, but in 2014 we were on the precipice of a cultural sea change. When Beyoncé performed at the VMAs the next year alongside a giant glowing "FEMINIST" sign and a sample from Chimamanda Ngozi Adichie's TED Talk "We Should All Be Feminists," it made me wonder if a column debunking stereotypes about feminist poetry was even still necessary. In a turn toward what writer Andi Zeisler calls "marketplace feminism,"[1] everywhere you looked people were suddenly wearing feminist T-shirts bought from indie retailers or from H&M, drinking from feminist mugs, meeting at feminist coworking spaces. There was also a huge influx of mainstream, corporate-funded feminist publications and content popping up online. *Broadly, VICE*'s women's imprint, launched in 2015. (I both was miffed by their tagline, "Women's news you thought would exist by now," and longed for them to hire me.) Lena Dunham and Jenni Konner teamed up to create *Lenny Letter* that same year. *Bustle, Rookie,* and *xoJane* had all launched a few years earlier, and the media landscape was suddenly flooded with women's personal stories and lists of "ten feminist novels to read this summer." Most of these publications folded by 2019—a testament to the tumult of the industry, but also to the fleeting nature of corporate interests in feminism as a cultural fad. Many of the original trailblazing feminist blogs and magazines of the 1990s and early 2000s—like *Bitch* and *Feministing*—have also since folded, a testament to the difficulty of sustaining an independent feminist project without sufficient funding.

But of course the cultural and social activism of the mid-2010s was about much more than just corporate co-opting of feminism, something that's been happening since the dawn of the women's movement itself. Between 2013 and 2015, in response to non-indictments of the murderers of Trayvon Martin and Michael Brown, the #BlackLivesMatter hashtag created by Alicia Garza, Patrisse Cullors, and Opal Tometi became recognized as a protest movement on a global scale. And #MeToo, the campaign started by Tarana Burke in 2006 to draw attention to sexual assault, was popularized as a viral hashtag in 2017. Around this time, my own writing community also began having vital conversations about inclusion, abuse, race, and gender on a scale I had never seen before. In 2015, for example, Marcelo Hernandez Castillo, Javier Zamora, and Christopher Soto founded the Undocupoets Campaign—and later a fellowship with the same name—to protest the discriminatory rules of many first-book publishing contests in poetry, which prohibited undocumented poets from applying. And after several high-profile conceptual poets were called out for racist performances, an anonymous collective of poets called the Mongrel Coalition Against Gringpo began sharing online manifestos lambasting what they saw as the white supremacist project of conceptual poetry (or "conpo"). When a number of instances of sexual misconduct came to light in the poetry and Alt Lit worlds, a proto–#MeToo movement, started by feminist poets including myself in cities across the US and beyond, undertook efforts to dismantle a widespread culture of sexual abuse and harassment in poetry and Alt Lit. Jennif(f)er Tamayo, whose literary activism was instrumental during this time in organizing "Enough Is Enough" meetings and discussions on sexism and accountability in the New York poetry community, writes about their commitment to "Being Unreasonable" as a locus for resisting entrenched forms of oppression in our particular literary communities (page 129). *Weird Sister* was created to encourage dialogue at the intersections of literature, culture, and social justice, and during this transformative moment it served as a space to document some of these conversations as they were happening in literary communities.

A feminist lit blog was never enough, would never be enough, to eradicate the world's injustices, but being one small piece of the puzzle trying to change things for the better was all we could ever really hope to be. Writing this in 2023, I can't say that I feel particularly hopeful about the state of the world. But I think about an interview with Jia Tolentino in 2022 where she says that she can accept hopelessness as a feeling, but never as a political standpoint, and I feel inspired by the continued work of all the writers gathered in this book and at work beyond it—all those "humorless" and hilarious and smart and radical and messy and groundbreaking literary activists that paved the way for us and continue to do so.

When I first launched *Weird Sister*, I loved the feeling of running a vibrant space where vital conversations about feminism, poetry, and pop culture could flourish. I stayed up late each night working on it between days at my copywriting job—high on the blend of excitement and anxiety—but naturally it was impossible for me and for all of the *Weird Sister* team to keep doing this work, at this rate, sustainably. And without a model for funding or time to make one, the blog slowly went from a rush to a trickle of occasional content. As Samhita Mukho-padhyay, former executive editor of *Feministing*, wrote for Barnard College's 2012 #FemFuture conference on the future of online feminism, "Blogging has become the third shift. You do your activist work, you have a job to make money and then you blog on top of that. It's completely unsupported."[2] The feminist blogosphere that Mukho-padhyay refers to is widely considered the hallmark of a whole "wave" of feminism, but—like so much activist work throughout history—it's had virtually no financial support. Still, in spite of the challenges that came with *Weird Sister*, it's amazing to look back on the vast and mind-blowing array of writing that came out of planting this weird little seed on the internet. I hear there's a movie about baseball where they say, "If you build it, they will come." I built *Weird Sister*, and out came all the feminist weirdos with their brilliant minds, and this incredible collaboration and community was born.

THE WEIRD SISTER COLLECTION brings together some of the most popular, insightful, LOL-funny, moving, and unforgettable posts from the blog between 2014 and 2022, along with some new work highlighting essential perspectives, figures, moments, and movements in feminist literary history. The book pulls out natural themes that emerged from the blog's eclectic archive: from bringing a contemporary feminist lens to historical literature and paying homage to the iconic writers that came before us, to shining light on current books, events, organizations, and conversations. And, of course, it includes writing about pop culture, both nostalgic and present-day. While never exhaustive, this book hopes to offer a snapshot of some of the vital conversations and commentary surrounding feminism, literature, and pop culture from the last decade, and those that led up to it.

Weird Sister was born out of a love for feminist books, from my longing for feminist books to exist, to line the walls; to read them all, to write them. So it makes sense that it is now a feminist book too. I want feminist literary writing to take up more and more space, both on the internet and in the physical world, on bookshelves where a teenager at a feminist bookstore café might stumble upon them, goddess willing, after bringing her tray up to the counter. And I hope that putting *Weird Sister*'s contents in a book will allow future generations to learn about the early twenty-first-century feminist blogosphere in a format that gives it the same legitimacy as the white male literary canon; the same weight as the copy of *On the Road* that my high school English teacher handed me because she thought I might like weird, emotional, experimental prose, and assumed, correctly, that I would ignore how it treated women. The impulse that propelled feminist bloggers in the first place was an interest in creating our own media, holding it up, declaring it real and legitimate and important amid a patriarchal culture that devalued it and gatekept it away. So this book is a reminder that *Weird Sister* happened, and of the powerful, cool shit you can do together as a creative community. It's proof that all these feminist writers read books by all these other feminist writers and wrote about them—and about music and movies and TV and art—and then became the feminist writers that others will write about someday. And actually, people are writing about them right now—go read it. Go write it. It's a never-ending cycle of influence, admiration, and creation. I hope that you find it weird and inspiring.

—Marisa Crawford
Brooklyn, NY
September 2023

Our Bookshelves, Our Selves

On Breaking the Bad Bitch Archetype in Toni Morrison's *God Help the Child*

Naomi Extra, June 2015

"GOD BLESS THE child that's got his own." In 1941, Billie Holiday sang these words on what would become not only an award-winning song but also creative fodder for generations of artists and writers to come. The tune, "God Bless the Child," is a moody blues that continues to speak to the realities of black life in America. It rings of class struggle and the bittersweetness of self-reliance. According to Holiday, the song was inspired by an exchange with her mother in which she asked for money and was flatly denied. In jazz-like fashion, Toni Morrison riffs off of Holiday's song lyrics in the title of her 2015 novel, *God Help the Child.* She also picks up on threads that have coursed through her previous work. Novels like *Jazz, The Bluest Eye,* and ultimately *God Help the Child* speak to Morrison's persistent exploration of the themes of colorism, community, love, and music. Both texts, Morrison's novel and Holiday's song, center on a black woman's experiences with rejection from her mother and the subsequent turn to self-reliance as a result. Morrison's novel, as a contemporary engagement with Holiday's song, offers a poignant take on what it means to be an independent and successful black woman of the twenty-first century—a quintessential bad bitch.

Bride, the novel's protagonist, is a thirty-something black woman who has worked to ensure that she's got it all in life—money, beauty, success. Rejected by her mother and abandoned by her father because of her "blue-black" skin, Bride sets out to make what she has work for her. She creates a cosmetics line called "YOU, GIRL" and finds a way to make her dark hue her biggest accessory. Bride seems to have gotten the memo from "God Bless the Child" and decides to make herself into one of the "haves" in the song. Bride's life is replete with blessings but not help. Her mother purports to "protect" and "prepare" her by treating her coldly and insensitively during her childhood. What Bride truly desires is her mother's love. As a young girl, Bride (who then goes

3

by her birth name, Lula Ann) helps herself by telling a lie that puts an innocent woman in jail in exchange for crumbs of affection from her mother. But as an adult, Bride prides herself on her self-reliance and drive. She becomes the prototypical bad bitch—attractive, strong, and self-reliant.

To be clear, what I mean when I refer to the bad bitch archetype is the "don't-need-nobody/I-run-this-ish" woman we see all over pop culture and on social media. The bad bitch is most often embodied by a black woman who gives zero fucks and gets what she wants. Our culture loves this type, and many of us seek to capture it in ourselves. Just think of Destiny's Child circa 2000 with the hit "Independent Women Part 1." Millennial women and girls everywhere bounced and swished as the group declared its catchy message in the form of call-and-response, singing along, "I depend on me." It was an anthem.

I think of the nineties as one of the major heydays of black independent woman images (although we can definitely look to the 1970s as well). The year before "Independent Women" was released, TLC put out their chart-topping hit "No Scrubs," a song expounding on the romantic desires of the independent black woman who wants a partner who matches (or surpasses) her economic achievements. This was also the era of Terry McMillan's blockbuster success as the author of two novels featuring successful single black women, both of which were turned into films: *Waiting to Exhale* (1995) and *How Stella Got Her Groove Back* (1998). In *Waiting to Exhale* we see the quintessential bad bitch embodied on-screen in Angela Bassett as she struts away from the smoldering flames of her cheating husband's personal belongings wearing a black negligee. These trends that appeared in music reflected some of the material changes in the lives of African Americans during the period. In the nineties, reports showed an upsurge in the number of black women graduating from college and entering into professional positions relative to black men. During this time, scholars and researchers began to write about an impending crisis in African American marital life. The bottom line of concern: black women had become too independent and wouldn't want to mess with black men as a result.

In *God Help the Child*, Morrison makes a point to let her readers know that Bride was born in the nineties. Also Bride names her cosmetics line "YOU, GIRL: Cosmetics for Your Personal Millennium." No coincidence here. Bride is a black woman millennial who is obsessed

with her body, her beauty, and her business. She is the quintessential independent woman of the nineties. In an article in the *Guardian*,
Morrison is quoted as stating, "I'm writing for black people." With
God Help the Child, I think the author is speaking not just to black
people but to black women. She asks us to carefully question what
freedom looks like and how it is achieved. Is it through self-reliance
and reclamation of beauty ideals, or is there something more that we
should be striving for? It's difficult not to think of the cultural narrative surrounding Lupita Nyong'o's skin when reading the novel. Like
Bride, Lupita is a dark-skinned black woman who was ridiculed as a
child because of her hue. Lupita is also a millennial who has managed
to benefit from the fetishization and commodification of blackness.
Where Bride's mother, Sweetness, sees her "blue-black" hue as an
impediment and a reason she needs to be protected, Bride is able to
see her complexion as a tool she can use to her advantage. This is the
Lupita moment fictionalized.

It's also worth pointing out that while Morrison may have chosen
a millennial voice through which to deliver her message, there's no
escaping the past in this novel. Part of its brilliance is in the timeless-
ness of the narrative, which speaks to pains of the present while also
engaging with the injury of a collective past. Sweetness seems like she
is several generations removed from her daughter, and the chapters
written in her voice float in an unidentifiable past. She captures the
still-present pains of colorism and the psychic remnants of the trauma
of slavery. Through this narrative, Morrison reminds us that the struggle continues and maps out the consequences of not confronting pain.
That map, in turn, presents us with a version of the bad bitch archetype to interrogate. Her writing urges us to think about the ways in
which capitalism has hijacked notions of female independence, especially for black women.

In Morrison's capable hands, the bad bitch archetype isn't just a
personality—instead it's revealed as a product that exploits and exports
a watered-down version of black femininity defined by strength and
control. Ultimately Bride must shed her armor of social prestige and
emotional disconnect to finally learn that she deserves love. She does
this by entering into spaces that challenge her value system when she
finds herself in need, embracing rather than rejecting her own vulnerability. Despite her focus on self-reliance, Bride is only able to heal
with the help of other people. It's a bumpy road through vulnerability for Bride to reach a place of love.

In the end, the bad bitch (like all archetypes) is just too small to contain an entire person. Morrison's response to this problematic cultural narrative demonstrates the absolute necessity of vulnerability. To be vulnerable is to acknowledge your human body, replete with its predisposition toward injury, whether emotional or otherwise. For black women, whose bodies have historically been already so prone to injury—be it through maternal and reproductive health disparities, carceral violence, environmental injustice, or the valences of everyday racism and sexism—it can be tempting to construct an airtight progress narrative that renders us untouchable. Still, as Morrison reminds us, pain and mortality tether every one of us to each other, irrevocably. They are realities we cannot hide from. We are all going to die someday, and we all get hurt—and we all need help sometimes. *God Help the Child* reminds us that being a bad bitch simply isn't enough to make a woman feel whole.

Best Literary Sex: *If Beale Street Could Talk* by James Baldwin

Camille Wanliss, February 2017

I COULDN'T HAVE been more than twelve or so when I first got my hands on *If Beale Street Could Talk*, James Baldwin's gut-punching 1974 novel about Tish and Fonny, young lovers struggling to fight a racist and corrupt justice system in 1970s New York. It had been placed in the mahogany bookshelf in the living room, right above the double rows of Encyclopedia Britannica. I remember flipping through it, scanning the pages until my eyes caught the passage about Fonny's "sex stiffening and beginning to rage against the cloth of his pants." In an instant, I had stumbled upon my first literary sex scene. I've come across a few since those days, but, my gosh, there's nothing quite like the first time.

I took the book back to my bedroom, absconded with it like stolen money, to read the pages that followed. In them, Tish explicitly describes losing her virginity to Fonny: "I screamed and cried against his shoulder . . . He moved back, but not quite out . . . then he pulled me against him and thrust in with all his might . . . A singing began in me and his body became sacred."

Can you imagine a twelve-year-old black girl from Brooklyn reading about being fucked so good it felt like teetering on the verge of death? About being awash in lust and love to the point that it felt as if you were drowning? And when breath finally filled your lungs, you couldn't tell whose it was? Here were naked bodies—black bodies—in simultaneous fits of agony and ecstasy.

Good Lawd, I still get goose bumps.

After picking the book up again for the first time in twenty years, I know now what lovin' like that feels like—freedom. Coming together in unconditional love; it's boundless. I think of Fonny before he was framed and caged for a crime he did not commit. Beautiful black Fonny. Free Fonny. With his future plans as a sculptor and his Tish. And the wind gets taken out of me 'cause freedom for black folks is always fleeting. In the forty years since the book was published, we're still grappling with the effects of mass incarceration. We certainly don't need the Justice Department to tell us what we've always known in Ferguson and Baltimore and Staten Island and Chicago and communities all around this country—that black folks are routinely and systemically targeted by police.

So in the novel, when Officer Bell goes after Fonny for protecting Tish from sexual assault at the hands of a stranger, I think of black love and how it's always been an affront to white supremacy—whether you're childhood sweethearts from Harlem or the first black couple in the White House. And then I think of me. Twelve-year-old me in my bedroom in Brooklyn. A few years shy of a first kiss but secretly reading about Fonny giving all that good-good to Tish.

The Books of Feminists Are in Every Place
(A Comic Diary)

Amanda K. Davidson, May 2015

I MOVE THROUGH the city at the same time as I move through narratives—in my headphones, on my pocket screen, in bed by the light of an iPad, folding open a borrowed paperback—and these stories lay on top of the visible world, making a third space, where I live.

The architecture of this year so far (a partial list): Elena Ferrante's *My Brilliant Friend*, Chimamanda Ngozi Adichie's *Americanah*, Tove Jansson's *The Summer Book*, Miranda July's *The First Bad Man*.

...to the door
of Don Achille's
apartment.

Elena Ferrante, My Brilliant Friend

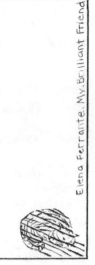

As they walked
out of the store,
Ifemelu said,
"I was waiting for
her to ask 'was it
the one with two
eyes or the one
with two legs?'
Why didn't she just
ask 'was it the
black girl or the
white girl?'"

Chimamanda Ngozi Adichie, AMERICANAH

Ginika laughed. "Because this is America. You're supposed to pretend you don't notice certain things."

Tove Jansson, THE SUMMER BOOK

"What is it you're doing?" Sophia asked.
"I'm playing," Grandmother said.
 Sophia crawled into the magick forest and saw everything her grandmother had done.
"Is it an exhibit?" she asked.

But Grandmother said it had nothing to do with sculpture, sculpture was another thing completely.

Miranda July, The First Bad Man

First he drank the day we made love; he gulped it all down. He drank the day we showed him off at Ralphs. He drank the cotton candy milk from the day at the pier. The last batch was from the morning she left and this milk was full of plans I didn't know about. When he finished that bottle she was really gone, every last drop of her.

The Nuclear Family / The Nuclear Bomb: Revisiting Kate Zambreno's *O Fallen Angel* in Trump America

Sam Cohen, January 2017

THE FIRST TIME I read Kate Zambreno's *O Fallen Angel* was in 2012, not too long after it was first released by Chiasmus Press in 2009, and it felt like something I'd been starving for: the story of a girl raised by a housebound Mommy whose constant care is a form of creepy control, whose love is both dollifying and cannibalizing. The girl—Maggie—is stifled and self-seeking and, with limited tools with which to construct a self, self-destructs instead.

O Fallen Angel is Zambreno's first book—she went on to garner a larger readership with her novel *Green Girl* and her critical book *Heroines*, both of which establish Zambreno as a formal innovator who is in constant conversation with dead critical theorists and Hollywood starlets, who returns from these conversations with new language with which to write the experience of the girl. Compared to *Green Girl* and *Heroines*, *O Fallen Angel* feels young, but in the best way—it's desperate, searing, hurting, angry, and unforgiving.

When I first read the novel, I loved it because I related so hard. Finally there was a mother in literature who wanted to "freeze [her children] when . . . they're at the age before they start disagreeing with you," who wanted to keep her self-harming girlkid out of therapy because psychologists "blame everything on the Mommy." Maggie's Mommy's dollification is so extreme it even leads her to fantasize about Maggie's death—in death, "finally Maggie will let Mommy dress her . . . and finally Maggie will be her girl yes her girl." Finally there was a girl in literature who, raised by such a mother and just like me, was so unequipped to live her own life that she was fired from all her waitressing jobs, that she sought self-worth in the beds of brooding, bohemian boys, that she got rejected from in-patient psychiatric care because even her suicide plan wasn't specific enough. And maybe it's true that we see girls like Maggie in stories from Mary Gaitskill and her acolytes, but *O Fallen Angel* is the first book I read that is some degree of diagnostic, that shows the reader how the girl got that way.

And maybe—like the therapist of Mommy's fantasies—Zambreno's narrator blames the Mommy, but Mommy's story gets told too, albeit judgmentally, and so *O Fallen Angel* gives us an intergenerational story of women teaching girls how to accept oppression, how to self-oppress, and why.

O Fallen Angel is told in the form of a triptych, narrated closely in turns to Mommy, Maggie, and the god Malachi. Mommy's sentences are long and smushed together, free of the constraints of commas and periods, often including rhyming folk-wisdoms and bits of Bible verses that seem to be Mommy's only external reference points with which to make sense of the world, but for Mommy they are enough. Maggie's references expand to include fairy tales and Hollywood movies from the fifties and sixties, clearly inherited from Mommy, which have taught her to be prince-seeking; that the only way out of her Mommy's American Dream is to latch her sense of self to a boy who looks like Marlon Brando and run to the other side of the proverbial tracks. Maggie's also got what she's learned from her brief stint as a psychology major. Maggie is drugging and slutting, but she's also reading desperately, reading in order to discover or assemble a self. But the thing is she's too young and too sheltered: She hasn't read enough to leave her hometown ideology behind for good. She hasn't read enough to enable her to know how to move around safely in Chicago, the city to which she's relocated.

In 2012, maybe I hadn't read enough, and I was reading desperately, self-seekingly too, and I glossed over the cultural differences between Maggie's family and my own, made the book into a book about me. But it's 2017 now and I've gone through my Saturn return, and *O Fallen Angel* is being rereleased by Harper Perennial the very same month that Donald Trump has been inaugurated into the US presidency, and it feels like a different book. It's no longer just a book for sad girls raised to be selfless dollies by controlling moms. It turns out to be a book about that 53 percent of white women voters so many of us were so shocked to learn about, and many others weren't; a book about the constant and attentive labor those women do to uphold patriarchy and racism and corporate capitalism and anti-environmentalism as the True American Values, the constant and attentive labor they do in service of their own oppression. If the election had gone another way, the characters in this book might seem quaint, obscure, like a dying breed. Instead the timing of *O Fallen Angel*'s rerelease fuckedly transitions it from Sad Girl Cult Classic to Great American Novel in écriture féminine. In Mommy's colliding sentences, we're able to see how thoughtless associations and oft-repeated phrases and rhymes take the place of logic:

> Mommy believes fullheartedly in the sacred institution of marriage. She believes strongly in family values and the importance of the nuclear family. It's the American way the nuclear family the nuclear bomb the white picket fence.

Though it was first released in 2009, *O Fallen Angel* feels painfully timely in its revelation of the ways in which the American Dream is a dream of white supremacy and masculine domination. In Zambreno's deft hands, it becomes clear that Daddy is a good American worker so that Mommy can live in her dream house in the country, that it is requisite that Mommy's dream be to live in that dream house in order to justify Daddy's robotic employment. Zambreno shows us that Mommy's job is not to cook (she gets takeout) or to clean (she has a brown-skinned immigrant woman to do this for her) but to oversee, to instill American values, to validate racism, homophobia, and environmental destruction—it is Mommy's job to keep everyone dreaming. It is a full-time job.

Zambreno is brilliant at getting inside Mommy's weird, oppressive logic. I know when I am in Mommy's brain that contraceptives and abortions are just means by which women can be selfish, which is to say that those women using contraceptives might not be working directly in service of the perpetuation of the American Dream, might not be doing their jobs; I know when I am in Mommy's brain that of course it *is* girls' fault if they're raped because what selfish thing are they getting up to outside the house? I know when I am in Mommy's brain that to be anti-racist or environmentally concerned is unladylike, because what then are you implying about Mommy's work of keeping everyone safe by moving them out to the white, white country or about Daddy's job of making SUVs?

Zambreno's Mommy-logic shows us how the Other—Mommy's cleaning lady who can't access an American Dream so that Mommy can have hers, Mommy's "faggot" brother—is a real threat. The threat is that the Other might, like Maggie's boy from the other side of the proverbial tracks, call into question whether Mommy and her family are *good* and might, more importantly, call into question whether

Mommy and her family are—the ultimate American value—*happy*. The Other might make Mommy's family start to stir in its American Dream. And if it were to stir enough, if it were to fall out of the dream, as Maggie has, the reality—terrible commute, isolation, boredom, meaningless and destructive work—might be too much to take.

When Mommy thinks about her children as babies, she primarily recalls their whiteness. They had "the whitest blond hair like glowing halos," but after this halcyon, angel-baby period, "their hair grew brown and darkened," and finally, Maggie's dyed her hair black. Maggie has followed the boy across the tracks to the wrong side, has pushed against Mommy's dollification. But the thing is, in a world which has decided that women are housebound providers and protectors of the American Dream, static and unwanting unless it's for a (white) picket fence, Maggie is sick, and Mommy can put her wherever Mommy wants.

What do we call it when Mommies teach their daughters to be stagnant dollies in service of a productive, consumptive, racist, destructive America? Is it misogyny? Is it white supremacy so deeply ingrained that one is willing to sacrifice herself for its continuation? Is it love? I'm not sure, but it's what I see when I look at Ivanka and Melania poised and posed behind Donald Trump, and it seems to be where Trump and his cabinet of monsters have promised to return us.

It's worth saying that, even with all the work it's doing, *O Fallen Angel* is slim and hurtling. It wraps you in its characters' compelling, charming voices and propels you forward to its sickening end.

White Space, Banana Ketchup, and Karaoke: A Review of Kimberly Alidio's *after projects the resound*

MT Vallarta, September 2016

I WAS INTRODUCED to Kimberly Alidio at Effie Street in Silver Lake, Los Angeles, at a quaint reading in the backyard of a professor's house. I was intrigued by the book Alidio held in her hands—a sky-blue volume with a longhaired figure on all fours, seemingly ingesting or expelling pink and orange confetti. Soon I was even more jarred and enthralled by the pieces she read aloud, poems speaking, stuttering, and singing about empire, migration, diaspora, and queerness—subjects I had become familiar with as a queer Filipina American and budding academic. *after projects the resound* not only interrogates these concepts but transforms them, remakes them, and melds them through reverberating wordplay, experiments with sound, and even the strategic use of white space. The final stanza in "All the Pinays are straight, all the queers are Pinoy, but some of us" demonstrates this:

> I will never not
> want to be violent with you (dare you to say
> this isn't love, queen)
> pray for
> her resurrection every easter
> "I'm just so bored and so pretty and not white"[1]

Although you may need to take a second to comprehend what is occurring, the sleek alliteration of the *w* and *n* sounds in the first two lines allows the poem to roll off your tongue, a slow, accentuated, but nevertheless pleasurable foray into the complexities and obscurities of Pinxy queerness. The enjambments, line breaks, and spaces in between help anchor and pace the reader, allowing us to appreciate the various intonations of sound. These rhetorical, sonic, and spatial devices showed me that I did not need the convenience of clarity to enjoy and appreciate Alidio's work. Her delightfully playful and musical words and sounds, for me, emulate the witty banter between Pinxys as we process the intersections of Catholicism, queerness, and brownness together in conversation.

The rest of *after projects the resound* is just as clever and pleasing to the ears. Alidio provides a critique of US empire through the terrain of pop culture and food, as illustrated in "Our lady of the banana ketchup":

> a UFC a Jufran a Mother's Best
> a torta a hipster a hotdog spaghetti
> a hater a sweeter tomato[2]

I'm sure all Filipinxs are familiar with the sweet, tangy taste of banana ketchup, but until reading Alidio's book, I was unaware of the hxtory of this cherished and highly popular condiment. Perfected during World War II by Pinay food technician Maria Y. Orosa, banana ketchup used an abundance of bananas to substitute the shortage of tomatoes for ketchup during the war. With this, Alidio shows how the squabbles of empires (WWII being one of many) can completely alter the course of culture in the name of production and survival. We can locate the hidden and subtle currents of US empire through everyday things, like the bottle of UFC banana ketchup sitting in my parents' pantry. In addition, Alidio alludes to how the concoction of Filipinx spaghetti (a banana-ketchup-and-hot-dog-infested dish of pure and undeniable goodness) has its roots in US colonialism. "Our lady of banana ketchup" makes us wonder what other artifacts of empire are hiding in our everyday consumption of food and culture.

Alidio continues her astounding play with the intersections of empire and popular culture with "I wanna be your dog," a reference to the Stooges' headbanging single. *after projects the resound*'s musicality is indisputable in the last few lines of the poem:

> So messed up I want you
> Here in my room I want you
> Now I wanna be
> Eaten by
> Igorots at St. Louis[3]

After finishing this poem, I had to read it again—or, rather, sing it this time to the groove of Iggy Pop. While singing about dog eating may be unsettling for a few folx, I enjoyed the mischievousness and deviousness this singsong poem afforded, and it is definitely one of the cleverest references to the 1904 St. Louis World's Fair I have encountered. Not many people are aware that indigenous Filipinxs (the Igorots) were exhibited like artifacts and animals at this world's fair. Easily becoming one of the most popular attractions with the Igorot people's so-called savage war dances and grotesque habits on display, dog eating rumored to be among them, the exhibit served to justify the colonization of the Philippines. What do we do when the darkest and most grotesque moments in Filipinx/American hxstory come to the surface? What do we do about the fact that dog eating has become so legible when others think about Filipinx/American-ness? The speaker of this poem encourages us to sing about it, to pronounce it, to reclaim it in creative and transformative ways that allow us to locate and critique the currents of US empire. And what better way to do it than through witty poetry and fun karaoke-esque tendencies? If we're going to talk about empire, we might as well do it through subverted pleasure.

after projects the resound is a metamorphosis, the aftermath of a dissertation-turned-monograph-turned-poetry. Alidio shows there is more than one way to produce cultural critique. The terrain of culture has the capacity to criticize, remake, celebrate, and eat itself in the most astonishing ways.

A Witch's Reading Report

Grace Kredell, October 2019

IN HER BOOK *Waking the Witch: Reflections on Women, Magic, and Power*, witch-ambassador Pam Grossman compares her feelings about witches going mainstream to the time when her favorite indie band blew up. While she's happy that their work is finally being valued and recognized, she also worries that their messages will be diluted. Grossman's mixed feelings resonate with my own apprehensions about this moment. As a psychic practitioner from a family of spiritual nonconformists, I embody this archetype publicly: the magic woman whose knowledge is feared, desired, and also scorned. A body on fire.

As I watch the witch ascend into the mainstream—everywhere from women's coworking space The Wing calling itself a "coven" to witch-inspired looks at fashion week—I'm forced to reckon with the suppressed witch legacy of my own family. While my family background is now increasingly considered "cool" or "different," as a child, I knew instinctively to distance myself from "The New Age" and ideas that would sound the alarm bells of the Reality Police. I kept my visions to myself. In school, I honed a comedic routine making fun of my psychic mom to classmates while quietly accepting my own intuitive experiences and letting them guide me. I never thought I'd be performing psychic readings until suddenly I was, unable to hide anymore. But my own resistance remains strong. There are many days I torture myself: *Do I really have to stand up for this ... represent this?* When I'm feeling particularly misunderstood, threatened, or unsupported, I fight the urge to take it all back. As sonic medicine, I've started to employ "Too Late to Turn Back Now" by Cornelius Brothers & Sister Rose, a jam that caught my attention in Spike Lee's *BlacKkKlansman*. I spin in my room and let the music gently soothe me onward.

While Grossman views the witch's rise as evidence of a paradigmatic sea change, I am more skeptical, though not entirely unhopeful. What I've noticed in my own life and in the lives of other mystic practitioners with whom I organize is that so far, this witch trend has not translated into meaningful public support or acts of institutional inclusion. The "What do you do?" question remains dicey for the working witches I know. Whether you get challenged on your worldview or asked for a free reading, it's a lot of labor and stress. There is a palpable hunger for psychic knowledge and insight, but at the same time, a deep accusation stands in the room with me when I announce this possibility out loud. *How can you tell me that magic is real?* Everybody knows that magic is fake, failed, dead. Gone.

Grossman's book, however, isn't just a book about witch practitioners like me, but a broader-based argument about why the symbol of the witch matters: to feminism, to spirituality, and to women's history, most importantly. As I was named and called myself a witch, I had to look at my own lineage and address how I got to this moment. Why was the knowledge that had been passed down to me through my family so culturally out of bounds, seen as devilish, even? Grossman discusses in her book how the devil was hardly mentioned in Christian theology until the church began to feel threatened by newly translated Greek and Arabic texts that described ceremonies and rituals outside of established doctrine. In response, the church produced propaganda espousing the dangers of what they labeled satanic practice. These magical discourses threatened the power of the church's own sacred discourses, a cultural contest that culminated in Pope John XXII declaring magic an act of heresy in 1326.

In short, over the next several hundred years, magic that was not church-state sanctioned became the devil's territory, and the devil in particular came to be theorized by powerful, state-allied theologians as living in women's bodies, minds, and imaginations. It was women more so than men who were charged with heretical beliefs as "witches." Grossman contextualizes a confluence of challenging conditions—crop failures, rampant illness, and economic instability—that led the church and state to leverage witchcraft as a convenient scapegoat. While we may be tempted today to cast these victims as magical practitioners akin to the contemporary witches now in vogue, this myth masks important historical contexts.

More so than Grossman, Italian activist and scholar Silvia Federici has worked to put the history of the witch into an economic context. In her book *Caliban and the Witch*, and more recently in *Witches, Witch-Hunting, and Women*, Federici links "witch" persecution to capitalism's rise in early-modern Europe. What her evidence reveals is that "witches" were mostly poor women, but also men, whose church- and state-sanctioned terrorization served as an effective measure of social control during a time of economic transition. Federici explains how capitalism came to control women's bodies and details the coincidence of the witch trials, the codification of a new sexual division of labor, and the rise of wage work more generally.

Federici narrates how as the land became increasingly privatized through the enclosure movement, people lost a relationship that was crucial to their independence and interdependence. People were forced to look outside of their own communities to sustain themselves. Social relations transformed in this erasure of "the commons," pitting neighbors against each other and, importantly, men against women. Federici found only one man in her archival research that stood up for his wife during one of the many witch roundups.

Another important piece of the witch-and-state puzzle can be found in Kristen J. Sollée's *Witches, Sluts, Feminists*. Quoting the often-criticized historian Anne Barstow on the witch trials, Sollée excerpts Barstow's findings that women were not considered independent legal entities prior to the witch trials, their public testimony not admissible until they were tried as witches. Thus, Barstow makes the case that women entered full legal status as witches. This legal history affects women in the United States, as our legal system has its roots in the English common law. These particular historical and legal legacies of persecution are why Pam Grossman chooses to address the witch as "she," although the witch transcends "she."

As an organizer, I continually go back and forth on my use of the word "witch" in my calls to action and support. Despite the witch's deep historical connection to renegade gender and sexual identities, when invoked in certain spiritual settings, this label does not always read as being queer and trans inclusive. However, gender-nonconforming folks were almost certainly targeted during the witch trials. More fundamentally, mainstream historical "witch" narratives have been woefully Eurocentric. Grossman acknowledges that much of the discourse she engages with focuses on the Western witch, leaving out countless other cultural traditions that have magical people of their own. This lopsidedness speaks to an ongoing erasure that must be remedied, but it is also impossible for any single author to construct a complete picture of witchcraft past and present.

It should be emphasized that the historic witch trials were concurrent with the European project of colonization, Indigenous land theft, and the enslavement of African peoples. For the colonized and enslaved, rejecting or resisting settler religion alone could tender lethal accusations of witchcraft. Remember that it was Tituba, an enslaved woman, who was the first to be accused of witchcraft in Salem. In 1986 acclaimed novelist, critic, and playwright Maryse Condé wrote *I, Tituba, Black Witch of Salem*, a book that employs mediumship to unearth a version of events entirely divergent from mainstream histories. By aligning ourselves with Tituba's perspective, the witch imaginary we've received essentially reshifts, with different truths coming into central focus. I found that while reading it, the sometimes-unfathomable events of Salem finally made sense to me.

In her essay "Bruja Positionalities: Toward a Chicana/Latina Spiritual Activism," scholar Irene Lara crucially asks, "Are women of color always immediately found suspect of using our magic?" Yes, profoundly more so than white women. In her book *Brujas: The Magic and Power of Witches of Color*, Lorraine Monteagut relays how the trauma of colonization causes suspicion to play out even between people who share the same culture: "When we are so far removed from our ancestral wisdom, we are attracted to those who have kept their practices strong—who we've called the brujos, the santeros and santeras, the *houngans* and *mambos*. We fear them as much as we're attracted to them." As Monteagut summarizes this dynamic in her discussion of the mythic La Llorona, "We've demonized the victim and projected all our fears onto her, while the colonizer rides away." Through the vehicle of popular myths and stories, the scapegoating of magical women continues, masking legacies of pain inflicted by those in power.

Many witches I know are desperate for a relationship to magical traditions we have been taught to fear, either within our own lineage or beyond them. As witches are drawn together through a mutual desire to reconnect to ancient ancestral practices, we must remind ourselves that this reclamation process is deeply unequal. While there are opportunities to heal long-standing wounds, it's only possible when we untangle and understand our own culpability. As Monteagut educates, "What if a reclamation of the occult looks like an apology for all the harm my ancestors might have done, for the harm I have done, even unconsciously?" Before we lay claim to a magical tradition, how can we acknowledge our role in suppressing the magic of others? Meeting Monteagut's challenge could easily constitute a lifelong project as we integrate repair work, redistribution, and reparations into our reclamation process.

Because of these unaddressed historical traumas, many people who might otherwise identify as "witches" cannot stand the word. Elissa Washuta, a member of the Cowlitz Indian Tribe, describes in her sobering essay collection *White Magic* that while "witch" seems a fitting moniker in many ways, she fears that using it would not only align her with a fad but set a dangerous precedent. As she explains, "I don't want the white witches I resemble to take my presence in their spaces as permission for theft. Really, I just want a version of the occult that isn't built on plunder, but I suspect that if we could excise the stolen pieces, there would be nothing left." Years ago, I worked at a Brooklyn witch shop with a popular Instagram account. It was owned by a self-identified "fake witch" who routinely trawled the internet for witch products she could copy and sell under her label. Like many similar white-owned spiritual businesses, she traded in white sage and crystals, providing customers with little context regarding the origins or sourcing of these tools. While I knew what was problematic about her business, I took the job because I needed the money to supplement my fledgling client practice, and I liked the other women who worked there.

Like me, this diverse crew of witches felt conflicted about the store's ethos, but we were all hungry for magical space and community. Together, we believed we could transform the business into something more aligned with our values. As a result, we stayed on, accepting an illegal wage structure and unreasonable working conditions—an exploitative environment where carrots were perpetually dangled with rewards never materializing. Eventually, the shop owner crossed a line, which sent us organizing against her. Washuta warns in her text that "the white women who dominate the online esoteric marketplace cannot hoard this power." As we prepared for our departure from the brand, we realized we had become a powerful coven. We performed a closing ritual and called the IRS. Our collective lives on to this day.

Mainstream media narratives continually reduce witchcraft to a marketing trend, focusing on consumable products and services, often spotlighting white-owned businesses like the one I worked for. Even when these stories include nonwhite practitioners who have made inroads in the consumer market, this coverage elides the origins and intentions of the multifaceted groundswell of participants who are fueling this movement. Monteagut pushes back against this misrepresentation in her work, affirming the rightful leaders of this magical moment: "In spiritual communities, Black witches and brujas are not minorities. They constitute the majority practicing ancestral traditions, just as Black and Brown people are the leaders of intersectional feminism." When mainstream commentaries chronically sideline these magical people and their deeply political motives in this whitewashing of witch culture, witchcraft can appear as a set of "empowering" consumer choices versus a collective call for the redistribution of power in our society and the abolishment of capitalism. Perhaps most insidious, these mainstream media sources are often the most accessible to the uninitiated, presenting newcomers with magic that is benign, consumer-driven, and plundered.

When people outside of witch communities say they don't get "the whole witch thing," there is a more universal point that I wish to hammer home: What has it meant for you to grow up in a culture where divine power is conceptualized predominantly as male authority? What human power structures are upheld through this visioning of the spiritual hierarchy? "In God We Trust" is printed on our money; God remains significant in so many of our public agreements, although we're told that church and state remain separate. It's so obvious, and yet it doesn't actually seem like a big deal to us. We're so used to it. We think it doesn't really mean anything anymore. But what would it feel like to walk around in a space where femme-, trans-, nonbinary-, and nonwhite-identified divinities were represented everywhere? What would your life be like if when somebody said "God" aloud (if we agree that that's even the word), "they/them" or "she/her" came to mind first? Or simply "us"? What would that world look like, where our collective magic felt like *The* power?

Where I experience the truest magic is in the alchemy of community, in the *interconnectedness*, which is how I conceptualize "God." Yet the reality is that we live and operate in siloed spaces (including digital realms), making it challenging for witch communities to bridge any number of boundaries, although *magic is boundless*. We are united by a legacy of persecution that, though experienced unequally, touches us all. In addition to the shared sense of having been dislocated from something essential to us as humans—the reality of broken lineages— what we "witches" may have in common is a collective ambivalence regarding that which has been marketed and sold to us as "magic." And yet, as a working witch, I must reckon with the ubiquity of this commercial "magic," occasionally playing into these outdated and offensive tropes to make a living.

When I first started giving psychic readings, I'd often wear a witch hat in sessions, in playful acknowledgment of the otherness that gets projected onto my body when I perform psychic work. My clients loved the getup, but it started to feel demeaning. Today, I don't want to wear the witch hat anymore. It feels complicit with the cultural dunk tank that's been assigned to the witch and witch history. What's more, it feels strange to me to be singled out as *the* witch when I've found that much of my client practice is about holding space for clients reckoning with their own experience *as witches*. Clients, for example, often confess to me that they talk to their dead, and that the dead talk back. *Loudly*. I say, "I talk to the dead too." We eye each other.

What are *we witches* to do? Recognize the power that we hold. Dedicate your individual power to a collective purpose and allow this to keep you in check. Lay your cards out on the table with the other witches you know and see what matches up—what is the work you have to do together? Interrogate the history of your practices and acknowledge how you and your ancestors may have misused this power in the past. There is no way forward without this reckoning. As Grossman says, "Whether as transformative spiritual figures, rabble-rousing cultural symbols, or bewitchingly complex characters in stories and histories that we read and watch and reimagine, I know this: witches are the future." As Monteagut declares, "The future is bruja." Speak your own words here, and let these spells intermix, amplifying each other. It is too late to turn back now.

Fifty Shades of Grey and
Why I Keep Defending Women's Trash

Caolan Madden, March 2015

IN THIS FANTASY he shows up at my boring job and we have an awkward but meaningful conversation. In this fantasy he just happens to walk by my house when I'm outside reading a Victorian novel and wearing a really flattering top. In this fantasy he shows up at the bar and I don't accidentally have my first kiss ever with the wrong guy. In this fantasy he wants me so much that it drives him insane. In this fantasy he can barely control himself.

I went to see *Fifty Shades of Grey* in NYC's Union Square at noon on a Tuesday. It had been out for ten days. The internet had said the stars had no chemistry and obviously hated sex. A lot of my friends had said I should boycott it because it romanticized an abusive relationship. Rory and Alison had told me the movie's sex scenes were incredibly boring, but the scenes where they do paperwork were delightful. Marisa had posted a photo on Instagram of her and Matt looking sad after they watched it. So I basically knew what to expect.

The movie made me pretty uncomfortable. Not because it was too sexy, not because I was offended, not even because I was a mom going to see some mommy porn by myself on a Tuesday afternoon. The *actors* were so uncomfortable! Poor Jamie Dornan's Christian Grey was the saddest, most vanilla boyfriend in the world. He's what would happen if that nice vanilla boyfriend's mom got kidnapped by the Jigsaw Killer and the Jigsaw Killer made him hit a girl with a belt to save his mom. That's how Jamie Dornan looked when he was hitting Dakota Johnson with a belt, like he was glad this was all going to be over and he hoped the Jigsaw Killer would give him his mom back but he really, really wished he didn't have to hit anyone with a belt; that's not how he was raised. He mostly likes kissing.

The audience made me uncomfortable too. There were three other women, all sitting alone, scattered throughout the theater, and one middle-aged bearded guy with something in his lap that made a

rustling sound. It might have been popcorn, and he had every right
to be there, but I wish he hadn't been there. I wish I had just watched
the movie with three other anonymous women. We would have made
a painfully cheesy ad for the franchise's universal appeal to women;
we were so diverse in age and race and sartorial style and probably
in the reasons we were free on a Tuesday at noon and maybe in the
reasons we wanted to go see *Fifty Shades of Grey* in Union Square. A
2015 version of a seventies Times Square porno, with the genders
reversed. Just some moms and grandmas eating popcorn and watching Jamie Dornan look uncomfortable and Dakota Johnson gasp and
writhe and throw back her head and otherwise look sort of dorky and
kind of cute.

*In this fantasy I have always been the most beautiful woman in the
world, I just didn't know. In this fantasy really loving a few Victorian
novels is enough to get me an amazing publishing job. In this fantasy I
never need to finish this dissertation because my love of Victorian novels
is as good as a dissertation. In this fantasy I love* Jane Eyre *so much that
the idea for a wildly popular and lucrative fantasy franchise just comes
to me in a dream. In this fantasy I love* Tess of the D'Urbervilles *and*
Twilight *so much that I become rich beyond my wildest dreams and make
millions of women come.*

All this discomfort—mine and Jamie's—says a lot about how *Fifty
Shades* works, what it does, who it's for. Whether or not you think E. L.
James's trilogy of novels is good for women, it's undeniably a women's
text, written by a woman for women, in imitation of another text written by a woman for women (*Fifty Shades* began its life as *Twilight*
fanfiction), as part of a long tradition of women's popular fiction that
includes mass-market bodice rippers about reformed rakes, edgier
women's erotica, and the Brontë sisters' obsession with bad boys.

I'm sure they could have cast a more enthusiastic actor to play
Christian Grey. And I'm sure there are lots of men, straight and queer,
who do find *Fifty Shades of Grey* at least kind of sexy. I mean, there are
sex scenes and boobs and men's and women's sexy butts, so there's
something for everyone! And in real life, men are as interested as
women in exploring and subverting gendered power dynamics. In
real life, BDSM is not specifically about masculine dominance and
feminine submission. But that's exactly what *Fifty Shades* is about.
As many brilliant women have pointed out, *Fifty Shades* is a terrible misrepresentation of the BDSM community; Christian Grey is
abusive, manipulative, and dysfunctional. The idea of a straight cis

man being turned on by that dynamic makes me uncomfortable. You probably don't belong here, bearded guy. You probably don't belong here, Jamie. But I'm really interested in the *Fifty Shades* novels as a space where women are trying to work something out among themselves, however clumsily. Something about desire and violence, and violence and reality, and what is okay to want, and whether there are real-world consequences to fantasy, and what our imagined relationship to power is, and what our *real* relationship to power is, and how power is expressed through sex and mobility and money and *stuff.*

On New Year's Eve 2013 I had a delightful drunken argument with another *Weird Sister* contributor about the *Fifty Shades* books. She was disgusted and saddened by the clumsy materialism in them, all the middlebrow brand names: Twinings Tea, MacBook Pro. We were both convinced Christian wore some specific middlebrow brand of body wash.

I admit to being just enough of a bohemian, just enough of a liberal elitist, to stand at an amused distance from middlebrow brand names, ham-fisted prose, "mommy porn," moms. I'm a cool mom, you guys. I'm *barely* a mom. I admit to chuckling deliriously at lines like "Double crap!" and "I don't make love. I fuck. Hard." I'm charmed by all this charming mediocrity, which is shitty and elitist of me, but I'm also charmed by the outsider position these texts take on sex, power, capitalism, wealth, America. The E. L. James who wrote *Fifty Shades* as *Twilight* fanfiction doesn't seem to know what it's like to be rich, *really* rich, and neither do I. On one level the text's pathetic fetishization of Wealth and Power is just another example of ordinary people failing to understand how power actually works, daring to dream they could actually get power, letting the rich people continue to make all the decisions and believing it will somehow work out for the best. On another level I can't help but be moved by that yearning to understand power, by the distance between these fantasies (women's fantasies, my fantasies) and the sad, boring violence of reality.

I've written elsewhere about how in the *Twilight* novels, vampirism is a strangely disappearing metaphor: it starts out as a stand-in for the destructive effect of male desire on women's bodies, but as the novels progress, Stephenie Meyer systematically removes every danger a vampire might pose to his human lover/victim. The *Twilight* vampires are literally, laughably defanged; to quote from my own essay, "The metaphor of bloodlust for sexual lust dissolves as the vehicle merges with the tenor; Edward's desire for Bella becomes . . . *merely* a boy's desire for a girl," and then, due to Edward's superhuman gentility and restraint, it's barely even that. And then in her fanfiction version, E. L. James replaced this nonmetaphor for male violence with an even more literal nonmetaphor. With, like, straight-up male violence. Holy crap, I don't know what to do with that. I don't think you do, either. Double crap!

In this fantasy he anticipates my every need. In this fantasy he can just tell which brand of tea is my favorite. In this fantasy he knows exactly which dove-gray chiffon halter dress will make me look the most exquisite. In this fantasy he knows exactly which dove-gray Italian tie will make me have the most powerful orgasm. In this fantasy I don't have to lift a finger. In this fantasy he has a lot of experience. In this fantasy it's the first time for both of us. In this fantasy he knows exactly what he's doing. In this fantasy it all just comes so naturally. In this fantasy he has a Dark Secret. In this fantasy he needs me to make him whole. In this fantasy he can hurt me. In this fantasy he will never hurt me.

I'm glad people have pointed out that Christian and Ana's relationship, like Edward and Bella's, is unhealthy. I'm glad members of the BDSM community have made it clear that real-life BDSM doesn't work the way it does in *Fifty Shades of Grey*. I'm glad people have pointed out that this stuff doesn't turn them on, that the movie is a valentine to materialism, that your love can't fix an abuser. We need to talk about this stuff. But let's also remember that *Fifty Shades of Grey* is itself another way of talking about this stuff. What if, rather than an inaccurate *representation* of BDSM, the *Fifty Shades* novels are trying to do the same work as BDSM: provide a space where people (in this case, specifically women) can safely, guiltlessly, ethically, pleasurably work through their complicated relationship to patriarchal power? In her BuzzFeed piece on the movie's "sly capitalist seduction," Anne Helen Petersen cautions us against the assumption that a film, or any text, is "a hypodermic needle that, once injected in its viewer, reproduced its values in its new host." Petersen argues that *Fifty Shades* viewers instead use the film to think through their own ideas and values: "That's how we consume media: We *digest* it."

Sure, the wild popularity of the *Fifty Shades of Grey* franchise might be a symptom of a diseased culture, in the same way that rape fantasies are surely symptoms of rape culture. If our culture were healthier, there would be fewer rape fantasies. But we understand that having a rape fantasy is fundamentally different from wanting to be raped. We understand that smart, healthy women can have rape fantasies.

The problem posed by *Fifty Shades of Grey*, maybe, comes from its flip-flopping back and forth between pure fantasy and an uncertain realism. It's uncomfortable with its own status as fantasy. It can't fully relax into pornography.

I love what Arielle Greenberg wrote about *Fifty Shades* in her essay for *Weird Sister*: "What we need in this culture are nonpathologized representations of masculinity and healthy, nonmisogynist depictions of masculine desire in action." I think that's how we make new fantasies: by imagining archetypes for desire that don't turn every text into a palimpsest with layers of real/fake/tamed/eroticized violence. I love that so many women have figured out how to do that already. I hate that we still have to ask questions like, "Do Housewives love all this submissive stuff because they feel like they don't have control over their lives? Do Career Women love all this submissive stuff because they feel like they have Too Much Control?" Oh, shut up. But I do still also kind of love that the whole world had to sit up and pay attention to thousands and thousands of words of ridiculous, dirty *Twilight* fanfiction.

In this fantasy power is always in the right place, always flowing in the right direction. In this fantasy all of this is for my own good. In this fantasy there's no conflict between my submission to a higher power and the possibility of my own free will, the possibility of free choice, individualism, my Inner Goddess, my feminism. In this fantasy I can have it all. In this fantasy that includes the kind of sex I've dreamed about having with Mr. Darcy, Mr. Rochester, Alec d'Urberville, Angel Clare, Tea Cake, Edward Cullen, Leo-as-Gatsby, President Fitzgerald Grant, the kind of sex I've read about on the internet, the kind of sex Sherlock has with Watson, Picard has with Kirk, Harry has with Draco. The sex that (straight, white, cis) men get to have with each other, sex between equals.

In this fantasy my lover has been blinded in a fire, my lover has been bitten by a rabid dog, my lover has been burned by cigarette butts, my lover has been shot by an assassin, my lover floats face down in a pool, my lover has been wounded by madwomen, by the proletariat, by drug dealers, by my mother, by his mother, my lover never had any power after all, women and poor people are the only ones with real power, I am an angel who can fix everything, I am driving the yellow Rolls-Royce, I am aiming the gun, I am lighting the fire, I am holding the riding crop, I am my lover's eyes, I am his hand, I am his voice, I am the wounded lover, I am the wounded landowner, I am the wounded imperialist, I am the wounded CEO, I am the wounded Republican president, I am the most beautiful girl in the world,

*I am a terrorist, I am what is wrong with America today. In this fantasy
if I could just suffer enough for him I could save him. In this fantasy if I
could just suffer enough for America I could save America.*

When I started writing this piece, I wondered why I feel such a
fierce need to defend all these trashy books that have been turned
into movies: *Twilight, Fifty Shades, Gone Girl.* Surely *some* of it is just
straight-up bad for women. Actual trash.

For example: In the fall of 2013 everyone was upset about Miley
Cyrus. Watching the "Wrecking Ball" video, I nursed my newborn
daughter and sang "You wre-e-ecked me." This is what I decided:

When I worry about what's going to mess up my daughter's relationship to sex and her body, I don't worry about stuff like Miley's
twerking. I worry about casual, unexamined assumptions and inoffen-
sive images and offhand comments about women's bodies and beauty
and agency and consent. That stuff will be everywhere: in the media,
at school, in our house. I do worry about what Miley's twerking could
do to my daughter's understanding of race. In her messy, over-the-top
performances of her own sexuality, Miley was really grappling with
the contradictory messages our culture sends to young women. That's
something I had to do all the time, still have to do. My daughter will
need to work through that stuff too; how can it be bad for her to see
another woman trying to figure that out? Marking it as a problem?
Miley's appropriation of Black culture as part of those performances,
though, seemed uncomplicated and thoughtless: of course that dance,
those dancers, were hers for the taking. It's going to be so easy for my
kid to accept that kind of gesture as natural, as the way things are.

Is it really eighties of me to be most afraid of the unmarked, the
unexamined, the natural?

I'm less afraid of big showy disasters like *Fifty Shades of Grey*, texts
whose confused metaphors and confusing narrative logic mark them
as urgent and contested and problematic, texts whose bulky knots of
questions and justifications and doubts and reassurances make them
feel unwieldy, unnatural. Maybe because that's how I think (have you
noticed, gentle reader?). Maybe because in not fully surrendering to
this punishing culture we love so much but still loving it so hard, these
works arouse my sympathy and my frustration and my shame. Those
big, clumsy, bulky knots can't cut off your circulation. They just make
you a little uncomfortable, show you where the ropes come together,
make you wonder if you might even be able to get out.

Talking Back to the Canon

The White Male Canon in Nineties Pop Songs

Marisa Crawford, December 2014

IN 2014 I spent two months trying to cram the entire white male literary canon into my militant gender studies–trained brain. I was studying for the GRE Subject Test in English literature, a dreaded admission requirement for most English literature PhD programs that is I guess supposed to measure your knowledge of what is widely accepted as the English literary canon. To have to learn the entire canon in a matter of months to prepare for a multiple-choice test felt like utter chaos and was made far worse by the fact that so few women writers and writers of color are included on the test. It felt like a cruel joke—having to find time between my full-time job and trying to launch this cool feminist website to make flash cards of basically all the writers that couldn't have been less relevant to my scholarly interests and life.

Then I got my test score back, and let me tell you, it was very terrible. Maybe you got your test scores back recently too, or maybe you took the test years ago and are still scarred by the experience. I decided to put my freshly sharpened knowledge of the canon to good use—by making a list of canonized works by white men and their nineties pop song equivalents. I offer this list in consolation for all of us who've spent hours uselessly cramming the white male canon into our brains and in celebration of all the other very cool stuff we all have in there. If there were GRE tests on nineties pop music or feminist history or *Saved by the Bell* trivia or contemporary women's poetry, I think I'd do really well on those, and I have a feeling that you, dear reader, would too. Unlike ETS, I think that counts for something.

From the Canon: William Butler Yeats's "The Second Coming"
Pop Song Equivalent: Nirvana's "Smells Like Teen Spirit"

"The Second Coming" begins with the extremely metal lines:

> Turning and turning in the widening gyre
> The falcon cannot hear the falconer;
> Things fall apart; the centre cannot hold;
> Mere anarchy is loosed upon the world,

My GRE study book calls this poem "probably the most quoted poem of the twentieth century," which I think means that its song equivalent held the number-one spot on every MTV video countdown throughout the 1990s. Also, remember how the liner notes for Nirvana's *Nevermind* included the lyrics "The second coming came in last and out of the closet," but those lyrics never appeared on the album? Other things "The Second Coming" and "Smells Like Teen Spirit" have in common: They both confuse me. Like, I don't really get either of them, but I take comfort in knowing that they both confuse a lot of people. They both also impart a kind of nihilistic cynicism about modern society. And they both make me wanna headbang in my bedroom until my brain falls out.

From the Canon: Walt Whitman's "Song of Myself"
Pop Song Equivalent: Jay-Z's "Izzo (H.O.V.A.)"

A fellow Brooklyn legend, Jay-Z seems like the obvious choice as Walt Whitman's pop star equivalent. But I also feel kind of like I could have chosen nearly any song containing braggadocious swagger to represent Whitman (he's so large and containing of multitudes and stuff):

> I celebrate myself, and sing myself,
> And what I assume you shall assume,
> For every atom belonging to me as good belongs to you.

Whitman's celebration of himself in "Song of Myself" also translates into a celebration of all people being connected as one, and "H.O.V.A." similarly presents itself as a kind of "song for the people." Both "Song of Myself" and "H.O.V.A." attempt—with great success—to hype up the human race. They're like, "That's the anthem, getcha damn hands up."

From the Canon: Christopher Marlowe's
"The Passionate Shepherd to His Love"
Pop Song Equivalent: Boyz II Men's "I'll Make Love to You"

Just like Boyz II Men, Marlowe's "Passionate Shepherd" wants to charm and woo his love object, but not in a creepy way—more in a chivalry-drenched proclamation of sweetness and devotion. These dudes are seriously invested in pleasing their ladies. Boyz II Men's speaker aims to set the stage for romance and make his female partner's every sexual wish come true ("Pour the wine / Light the fire / Girl your wish is my command"), and Marlowe's speaker spends the whole poem promising to handcraft for his love all the sweetest of objects ("And I will make thee beds of Roses [shout-out to Bon Jovi] / And a thousand fragrant posies, / A cap of flowers, and a kirtle / Embroidered all with leaves of myrtle"). Yes, the woman is the love object in both of these works—a trope that's tired at best—and it would be nice if the poem and the song made a leap to seeing their "love" as an equal, a person with her own ideas. But at least these male speakers are in adoration of the women in their lives, ones that sound on paper like they could make pretty good boyfriends. Maybe even Salt-N-Pepa's "Whatta Man"–worthy.

From the Canon: Thomas Gray's
"Elegy Written in a Country Churchyard"
Pop Song Equivalent: Guns N' Roses' "November Rain"

This banger and epic meditation on death can only be the eighteenth-century equivalent of "November Rain," and in particular it is the span of minutes in the "November Rain" video, beginning around 8:36, during which Axl's wife, played by Stephanie Seymour, throws her bouquet on her wedding day in one scene, and it LANDS ON HER COFFIN IN THE NEXT SCENE. From what I gathered via my GRE prep book, Gray's poem is sort of considered the elegy to end all elegies. It's on the longer side and deals in particular with the idea of death without recognition, worldly fame, or a full expression of one's talents in life, an idea which comes across quite succinctly in the irony of throwing one's bouquet only to have it land on one's coffin. Take a look:

The boast of heraldry, the pomp of power,
And all that beauty, all that wealth e'er gave,
Awaits alike the inevitable hour.
The paths of glory lead but to the grave.

Nor you, ye Proud, impute to these the fault,
If Memory o'er their tomb no trophies raise,
Where through the long-drawn aisle and fretted vault
The pealing anthem swells the note of praise.

I am a little torn calling "November Rain" the pop song equivalent of "Elegy" because the song itself doesn't speak to death for me as much as the music video does, and the music video is about Axl's Love Object/Wife dying and shows her death very much through her male lover's experience of it, night sweats and all. This reading of the "November Rain" video aligns it more with Poe's "Annabel Lee" or "Lenore" (and with Poe's whole dead-woman-as-beautiful-object thing in general). But since we're dealing with the elegy of all elegies here, its musical counterpart has to be the finest epic elegy that pop music has to offer—eight-minute-long, Slash guitar solo–laden, sweeping orchestra–backed "November Rain."

From the Canon: John Keats's "La Belle Dame sans Merci"
Pop Song Equivalent: Bell Biv DeVoe's "Poison"

Two classic ballads of the dreaded femme fatale. Wikipedia says, "With a few skillful touches, [Keats] creates a woman who is at once beautiful, erotically attractive, fascinating, and deadly." Bell Biv DeVoe says, "That girl is poison. / Never trust a big butt and a smile."

From the Canon: John Donne's "Holy Sonnet 14"
Pop Song Equivalent: Madonna's "Like a Prayer"

To be clear, you guys, this poem is fucking *hot*. "Like a Prayer" is less hot, though much more danceable, but still touches on the erotic in relation to religion (a theme that's present in much of Madge's earlier work). My Princeton Review study book calls Donne's Holy Sonnet series "marked by passionate, original, and searching thought regarding the Divinity and Christian faith." Addressing God directly, "Sonnet 14" is the one that starts, "Batter my heart, three-person'd God" and ends with these lines:

> Divorce me, untie or break that knot again,
> Take me to you, imprison me, for I,
> Except you enthrall me, never shall be free,
> Nor ever chaste, except you ravish me.

Donne's evangelical S&M-style relationship with a fire-and-brimstone God takes the form of sexual innuendo and double entendre in "Like a Prayer," with the added subversion of a female speaker (i.e., "I'm down on my knees, I wanna take you there").

From the Canon: Robert Herrick's
"To the Virgins, to Make Much of Time"
Pop Song Equivalent: Billy Joel's "Only the Good Die Young"

This poem is one of several Very Important Literature, GRE-worthy poems in the voice of dudes pressuring women to have sex with them, because time is of the essence and we're all gonna die soon and stuff. Another popular poem in this category is Andrew Marvell's "To His Coy Mistress" (lol forever at the opening lines "Had we but world enough and time, / This coyness, lady, were no crime"). These poems remind me a lot of being shamed for not being "spontaneous" enough by a guy in college who was pressuring *me* to have sex with *him*. Herrick's poem, which you probably recognize by its opening lines, "Gather ye rose-buds while ye may," doesn't urge the "virgins" to engage in sexual relations with his speaker as much as he urges them to "marry" because "this same flower that smiles today / Tomorrow will be dying." I think this poem is "Only the Good Die Young"—not exactly a nineties song, I know, but a lot closer to the 1990s than the 1600s—because of the "Virginia/Virgin" connection, as well as the song's overall message: let's have sex ASAP because waiting is for suckers (Catholic suckers, specifically), and you're not getting any younger. Of course 1970s bad-boy Billy Joel mocks Christianity and the importance of women saving themselves for marriage (making "Only the Good Die Young" more subversive and a favorite of suburban fifteen-year-old Marisa as she questioned participating in her Catholic confirmation), while seventeenth-century Herrick conflates sex with marriage. But the "live life to its fullest via doin' it with me" message is still the same.

From the Canon: William Blake's "The Lamb" and "The Tyger"
Pop Song Equivalent: Whitney Houston's "Greatest Love of All"

Houston and Blake both believed that children are our future. "The Lamb," from Blake's *Songs of Innocence*, and "The Tyger," from his *Songs of Experience*, create a weird diptych that addresses childhood, God, creation, and good and evil, all within a style that Princeton Review calls "childlike simplicity." "Greatest Love of All" is also a song of both innocence and experience (an idea that the music video really goes for with its simultaneous portrayals of Little and Grown Whitneys). To this day I have a hard time accepting that the "I believe the children are our future" bridge is really part of this song about finding love within yourself—it feels like two songs within one to me.

> Did he smile his work to see?
> Did he who made the Lamb make thee?
>
> Tyger Tyger burning bright,
> In the forests of the night:
> What immortal hand or eye,
> Dare frame thy fearful symmetry?

Blake's poems asks a lot of big questions, ones that I think Whitney has the answers to.

From the Canon: William Wordsworth
and Samuel Taylor Coleridge's *Lyrical Ballads*
Pop Song Equivalent: Blind Melon's "No Rain"

Considered the book that launched the British Romantic movement, *Lyrical Ballads* was written by Wordsworth and Coleridge together as buds, which is Bee Girl finding her people in the "No Rain" video-style cute. The Princeton Review English Literature GRE study book advises to "note Wordsworth's values of rustic people and rural settings, as well as his nonacademic language." He's all, "All I can say is that my life is pretty plain / I like watching the puddles gather rain." I also learned from my study book that Wordsworth and Coleridge were called "The Lake Poets" because they hung out in the Lake District of England and were characterized by a "muddy-boots-and-daffodils joy." I rest my case.

From the Canon: T. S. Eliot's
"The Love Song of J. Alfred Prufrock"
Pop Song Equivalent: Counting Crows' "Mr. Jones"

Eliot's dramatic monologue begins, "Let us go then, you and I, / When the evening is spread out against the sky." Both this song and this poem have an epic feeling to them of stumbling through the world aimlessly, filled with passionate desire to be more than you are, a self-important feeling of grandiosity that we can all relate to. Both seem to be making huge, important statements about the human condition and, in Eliot's case, about modernity, but both are also very much about being grumpy over wanting girls to pay attention to you. The entire poem, which meditates on the male speaker's feelings of disillusionment and isolation, is organized around the repeated refrain, "In the room the women come and go / Talking of Michelangelo." (If only they would just stay in the kitchen where they belong, talking of, like, dinner.) I'm putting it out there—I *LOVE* "Mr. Jones," and I feel the need to clarify that, 'cause I don't really love "Prufrock." Maybe it's just 'cause I encountered "Mr. Jones" when I was only eleven years old and it burned itself onto my young, impressionable soul, whereas I read "Prufrock" for the first time in a grad school class about modernist women writers, where we talked specifically about the role women play in the poem (call me if you wanna talk more about that for hours). In early drafts, the Eliot poem even included the subtitle "Prufrock Among the Women." Actually I considered the classic bitter-dude anthem "Cumbersome" by Seven Mary Three as a stand-in for "Prufrock," since it's so much about feeling emasculated by a disinterested female love object (and because the lyrics "She calls me Goliath and I wear the David mask" are so epically hilarious and kinda Eliot-esque in their dark, biblical allusion). But comparing Eliot to a nineties one-hit wonder seemed slightly too cruel.

My Feminist Literary Grudges

Olivia Campbell, November 2022

AS IF BY conjuring, the minute I sat down to work on an essay about being a writer who is also a mother, my youngest son, five, burst in and dumped his tub of RC cars on the end of my bed, demanding we play together. Had I waited until my husband was off work to write? Yes. Still, my children have always seen me as the first line of assistance. I am a professional writer whose words put food on our table. But am I the one who's expected to drop everything when one of our three kids needs something? For the most part, yes.

As a writer who longs for solitude and relief from domestic drudgery, you'd think I would relate to historical male writers who sought the same. But in fact, the opposite is true. I see how much their selfishness in the name of art cost the women and children in their orbit, how the more responsibilities they neglected, the more their wives had to pick up, the more their children suffered. I carry a torch of feminist rage for so many dreadful yet long-dead men whom we laud as genius authors because of double standards that still exist today. I mean, honestly, has anyone ever used the term "writer-father," while a quick Google search for "writer-mother" brings up pages and pages of articles? Society always seems to look for an excuse to loudly point out how women have failed at doing it all while simultaneously twisting themselves into convoluted knots searching for a way to excuse men for their every transgression. From quaint to downright evil, here is a brief accounting of my most fervently held feminist literary grudges.

1. While history remembers Henry David Thoreau as one of the world's greatest writers on nature and philosophy, I'm still salty that his mom was doing his laundry and making him sandwiches while he was purportedly roughing it in the woods writing *Walden*. In the book's introduction, Thoreau notes, "When I wrote the following pages . . . I lived alone, in the woods, a mile from any neighbor, in a

house which I had built myself . . . and earned my living by the labor of my hands only." His mom doing his chores wouldn't be such a big deal if he hadn't made such a to-do of pointing out that he was a self-sufficient, rugged survivalist. I mean, it's kind of the book's whole conceit. Unfortunately, Thoreau is far from the only Great Male Author who could only carve out the time and space to create great art by exploiting the labor of the women in his life. And his tale is actually one of the least rage-inducing.

2. Great works like *War and Peace* and *Anna Karenina* firmly ensconced Leo Tolstoy in the literary canon as one of the greats of Russian literature. But without the hard work of his wife, Sophia, a prolific diarist herself, we may never have read these stories. Sophia bore thirteen children, nine of whom survived. In addition to caring for them and managing all of the household duties, she, like many great literary wives of the time, transcribed and edited her husband's manuscripts. In the case of *War and Peace*, Sophia copied down, then rewrote the manuscript seven (!) times by hand. She also acted as his secretary and financial manager. Not even a postpartum infection that nearly killed her could keep Sophia from her duties; Leo oversaw the installation of a tray enabling her to write in bed while recovering. To repay his wife's selfless dedication, Leo regularly cheated on her.

3. Then there's Charles Dickens, who was one of the rare authors in history who got to enjoy commercial success and fame in his lifetime. He wrote sentimental novels about family values like *Oliver Twist*, *A Christmas Carol*, and *Great Expectations*. Yet in his own life he is thought to have fathered several children outside his marriage and refused to participate in raising or providing for them. While his wife, Catherine, endured twelve pregnancies (and several bouts of postpartum depression) in just fifteen years, Charles, at forty-five, became infatuated with eighteen-year-old actress Ellen Ternan. Before long, he and Ellen were an item, and Charles had banished Catherine from the family home, blaming the failure of his marriage on Catherine, whose "mental disorder" left her unfit as wife and mother.

4. Esteemed British Romantic poet Lord Byron was much more interested in the process of making babies than in dealing with the

results. Byron had two children he acknowledged and two others he is suspected of fathering (one born to his young maid and the other to his half-sister). Far from a supportive husband and father, Byron tormented his first wife, Annabella, when she was pregnant, bragging to her about his extramarital conquests. Once their daughter Ada was born, Byron left England for good to cavort around Europe and write. Byron's next child was born to eighteen-year-old Claire Clairmont. He told Claire he would raise the child if she relinquished all parental rights, which she agreed to, but before long, Byron sent the child to a convent where she died of a contagious illness at age five. Truly, how could such a man claim to know love well enough to write poetry about it?

5. Remembered as a reclusive genius, *The Catcher in the Rye* author J. D. Salinger is less known for largely ignoring his family, choosing instead to hide in the writing cabin on their property for months at a time while his wife, Claire Douglas, trekked the half-mile round trip from the house to the cabin to bring him his meals. It also bears mentioning that Douglas was just nineteen when her relationship with then-thirty-five-year-old Salinger began and that the author regularly preyed on teen girls throughout his lifetime. At age fifty-three, Salinger began a relationship with eighteen-year-old Joyce Maynard, who, after writing about her experience with J. D., was widely seen not as the victim of a predatory groomer but as a vindictive jilted lover, a celebrity seeker.

6. John Steinbeck's work earned a Nobel, a Pulitzer, and the Presidential Medal of Freedom. Among his best-received books were *Of Mice and Men* and *The Grapes of Wrath*, the latter considered a true masterpiece. In a posthumously published memoir, Steinbeck's second wife, Gwyn, claimed that being married to John was utter misery. When she experienced complications during one of her pregnancies, John snapped at her that it was *she* who was complicating *his* life by being ill during what was an incredibly productive writing time for him. I mean, the nerve of her! After their divorce, he spent a decade fighting her in court so he wouldn't have to pay child support. What's more, he sought literary revenge on her by claiming to use her as the basis for the nefarious alcoholic character in *East of Eden*. Still, the most strongly worded title pundits can muster for John today is "flawed genius."

7. What about those few times when the shoe has been on the other foot? Okay, let's go there. Let's talk about Doris Lessing. First of all, she's probably the least well-known writer I've mentioned, even though she won the Nobel Prize in Literature in 2007. A phenomenally prolific writer, Lessing published some twenty-six novels, twenty-three story collections, thirteen nonfiction titles, and several operas, poetry books, and plays. She also abandoned two of her three young children and moved thousands of miles away in order to pursue her writing career. In a 2013 article, the *New Yorker* excused bad author-fathers of the 1950s to 1970s as "a generation of (mostly male) American writers who held a romantic idea of what it meant to 'be a writer.'" The *New Yorker* goes on: "But theirs was also a notably vulnerable time in American society: a moment of utmost domestic conventionality that coincided with the waning of American patriarchy." As for Lessing, a 2019 article in the same publication describes her as "notorious" for abandoning her kids, and the entire piece revolves around her "maternal ambivalence." Show me one essay focusing on—or even mentioning—a male writer's "paternal ambivalence." Women are expected to want to have and care for children and spouses; men are not.

What of what these wives wanted for their lives? Did they have dreams before being relegated to the posts of baby factory, household manager, and unpaid copyeditor? Might they have been capable of producing great works of literature of their own given similar support from their spouses? I mourn all of the books and other creations that don't exist because so many women were not given the freedom from caregiving or other domestic duties to write, to be creative and intellectually curious, or to pursue advanced education.

But if this is my conclusion, I have to be prepared to address the opposite: Would I be okay if some books written by men no longer existed because they instead were sharing in their domestic responsibilities? Is it okay for one gender to be stifled creatively but not another?

I'd like to think no one need be denied their creative well-being in relationships where all parties participate equally and are truly valued. And at the very least, I believe everyone's work and behavior should be judged by the same criteria, regardless of their gender. *New Yorker* writers may try to convince us that being an asshole husband and absent father was just male writers' way of asserting their masculinity, but not every asshole deserves an excuse. I think father-writers should warrant just as much scrutiny as mother-writers for their participation—or lack thereof—in domestic responsibilities. And women deserve just as much grace as men when evaluating their personal versus artistic legacies.

Sister Souljah's *The Coldest Winter Ever*: A Coming-of-Age Tale and Hip-Hop Opera

Vanessa Willoughby, January 2016

WINTER SANTIAGA, the protagonist of Sister Souljah's 1999 debut novel *The Coldest Winter Ever*, is anything but a wallflower. The equally beautiful and selfish favored daughter of Brooklyn drug kingpin Ricky Santiaga, Winter is sixteen going on twenty-five and accustomed to the luxuries bought with dirty money—her biggest concerns are looking fly, getting off, and having fun. When things are good, Winter's life is a label-flashing Hype Williams video. Her father expresses his love through expensive gifts, from 14K gold and diamonds to head-to-toe Chanel and Gucci outfits. Winter admires Ricky's hustle, confusing wealth for the promise of unshakable stability, social status, and security. Unfortunately Ricky's empire implodes when jealous rivals snitch to the feds. He is arrested and shipped off to Rikers. Child Protective Services snatches up Winter's three younger sisters, and her mother is arrested for being an accessory to her husband's felonies. Without hesitation, Winter snaps into soldier mode, plotting and scheming ways to make some quick cash while remaining in hiding. She's not above using sex to get what she wants, whether that be funds, transportation, or a place to crash for the night. She says, "To be able to shit on people before they get a chance to shit on you. That's power."

Including her fiction debut, Sister Souljah's books continue to sell well year after year. Despite the staggering success, mainstream publishing has been quick to categorize her work as Urban Literature or Street Lit. The origin of the name is literal and, according to scholars such as Keenan Norris and authors such as Omar Tyree, refers to stories around the plight of urban life, ranging from Teri Woods's *True to the Game*; Stephen Crane's *Maggie: A Girl of the Streets*; Iceberg Slim's memoir, *Pimp: The Story of My Life*; and Richard Wright's *Native Son*. Yet mainstream publishing, which is typically not a reflection of diversity but racial and often gender uniformity, uses this label as a code for Black, as though all work revolving around Black characters in urban environments repeats the same stories. One look around your last standing Barnes & Noble, or even while browsing the endless genres on Amazon, shows this race-based categorization and exclusionary hierarchy of literature. Souljah's novels routinely address the trials and tribulations of Black and African American people, but this does not mean that her work cannot also embody a category not defined by Otherness. This would otherwise simply be known as Fiction.

Souljah herself isn't comfortable with the label. She confesses to *Time* in a 2015 profile, "I'm a college graduate, and if I read something like *Romeo and Juliet*, I'm reading about a gang fight, I'm reading about young love, young sex, longing. I'm reading the same themes that I'm writing in my books. So if somebody comes along and says, 'Yours is street literature'—what was Shakespeare's?" Street Lit is a label conjured by a very white, male, privileged publishing industry. Thus, it carries a different, even class-based, connotation from Fiction. Such a label does a great disservice to the novel, relegating it to Other, separating it from Literature (a.k.a. work written by white authors). Why must it solely stay in the African American Literature section of bookstores? What is it about Souljah's novel that disqualifies it from Fiction?

In a 2011 interview with *The Root*, the author says, "I'm not in sync with this street-lit genre. I think that when European authors or Euro-American authors write about urban, suburban, or rural areas, it's just called literature." Unfortunately her argument is nothing new; this critique of diversity (or the lack thereof) in mainstream publishing has been echoed by Toni Morrison and all corners of social media, namely with the #WeNeedDiverseBooks campaign. In an interview with *Urban Times*, Souljah elaborates on the marginalization of works written by Black authors. The labels of Urban Fiction and/or Street Lit, as Souljah puts it, stem from "fear and power." There is an inherent privilege in being a white author, as "making books by African American authors have a segregated place in bookstores with very little advertisement and even less copies available to the customer allows the 'mainstream authors,' white authors, to remain dominant in sales, presence, and imagery." The authors that seem to implode this glass ceiling are proof of the need for diversity in publishing. According to *T Magazine*, husband and wife writing team Ashley Antoinette and JaQuavis Coleman "have earned millions of dollars, almost exclusively from cash—for manuscript deals negotiated by independent publishing houses." Yet even if Urban Lit authors can push past the obstacle of representation, there are certain advantages denied to authors on the so-called fringe. For the Colemans, their prolific work ethic hasn't necessarily attracted traditional publishers. In fact, the article notes, "the pair had no literary agent; they sold hundreds of thousands of books without banking a penny in royalties."

Studying the *Publishers Weekly* 1999 review of *The Coldest Winter Ever*, it's easy to see why Souljah dislikes being marketed solely as "Street Literature." It implies that the genre lacks a certain finesse and elegance, even literary merit, in comparison to that which is regarded as Fiction. The review commends her for using "a raw and true voice," but then, in the same sentence, goes on to say, "Though her prose is rough and unsophisticated." The review also criticizes using African American vernacular and slang rooted in hip-hop, calling it "potentially offensive prose." Such comments are a reflection of the reviewer's inherent bias and not the structure of Souljah's narrative. Hip-hop is integral to the story, and to dismiss this obvious correlation is evident of cultural and racial ignorance. *The Coldest Winter Ever* is much more than Urban Lit; it's a literary bridge to a kaleidoscope of human behavior.

Contrary to what the *Publishers Weekly* review posits, the prose is a reflection of how speech patterns are influenced by hip-hop culture and Black slang. Why is Souljah's prose "unsophisticated" when authors such as Mark Twain and William Faulkner can write in Southern dialects and, in Faulkner's case, sometimes long, twisty, confusing streams of consciousness, only to be labeled literary geniuses? In both Faulkner's and Souljah's works, a person's voice is a window into their character, serving as the imprint of both cultural and historical influences. Souljah's novel is strictly told from the perspective of Winter, and thus the prose vividly showcases a mixture of the arrogance of youth and the entitlement of a pauper turned princess. If writing in vernacular can be considered high art when executed by white authors like Faulkner, why aren't the code-switching skills of Souljah's characters worthy of the same esteem? Just as Faulkner wrote unflinchingly brutal depictions of human relationships, Souljah does not present a sugarcoated version of victories and failures in her prose. In this world of "trust no one," love can be a shield or an Achilles heel.

Winter's voice is that of a young, mostly streetwise girl who thinks she's older and wiser than anyone in her peer group. When her friend Natalie declares, "The block is hot," Winter quickly dismisses Natalie's concerns, arguing that the compliance of the cops can be easily bought.

Winter's voice can easily switch from street slang to the familiarity of a confessional yet unapologetic narrative guide. When Winter runs into an old hookup buddy, his usage of street slang indicates the depth and the seriousness of his commitment to the hustle. Bullet boasts, "A nigga been stacking chips, I'm about to cop something lovely."

Although *Publishers Weekly* doesn't fault Winter's narcissism and materialism, other mainstream publications, such as *Booklist* and *Kirkus*, deliver backhanded compliments relating to the strength of the novel's context. The former says, "The audience to whom this book is written will find the language real and raw, yet the story could have been told with less obscenities and vulgarity." The latter assesses, "This is a tour de force of black English and underworld slang, as finely tuned to its heroine's voice as Alice Walker's *The Color Purple*. The subject matter, though, has a certain flashiness, like a black Godfather family saga, and the heroine's eventual fall develops only glancingly from her character." Why does the "flashiness" of the characters' life-styles demote its literary meatiness? Both Mario Puzo's novel and Coppola's *Godfather* clearly follow the American fairy tale of attempting to make it in the land of milk and honey. Materialism and hustling aren't viewed as immoral offshoots of debauchery but as a means to an end, a way of survival. Hip-hop and rap culture are the heartbeat of Souljah's novel, never romanticizing the lifestyle but depicting the extremes of the spectrum. It pointedly touches upon the everlasting and all-around destruction caused by HIV/AIDS, using Winter as a cautionary tale without succumbing to a puritanical treatment of sex. Winter's sexual politics channel the unapologetic bravado infused throughout Lil' Kim's 1996 debut album, *Hard Core*. Winter and the former Junior M.A.F.I.A. member challenge, and to an extent mock, the double standards imposed by patriarchal rule. Winter is fearless, and even when she can't ward off feelings of anxiety or insecurity, she clings to the tough-girl persona exhibited in the rhymes of the afore-mentioned MCs.

In a 1997 interview for *Paper* magazine with renowned feminist, scholar, activist, and author bell hooks, Lil' Kim shares her thoughts about sex and sexuality. hooks mentions that critics, especially right-wing advocates, have said that the rapper talks too much about sex and that her music is anything but liberating for women. Kim says, "I don't think that either. You wanna know why? Because we have people like Too Short, Luke Skyywalker [of 2 Live Crew], Biggie, Elvis Pres-ley, Prince, who are very, very, very sexual, and they don't get trashed because they like to do it. But all of a sudden, we have a female who happens to be a rapper, like me, and my doin' it is wrong." There's something undeniably refreshing about Winter's cutthroat philosophies and her refusal to feel shamed for not being, as Drake would say, "a good girl." Being "likable" is irrelevant. The narrative is compelling and exciting precisely because Winter is no damsel in distress; she's a female Michael Corleone. On the other hand, Winter is only sixteen and considerably sheltered from the more hardcore aspects of her father's intricate drug empire, thus making her sexual freedom more of a fall from grace than a feminist manifesto. Later on in the interview, Kim elaborates on how money embodies almost the same transgressive properties as sex. She explains, "I feel money is power in certain senses. A lot of women out there are just givin' it away. And then there are the women that're selling their bodies. But they chose to do that. But this is how they make their money. And I don't see anything wrong with that." Winter is the daughter of hip-hop, heavily influenced by both her street-smart father and the boss-bitch mentality of the few women rappers in the game. In "My Life," a track off Foxy Brown's sophomore solo album *Chyna Doll*, she takes a moment to show equal parts blunt vulnerability, regret, and unapologetic bravado. Like Sister Souljah's protagonist, Brown discusses the double-edged sword of materialism and the pursuit of financial prosperity, name-dropping designer labels as markers of status, class, and exclusivity. The high-price life is regarded as an escape hatch, utilized to gain autonomy.

The labels of Urban and African American Fiction fail to tell us anything relevant or tangible about these novels. Fiction can deal with a variety of topics, people, places, and time periods. When publishers use the aforementioned genres, it prescribes a one-size-fits-all set of expectations onto a novel that just so happens to feature Black characters. A coming-of-age novel doesn't have to resemble the lily-white versions of New York as seen in *The Catcher in the Rye* or the Manic Pixie Dream Girl wonderlands of a John Green novel or the coke-snorting, pretentious exclusiveness of Bret Easton Ellis's *Less than Zero*. By placing Winter Santiaga as the protagonist, *The Coldest Winter Ever* demands that readers not think exclusively in absolutes. Winter's narrative is very much a coming-of-age story without overt preaching. There is a lesson to be learned, but the way in which Winter reaches such a conclusion is not cut and dry. If anything, the events of the book portray an inverted fairy tale; Winter's fall from royalty not only enrages her but makes her anxious to regain her title. She thinks it's her God-given right to reclaim what's destined. Winter's narrative may not be universal, but its grittiness matches the hip-hop soundtrack threaded in the prose. For mainstream publishing, *The Coldest Winter Ever* may not be a "traditional" coming-of-age novel, but this kind of praise seems irrelevant when "traditional" typically means white, heterosexual, and male.

Writing the Wound: A Letter to Hélène Cixous

Zoe Tuck, July 2022

DEAR HÉLÈNE,

I want to pull up a chair for you to sit in. The table is set. Outside the window, pigeons perch on ledges or wheel through the sky. The meat of the moment steaming on the plates. Does that image have an implicit violence to it? I love what you write in light of one of Kafka's letters: "I too believe we should only read those books that 'wound' us and 'stab' us, 'wake us up with a blow on the head' or strike us like terrible events."[1] In deference to the taste we share, I'm serving you a letter that has my wound in it.

I imagine us sitting at a scaled-down version of Judy Chicago's *The Dinner Party*. Have you ever seen it? It's a permanent feature of the Brooklyn Museum—a big triangular table with place settings for famous women from history, each setting featuring a vulvic plate. It's what used to be called an imbalanced table. I've heard that at dinner parties, people were traditionally seated *man woman man woman*, and here we are all women (you, me, and Chicago, followed by a rotating cast of interlocutors).

As soon as Chicago made it, *The Dinner Party* signified incompletion. None of the ceramic vulvas look like mine, nor can the triangular table—one degree more symbolic, but still genitally allusive—seat all women. Why do I imagine our conversation happening in a place where my presence throws off the balance? The writer's wound is her way in. When I was younger my wound was feeling like I could never truly be a woman. Art like this compelled me because it constructs femininity in the realm of the mythopoeic, which is a realm I was initiated into early and have dwelt in since. For this reason, it was also excruciating. I grew around the gap I perceived between what I was and what I ought to be. Discovering that it wasn't irremediable made it less excruciating over time, but the gap is always within reach.

IN 2021, I decided to teach a class called Écriture Trans-Féminine. The title is a nod to your 1975 essay "The Laugh of the Medusa,"[2] a call-to-arms for women to write a new literature into being—which you call "écriture féminine," or "women's writing"—by writing against the prohibition of women writing from their full personhood. In my case, I was quoting Juliet Jacques quoting you in her 2018 essay "Écriture trans-féminine?"[3] I first came to the notion of women's writing through a palimpsest of secondhand opinions. I had a vague sense that it was not for me, did not belong to me. A misconception suggesting that if perhaps there was an "essence" to women's writing, then perhaps there was an "essence" to women.

From my assumptions above, it followed that "The Laugh of the Medusa" would be an essentialist text. Delving in, I found what Jacques describes as "a strong focus on the cisgender (nontrans) female body: it advocated the discussion of menstruation, lactation, pregnancy and clitoral pleasure." But I also found an "intoxicating blend of poetic prose, postmodern theory, and feminist activism . . . [which] called for women to engage with their designated 'otherness' in the established patriarchal order." It still carried a charge and was porous in a way that left room for women like Jacques and me to think and write into the countertradition you opened up.

In planning for the class, I wanted to find works that seemed to have been written in response to Jacques who, following you, advocates for "no longer excluding the reality of sex and sexuality from the picture; incorporating it into an expanded *écriture trans*." Will Jacques's conjecture—that writing about sexuality as trans people "may help us to overcome any fear of transphobic detractors, and take the creativity unleashed by Cixous, [Sandy] Stone and others into unprecedented places"—bear out?

Whether it does or not, there is a spate of recent work that treats sex and sexuality from a trans perspective. The older I get, the more comfortable I feel delving into the erotic in my work. With my class, I hoped to discover if there were other commonalities in the field of contemporary trans women's writing. As a practitioner I can only speak for myself, and I wanted to know how I, my friends, and my favorite authors fit within this field.

Although they are familiar tropes, the girl that I never was isn't done with the sad trans, the monster, and the witch yet, and I'm accountable to her. Not only that, I wanted to understand where we were and how we had gotten here. For the class, I had in mind a series of general modes or categories: precursors and how we claim historical figures as trans avant la lettre—before the term "trans" existed, trans mythmaking, trans spirituality, trans political economy, and writing trans childhood. You'll understand that these categories are blurry and comingle.

TO WRITE THE name "Hélène Cixous," I must also write the name "Clarice Lispector," the Brazilian writer whose work so frequently inspires your own. All the things you were calling out for in "The Laugh of the Medusa" Lispector's writing not only embodies but expands, such that in your career you proceed with her textual presence at your side, conversing in a kind of transtemporal telepathy. You write about her book *The Passion According to G.H.*, whose protagonist crushes a cockroach, provoking a spiritual crisis. About G.H.'s "He-Bible," you clarify that this patriarchal force positions itself against what it finds "unclean and abominable," which you associate with women, writing, and some men—"those who belong to the birds and their kind."

"Some men": Jean Genet is a member of this company, as are Franz Kafka, Paul Celan, Edgar Allan Poe. Extend this to, say, trans women too. There's something in the writers you assemble around yourself that interests you more than binary gender, and it is in part through this gap that I've come to feel at home in your work. You've populated your writing not just with characters in your drama and fiction but with fellow travelers in whose company you remain other but not alone.

After all, as early as "The Laugh of the Medusa," you are troubling one side of that binary by writing into the rich heterogeneity of female sexuality. It's not simply that gender seems not to be so tightly genitally delimited in your work, but it helps me get through the door. And I have felt myself to be, quite transnormatively as I've learned, an abomination, a monster, and a witch. Being abominable and monstrous means that I write from an excluded place. Taking my power from that and refusing shame make me a witch. You make a place for those whose writing is powered by their exclusion. The exile's shared lot becomes the shared dream of the reader. Reading you, I feel invited in.

MAYBE THIS IS also what I wanted to do with my class: to populate my reading and writing life with fellow travelers, both on the roster and on the syllabus. And so in my class we read from John Wieners from *Troubling the Line: Trans and Genderqueer Poetry and Poetics*, as

well as editor Trace Peterson's rationale for Wieners's inclusion from
her introduction; some of kari edwards's *Bharat jiva*, as well as writ-
ing about edwards from *No Gender: Reflections on the Life & Work of
kari edwards*; some of Never Angeline Nørth's *Sea-Witch*, Kai Cheng
Thom's *Fierce Femmes and Notorious Liars*, Jackie Ess's *Darryl*, Torrey
Peters's *Detransition, Baby*, Joy Ladin's *The Soul of the Stranger*, and
Siobhan M. Kelly's essay "Multiplicity and Contradiction: A Literature
Review of Trans* Studies in Religion"; *Transgender Marxism*, edited
by Jules Joanne Gleeson and Elle O'Rourke, specifically Nat Raha's "A
Queer Marxist Transfeminism: Queer and Trans Social Reproduction,"
Farah Thompson's "The Bridge Between Gender and Organising," and
"Cosmos Against Nature in the Class Struggle of Proletarian Trans
Women" by Anja Heisler Weiser Flower.

The aesthetic sensibilities of the participants in Écriture Trans-
Féminine were as varied as the list. Any illusions I had about a shared
grammar of trans lit was punctured by the experience, leading me back
to your "The Laugh of the Medusa," in which you refute the idea that
you can talk about *the* female experience.

We ended on Jules Gill-Peterson's *Histories of the Transgender Child*.
I hadn't read it before the class, so I didn't know what kind of book
it would be. Gill-Peterson demolishes the book I had imagined in a
swift parenthetical: "(and not, say, a retrospective desire for a trans
childhood that I or anyone else might have had)."[4] What we found in
Gill-Peterson's book was urgent, necessary, but left me wanting something else too.

For Jacques, as for you, Cixous, honest writing about sexuality is a
taboo topic, and both authors see immense liberatory power in breaking the taboo. I also read it as standing in for other areas where speech
has been constrained, like trans childhood. What could communicating retrospective desires for trans childhood open up? Finding out
necessitates going through a portal into the kind of space you describe
in *Philippines*, a "twilight zone" where playful liminality is the order
of the day and where not just gender but almost everything might be
mutable.[5]

I wanted to know, yes, what the fate of trans children has been,
what it could be, what it ought to be (and how to make it so), but I
also wanted to know where my trans childhood had been. I wanted to
remember what my childhood had been and to remember it otherwise:
literally re-membering it, in the sense of reclaiming its vast, spectral
unlived areas. How? Your book *Philippines* turns on the premise that

the beloved childhood book (Proust's, Freud's, your own, mine) now, from a great remove, can be a portal back into that time.

From the beginning of *Philippines*, you rhyme rêve (dream) with revenon (return), describing your "melancholy enthusiasm," a phrase that succinctly characterizes the nostalgic's affect. Svetlana Boym describes nostalgia as having restorative and reflective dimensions.[6] And I think that reflections on girlhood, from those of us who didn't, or didn't exactly, have one, are significant both in and of themselves— no two exactly alike—but also as waypoints one must return to and dream through to proceed, in the process converting an active wound into a site of "melancholy enthusiasm" and finally a spur to action.

What kind of action? The world can't be transformed without action in the symbolic realm. I learned it from you. And that's why I'm

Gratefully yours,
Zoe

Emily Dickinson: Subversive Kin

Christina Olivares, October 2022

THESE WERE THE things I knew about Emily Dickinson from school: She was a woman, fragile, who wore a white dress and rarely left the house. She wrote tons of poems, most of which were not published during her lifetime. She was a genius. Each of her poems encodes meaning, and each meaning can be decoded with study. She preferred asceticism to her few (ardent) suitors. Her reclusiveness and fragility disinclined her to marriage and motherhood, but actually in retrospect maybe it was her genius that disinclined her to marriage and motherhood. She's white, but we don't talk about it.

This Emily's ways are eccentricities caused by or resulting from her writerly habit. Her ways are involuntary. This Emily's strangeness does not exceed the limits of permissibility conferred by her genius. She's strange, but she's not other. This Emily's exceptional fragility compensates for that strangeness, keeps her a lady and not a freak.

When I was eight or so, I went to the Emily Dickinson Museum, which is composed of Emily's father's and brother's restored houses. She lived in her father's. Bored by the tour but at once enraptured by late sunlight spilling over the aged wood floors as it concluded, I had an epiphany. *If I'm perfect, when I'm dead, people will publish my poems in dozens of languages and tour my home and I can haunt them all.* But even as I daydreamed about lounging in her sun, I didn't recognize Emily as kin. I conjure another Emily now, waving her flour pin above me as I visited her home as a child, saying, *Get up, it's almost 1990, you don't need little sad-ass poems. Go out and wear pants! Go out and get gay married to your mutual crushes!*

In 2017, the poet Yesenia Montilla, for a writing conference panel, invited three women of color poets—Mariahadessa Ekere Tallie, Elisabet Velasquez, and me—to explore what Emily Dickinson meant to us. Yesenia titled our panel "Clap Back." Her love for Dickinson's work, and for us—our different ways, knowings, and imaginations—grounded our collaboration and challenged me past the resistance I once had to Emily's mythic extremes.

In the time since our panel, which prompted this writing's first iteration and its publication here, a revised Emily has appeared onscreen. In the movie *Wild Nights with Emily* and the TV show *Dickinson*, Emily 2.0, still unselfconsciously white, is agentic and uninhibited, funny, and unapologetically queer. The reimagining of Emily offers an American past in which (white) queer love not only existed but, even in secret, was reciprocal, healthy and healing, sustained and joyful.

I revisited Emily's home for the second time in my life just before our 2017 panel discussion and before the show and movie. I arrived late, wandered through the gardens, then through all the rooms, her bedroom last. The setting sun wiped dusky, saturated light all over the lace curtains, over her bed, over her famous little writing desk, over me.

During that visit, I learned about several possibilities. First, that Emily's penchant for white house dresses could be a matter of practicality: she spent time in her garden and she got dirty, and white dresses can be easily bleached. I learned that she preferred her niblings call her Uncle when they played, probably because they tended to be too careful, less rowdy, when they called her Aunt. I learned she may have had a thing with, or maybe just for, her brother's wife.

Each fragment is of a life wholly lived, pointing to feelings, memories, and logics that are hard to fully know even in ourselves when we are alive. It is impossible to create a coherent and narratable Emily, because even living people are not coherent or narratable. Emily 2.0 is relatable: stealing joyful kisses upstairs at a party, writing feverish letters to a beloved, wandering disheveled in the woods as poems appear out of thin air. She is, of course, as unreal as my original Emily, the haunting, haunted one whom I imagined at eight years old to be as moved as I was by the sunlight making its way through her house. My then-imagined Emily served me: she taught me, I understood later in my life, to accept my pace—very slow—and to accept daydreaming as a crucial doorway to any significant insight writing might reveal. It was there in the child-me/child-Emily I imagined the first visit, lying on her belly gazing off while wor(l)ds fit and refit themselves inside of her.

Emily often wrote alternate word options, known as variants, into her poems—words above or below certain words, multiple beginnings, middles, and endings. She often built and refigured poems without choosing a single version as definitively better than the rest. While it might be clear from the physical document of the poem which lines were the first lines, it is not usually clear which were her preferred. Perhaps there was no preferred.

Emily's manner of writing was, perhaps, subversive in its rejection of singularity. But for much too long, Emily's multiplying poems were published as singular poems, variations excised. Her editors chose words, phrases, and ordering for her, typesetting linear, unbranched versions of her poems that are the versions we are familiar with now. The recent digitization of her surviving manuscripts into a freely accessible online archive makes clear she really did like to dwell in possibility. Most revelatory, her poems-on-poems are complete even as they eschew completion.

Imagine knowing Emily made all these poems at once. What, given her fame now, might that have done to poetry and to writing and publishing? What is a literary landscape, the publishing-and-prize complex, that understands flocks of variants as standard practice for any poem, should the poet choose to make many instead of one? I imagine it complicates things a bit, and I imagine it complicates those things—particularly how we construct our making and our being—in productive and surprising ways.

In the poems composing the middle of my book *Future Botanic*, I write about whiteness's relation to me: what it destroys, what it denies, how it attempts to claim or reject, its embeddedness, familiarity, and incompatibilities. Those poems are not linear and aren't supposed to be without contradiction. Whiteness converges and empowers chaotically, even as its ubiquity and narrativizing present as singularly clean and normal. I interpreted Yesenia's call to us as an invitation to encounter Emily without putting ourselves, our preoccupations, or our realities away. To occupy ourselves fully at the point of contact in order to see what new might happen. I don't know what sense Emily made of race, and I am not invested in whether she was good or bad as a white person. I encounter her in myth, and I do not know her. What I see is what I recognize in myself.

The Honesty of Jean Rhys

Kristin Sanders, September 2016

I RECENTLY HAD a conversation with a man about Bukowski. Had I read much Bukowski? I said I've avoided a lot of the bro-writers: Bukowski, Burroughs, Miller, Kerouac (though I've come to love Miller and Kerouac). He said, Yeah, those guys are great writers, but, you know, they're not really great toward women.

It's not surprising that we have a whole genre of literature by men who disrespect, objectify, reduce, and silence women. A more interesting question is, Who are the women—especially the early women writers—of whom we might say the same? They aren't *really great* toward men, you know, but they're still worth reading.

I posed this question to a brilliant poet friend, who responded that while male writers are often being *sexist* when they write about women, women are often being *honest*. So the comparison doesn't really work, she said, laughing. She then made some contemporary suggestions: Dodie Bellamy. Kathy Acker. Myriam Gurba. Rebecca Solnit.

But what about going further back into the archives?

I've been on a Jean Rhys kick lately. I blame it on Kate Zambreno's *Heroines* but also on a writer girlfriend who, when I recently went through a breakup while traveling in a foreign country, emailed to suggest I *imagine myself in a Jean Rhys novel.*

There's something very contemporary about Jean Rhys's novels. Through fictional female protagonists (thinly veiling her own life experiences), she provides an unflinching, searing view of sex and relationships in the 1930s. The men are pompous jerks. The female protagonists are struggling, financially and emotionally, often dependent on men for money; they are women caught in the negative cycle of beauty standards—afraid of aging, afraid of being unattractive, vulnerable to the abuses of men.

Despite publishing *After Leaving Mr. Mackenzie* in 1931 and *Good Morning, Midnight* in 1938, Rhys's observations are so timeless and astute that they could easily be describing our society's obsession with presenting ourselves (and our personal "brands") on the internet, our social media following, and the self-objectification and consumerism that women are especially vulnerable to as we try to assert agency through various means. For example, in *After Leaving Mr. Macken-zie*, the infamous Mr. Mackenzie, who has just dumped protagonist Julia Martin, wonders if his travels in Spain and the south of France were worth it, as they didn't solve his problems or fix his misanthropy after all—yet this might as well be Rhys musing on every 2016 dude's dating app, with its bevy of seemingly obligatory travel photos.[1] Rhys's protagonist in *Good Morning, Midnight*, Sasha Jensen, observes of her fellow humans that everything they do, everything they believe, is a cliché—and who, scrolling through their social media feed or poten-tial matches on a dating app, hasn't wondered the same?[2]

Later in *Good Morning, Midnight*, Sasha reflects on how hard she tries to "succeed" as a woman, which includes the exact number of hours she takes to get ready in the morning (one and a half), the number of hours she takes to buy a hat (three), and how, weighed down by society's expectations, she is only triumphant in her performance of femininity when she manages to look like all the other women.[3]

Long before the Gurlesque, Rhys was writing about makeup, shop-ping, and femininity. Her observations on being an aging woman and the beauty and fashion industries are wry while simultaneously celebrating the ceremonial power and possibilities for connection with other women that these subjects offer. Rhys's protagonists, ever exhausted and distraught, apply makeup religiously, mechanically, and the process is likened to a ritual meant to defeat time, defeat age, and gain power over the men who have hurt them.[4] Afraid of growing old and of being single, Sasha Jensen describes shopping as a neces-sary and transformational act.[5] At the hat shop where she is the only customer and the shop girl helps her pick out the trendiest hat, despite Sasha fearing she looks ridiculous in it, the intimate moment is an "extraordinary ritual."[6]

Sitting at a hair salon while her hair is dyed blond, Sasha reads in a women's magazine a litany of ways to become thin, find a husband, and reshape her breasts, amid of chorus of reminders that life is diffi-cult and nothing is easy—for women, that is.[7]

The only disappointing thing in *Good Morning, Midnight* and *After Leaving Mr. Mackenzie* is that Rhys's protagonists aren't writers like Rhys herself. Still, these characters are clearly sharp women, obser-vant of society and critical of the particular social pressures facing intelligent, driven women. In *Good Morning, Midnight*, for example, Sasha Jensen has a conversation with a young man she's befriended. He calls her a "cérébrale," and they begin to debate the term's definition with a lively back-and-forth, each expanding on the other's definition: a woman who doesn't need or like men, a woman who is an independent thinker, a woman who neither needs nor likes anyone besides herself.[8] In other words, a woman who risks the societal repercussions of being seen as selfish. Sasha Jensen ends the conversation with a curt observation about how society sees this type of intellectual and independent woman as, in fact, a "monster,"[9] which feels perhaps as true today as it must have felt in 1938.

And yet despite these moments when Rhys seems to champion feminism, her power as a writer lies in her egalitarian perspective. Men, women, herself, all of humanity: no one escapes her cutting gaze. Characterizing humans as vicious "hyenas,"[10] Rhys's pessimistic worldview practically prophesied the phenomenon of online social shaming.

As honest as they are about the social pressures women faced at the time, Rhys's novels sidestep sexual content. Rhys dances around a sexual assault in *Good Morning, Midnight* with language that suggests he does, he doesn't, she fights him off? (It reminds me of the sexual assault scene in Plath's *The Bell Jar*, when Esther is suspiciously successful at fighting off her rapist by punching him in the nose.) Trapped in an era when sexuality could only be veiled (with exceptions, of course, like the writing of Anaïs Nin and Violette Leduc), Rhys can only *evoke* the dark sexuality of a woman both independent and reliant upon men, especially at the end of *Good Morning, Midnight*, in two uncomfortable encounters with a young "gigolo" and her hotel neighbor, neither of whom the protagonist seems to actually want.

In her 2016 piece for the *Paris Review*, Lauren Elkin, author of *Flâneuse: Women Walk the City in Paris, New York, Tokyo, Venice, and London*, defines the flâneuse (a female flâneur) as "someone who gets to know the city by wandering its streets, investigating its dark corners." "Rather than wandering aimlessly," writes Elkin, "the most salient characteristic of the *flâneuse* is that she goes where she's not supposed to."

Rhys writes the flâneuse, who is, indeed, a woman who "goes where she's not supposed to"—into the mind of the single, aging woman—with her self-criticism and her keen eye trained on men. Rhys's radical honesty set the path for the Ackers and Bellamys and Zambrenos of today.

Calling On Our Feminist Elders

The Many Names of Barbara Grier: On Naiad Press, Lesbian Publishing, and Pseudonyms

Megan Milks, November 2022

I FIRST LEARNED of writer, editor, and publisher Barbara Grier when I looked up one of her pseudonyms. In my queer studies class, I assigned a pre-Stonewall primary source, "Living Propaganda" by Marilyn Barrow, included in our textbook. Published in 1963 in *The Ladder*, the monthly magazine put out by the first US-based lesbian rights group, Daughters of Bilitis, the piece makes the case for coming out in the workplace and beyond. "We are all living propaganda," Barrow writes. "Everyone we meet who knows we are gay, and likes and respects us, is a potential weapon for our struggle."

I assigned Barrow's column as an example of homophile-era arguments that viewed respectability as the path to queer acceptance. But I'd never heard of this writer, and the textbook offered little context. An online search of "Marilyn Barrow" got me nowhere. I added "lesbian," which brought me to the Wikipedia page for Barbara Grier. Turns out Marilyn Barrow was one of at least nine of Grier's pseudonyms used in *The Ladder*.

Nine pseudonyms! I was intrigued.

I'd been in my own process around names for some years. I'd gone through M., M. Henry, Maybe, Maybe Henry, Mayes, then reverted—or recommitted—to Megan. Though it's connected to trans identity for me now, this problem of self-naming is not new. As a softball player in middle school, I struggled to come up with a decent nickname to plaster onto the back of my jersey. As a radio DJ in college, I failed to generate a flashy on-air persona. A friend who was also DJing avoided names altogether. "Hi everyone," she would say. "It's . . . me." I stewed, wishing I had thought of that.

I know. People do it all the time: change their names or invent new ones for specific spheres—e.g., publishing, radio, sex work, dating profiles, sports. Other people's naming skills fill me with awe and respect. So I was impressed by this "Barbara Grier" who had made up a whole crew of alter egos. Who was she, and why did she need all these names?

BARBARA GLYCINE GRIER was born in Cincinnati, Ohio, in 1933. According to Joanne Passet's *Indomitable: The Life of Barbara Grier*, when she was thirteen and living in Detroit, Grier developed feelings for a close friend named Barbara Shier. Understanding the unconventional nature of such feelings, the two Barbaras went to the library and requested books about homosexuals. Grier came home and came out to her progressive mother, who took the news in stride.

It's fitting that Grier's coming-out story involved books. Whether attained through libraries, used booksellers, or her mother—who gave her a copy of *The Well of Loneliness* when she was a teenager—books were vital resources for Grier, especially those with lesbian content. By her early adulthood, she was already a dedicated collector of lesbian literature and a grassroots historian of lesbian life; later, she became a critic, then a publisher, of lesbian books.

Grier recognized the importance of literature for women who did not have access to queer culture, history, and community. "Every sixteen-year-old in the world," Grier said in a 1987 interview, "when she comes out, should be able to walk into a store and find a book saying yes, you're a lesbian, and you're wonderful!"[1] It was her life mission to bring lesbian books to lesbians who needed them, and she did this through her contributions to *The Ladder*, by compiling three editions of her book-length bibliographical index, *The Lesbian in Literature*, and by publishing hundreds of books as cofounder of Naiad Press.

Established in 1956, *The Ladder*'s first issues were edited by Phyllis Lyon, who founded the Daughters of Bilitis (DOB) with her partner Del Martin in 1955. In Grier's first letter to *The Ladder*, signed as "G.D." and published in Readers Respond in 1957, she shared her enthusiasm for the magazine: "I have now received and thoroughly read (and reread) five issues of THE LADDER, and I feel I must write and congratulate you on your magnificent work for us all."[2] She was especially thrilled by the "Lesbiana" column, a compilation of short, reader-submitted reviews of lesbian-related books, and enclosed a few of her own reviews. Within a few years she was writing—as "Gene Damon"—the majority of the Lesbiana content herself and took over the column in 1966. While Lesbiana was her mainstay, she also, writing as Damon and under other pseudonyms, contributed an abundance of other content to *The Ladder*, including in-depth book reviews, profiles of writers and historical figures, commentaries, short stories, and letters. She became editor of *The Ladder* in 1968.

Grier's comprehensive knowledge of lesbian-related literature made her the perfect person to produce a comprehensive bibliography of books featuring lesbian content—and that she did. Grier compiled the first edition of *The Lesbian in Literature* in 1967 and updated it twice over the next fourteen years. The bibliography was circulated avidly among lesbians, and its rating system became known as "Grier Ratings." According to this system, a book rated "A" contained "major Lesbian characters and/or action." A book ranked "B" contained "minor Lesbian characters and/or action." A "C" ranking indicated "latent, repressed Lesbianism or characters who can be so interpreted." And "T" meant trash—that is, of "essentially poor" quality, regardless of the degree or type of lesbian representation. A tiered asterisk system conveyed the quality or significance of the book to lesbian literature.

After *The Ladder* folded in 1972, Grier infamously "stole" the DOB's list of names and addresses to build her next venture, Naiad Press, the following year. A joint publishing project involving Grier, her partner Donna McBride, the novelist Anyda Marchant (whose pen name was Sarah Aldridge), and Marchant's partner, Muriel Crawford, Naiad was part of the vibrant Women in Print (WIP) movement—the feminist print culture that emerged during the 1970s, drawing on the energy and activism of the women's liberation, civil rights, and gay liberation movements. Part of the larger rise of independent media, the WIP movement aimed not simply to publish women's and feminist literature but also to create an alternative, women-led network of publishers, editors, writers, readers, and bookstores circulating outside of patriarchal capitalism. Feminist periodicals and women's presses—including Firebrand Books, Diana Press, the Women's Press Collective, Aunt Lute Books, Kitchen Table: Women of Color Press, and the Feminist Press—proliferated.

Focusing exclusively on lesbian literature, Naiad was unique in its egalitarianism when it came to quality and aesthetics. At Naiad, pulpy romances were published alongside reprints of classic works by authors including Patricia Highsmith and Gertrude Stein. Here, it seems, Grier's commitment to "living propaganda" and respectability politics receded in favor of her relentless enthusiasm and support of all things lesbian. Whereas other presses, such as Daughters, Inc., saw themselves as enacting a radical feminist politics through their aesthetic choices,

Naiad's primary political impulse was to support a diverse lesbian literary culture. In fact, Grier's decidedly apolitical aesthetic taste— and her desire to turn a profit—were off-trend in the WIP movement at large, which led to some division and controversy. Grier's decision to reprint, without its contributors' consent—for example—excerpts from its best-selling anthology *Lesbian Nuns: Breaking Silence* in a soft-core men's magazine incited a storm of criticism, mostly directed at Grier, who was accused of being capitalistic and exploitative. But she had never made her goals of market success a secret, and for a small press, Naiad was unusually successful and enduring. When it closed in 2003, transferring many of its authors' contracts to Bella Books, it was the oldest and largest publisher of lesbian literature in the world.

IT WASN'T UNCOMMON for queer writers to use pen names, as Grier did, during the era of *The Ladder*. In fact, before the 1969 Stonewall Uprising and the birth of the queer liberation movement, queer discourse was built on pseudonyms. It simply was not safe to be a known gay or lesbian during a time when anyone—even straight people—could be fired from a job if suspected of engaging in homosexual acts. In the 1950s and 1960s, lesbian and gay writers and publishers were held in check by the US Postal Service's reactivation of the Comstock Act, which prohibited the circulation of obscene materials through the post office. This act permitted the post office's federal law enforcement unit to infiltrate the mailing lists of publications thought to be associated with homosexuality, using them to search the homes of subscribers for more materials that could be considered obscene. Post office feds then paid "educational visits" to subscribers' employers, informing them of what kind of mail their employees were receiving.

Within this fraught context, many lesbian and gay writers took cover under pen names. Patricia Highsmith published *The Price of Salt* (now *Carol*) as Claire Morgan in 1952. As Isabel Miller, Alma Routsong published *A Place for Us* (now *Patience and Sarah*) in 1969. Eric Garber, who came of age in the 1950s, continues to publish as Andrew Holleran.

Then there was Grier, who took a more Pessoan approach. Like many of her peers, Grier came up with her primary pseudonym, "Gene Damon," as a form of protection. Her first partner, Helen Bennett, had expressed nervousness about all the "weird stuff" that Grier was ordering in her quest to collect as much gay and lesbian content as she could. To allay her partner's fears and protect them both from police entrapment, Grier invented this fake name and sent mail to a general delivery address. (The alias and alternate address later allowed her to keep correspondences a secret from Bennett and develop a few romantic pen pals through her *Ladder* work as Gene Damon.)

But she didn't stop there, generating at least eight other noms de plume, including Barrow, for her contributions to *The Ladder*. The others were: Vern Niven (sometimes printed as Vern Nixon), Lenox Strang (sometimes printed as Lennox Strong), Irene Fiske, Dorothy Lyle, Malvina Creet, Gladys Casey, Theodora, maybe more. In the pages of the gay magazines *ONE* and the *Mattachine Review*, she used the masculine-sounding names Gene Damon and Larry Marvin.

Why did she need so many names? Grier's terrific enthusiasm for *The Ladder* compelled her to unreservedly flood its editors with letters, reviews, and essays. "I shall undoubtedly bombard you," she wrote to Martin in 1957, "with or without reply." As Gene Damon, Grier eventually took over the Lesbiana column, covering hundreds of books over a few decades. Damon's reviews were pithy and forthright, warmly generous when they weren't witheringly blunt. Here's a sample of the latter, about a novel called *Tomboy* by Arline McNamee Hammond (Comet Press, 1960): "Reviewed primarily for its inherent idiocy. A vanity published novel about a girl who apparently believes her 'ductless glands' are turning her into a Lesbian. It has to be read to be believed."[3]

Grier also wrote longer reviews, profiles of historical figures, letters, and political and cultural commentary like "Living Propaganda." As she contributed more and more writing, she came to understand it was not in her beloved magazine's best interests to be perceived as univocal. Another person might have responded to this realization by simply taking up less space. Grier continued her bombardment—now deploying an array of different names. And so her aliases proliferated, adopted as a way to hide from *Ladder* readers just how many articles she had written—er, how many Gene Damon had written. While Grier did not appear in every issue, she often contributed a third or more of the content, sometimes manufacturing her own point-crosspoint debates within its pages. The goal was to present a pluralistic and vibrant magazine—more, perhaps, than *The Ladder* actually was.

BY THE TIME she cofounded Naiad Press, Grier had peeled away her Gene Damon persona—a response to a changing context. The younger feminists of the 1970s had a different attitude toward pen names—they felt it was a form of hiding and preferred to emphasize authenticity. With the birth of Naiad, she stepped into the world as Barbara Grier.

Still, Grier stacked Literary Market Place's 1981 entry on Naiad's debut with a number of made-up staff names—she wanted to suggest that the press had a more sizable staff than it did.

IN THE FIRST half of the twentieth century, "Barbara" was among the most popular given names in the English-speaking world. It was a common name among lesbians of the 1970s and 1980s, who included Barbara Grier, lesbian film pioneer Barbara Hammer, *The Ladder* editor Barbara Gittings, and Combahee River Collective member and Kitchen Table: Women of Color Press publisher Barbara Smith.

In 2022 I watch the recording of an online event celebrating lesbian publishing, part of a digital exhibition devoted to Naiad Press. Barbara Smith is one of the participants. "I almost didn't do this panel because it focused on Naiad," she shares. "I have had such haunting experiences dealing with people—I don't have to say the names. It was very painful."[4] She goes on to describe the racism she and other women of color publishers experienced within the Women in Print movement. I'm not surprised to hear these charges: despite the arrival of groundbreaking WOC anthologies like *This Bridge Called My Back* and *But Some of Us Are Brave* during this period, the WIP movement was lamentably white. And although Naiad did publish some important works by and about lesbians of color (e.g., Ann Allen Shockley's *The Black and White of It*; Anita Cornwell's *Black Lesbian in White America*; *Black Lesbians: An Annotated Bibliography*, which was edited by a white woman using the pseudonym J. R. Roberts), their work as a publisher was, as Julie R. Enszer argues in a 2014 essay on Grier's publishing record, not in keeping with the emerging standards of the 1980s, especially the turn toward coalitional intersectional politics.

Grier believed the ideas she espoused writing as Barrow in "Living Propaganda" and lived according to the belief that the way to win social acceptance for lesbians and gays was through respectability. For her, that meant commitment to long-term monogamous coupledom. It meant putting stories into the world. It didn't mean commitment to intersectional feminist politics or even necessarily accountability to certain truths. As part of her "living propaganda" agenda, Grier stayed in an unhappy partnership with Helen Bennett for two decades, simply to maintain what she felt was model lesbian behavior.

Were her many pseudonyms part of this project? Did she feel so adamant about spreading "living propaganda" that she needed to make more of her? In a subsequent issue of *The Ladder*, a writer named Ginny Farrell supports Barrow's philosophy by narrating a scene in which she overhears two married couples in a New York café speaking negatively about gay people. She happens to have a copy of *The Ladder* with her and approaches the table "with a propaganda smile" and the magazine outstretched. "If you really want to know more about homosexuality," she tells them, "you might consider subscribing to this magazine."[5]

Implausible scenario plus incorrigible enthusiasm for *The Ladder*? Sounds like Barbara. Was "Ginny Farrell" a tenth pseudonym? I suspect so.

I don't know quite what to make of the fact that Grier concocted so many fake bylines even as, in "Living Propaganda," she made the case for being known. As a fiction writer, I understand that characters can provide space to explore hidden or aspirational selves. I don't know which, if any, of Grier's personas were more or less authentic selves, but together they gave her a voice—and access to the readers through which she would come to build her complicated legacy.

ALL THE FEMINIST BOOKS:
Midwinter Day by Bernadette Mayer

Becca Klaver, December 2014

BERNADETTE MAYER'S *Midwinter Day* (1982) has everything: dreams, daily life, memories, poetry, prose, rhyming, abstract concepts, proper nouns, flights of fancy, pure mundanity, the plots of children's books, "Lives of the Poets"–style histories, and many epic catalogues of everyday life: grocery lists, titles of "all the current books," names of the town stores, a list of people Mayer would buy "Xmas presents" for if she had any money (which ends up being a snapshot of a poetic circle), and a list of the contents of every room in the house in Lenox, Massachusetts, where she was living with poet Lewis Warsh and their two small children, Sophia and Marie, on December 22, 1978—the day she wrote *Midwinter Day*, which Alice Notley calls, on the back cover, "an epic poem about a daily routine."

Mayer and Notley are two of the poets in the dissertation I'm writing, "Include Everything: Contemporary American Poetry and the Feminist Everyday." The impulse to "include everything" wasn't limited to women poets in the second half of the twentieth century, but it's in their work that this impulse achieves its most brilliant, groundbreaking effect. As Notley writes in her lecture *Doctor Williams' Heiresses* (1980), in which Mayer is one of the titular "heiresses," "Too many people have always already been telling you for years what your life includes." In books like *Midwinter Day*, we watch women poets taking inventory of what their lives include and deeming even the most banal details worthy of poetic attention. It's a poetics of radical inclusiveness, feminist in its insistence that women's everyday lives belong in poetry—not only women's lives made to sound lofty or "universal," and not only women's secrets or confessions, but also friends' names and spaghetti-sauce making and folding clothes and a family dance party to the music of the Talking Heads.

In 2014, I cohosted a solstice reading of *Midwinter Day* at Berl's Brooklyn Poetry Shop, their last event of the year and a felicitous send-off for the other hosts, Berl's owners Farrah Field and Jared White, who were about to have their second child and begin an even more *Midwinter Day*–style life made up of two poets with two small children. (In another echo of the two-poets-with-two-children pattern, early in the reading Anselm Berrigan read pages full of references to his parents, Notley and Ted Berrigan, and to himself and his brother: "So even if the two men were Ted and Alice's two sons / It's clear the women they became were my two daughters," Mayer writes at one point, analyzing a dream.) It's sometimes difficult to sustain attention at a marathon reading (even though, heads-up to future event planners, *Midwinter Day* only takes three and a half hours straight through, which led Jared to dub our event a "*Midwinter Day* 5K" rather than a marathon). But hearing *Midwinter* read aloud was consistently exciting: it's a book packed with pleasurable swerves in content, rhythm, and tone, and full of humor, wisdom, and anecdotes. Perhaps what the event most resembled was, fittingly, childhood story time, with Mayer as mother-bard, reanimating our wonder at everything that a single day can include.

Revisiting Raven: Thoughts on Zora, Nina, and Take-Down Culture

Naomi Extra, January 2015

In 2014, Raven-Symoné said the notorious words, "I want to be labeled a human who loves humans, [and] I'm tired of being labeled. I'm an American; I'm not an African-American, I'm an American," and the internet exploded. I know, so passé to revisit a moment that's so firmly exited the news cycle. But I want to make a plea for thoughtful and sisterly discourse on the internet (and in general). To me, this means returning to old conversations where we may have responded impulsively; it means thinking twice—and then three or four times more about things. In this spirit, let us return to the scene of action: *The Oprah Winfrey Show* on October 4, 2014.

You might need a quick memory jog on the controversy around Raven's statements. Most of the criticism was aimed at her perceived rejection of the ethnic category, African American, in favor of the ostensibly more privileged label, American. Folks didn't miss a beat before staging an online take-down of Raven. The take-down is a very particular way of telling someone they've done wrong by negating their point of view. It can be subtle in the tone of an online article, a joke, a passing microaggression, or it can come in the form of an all-out verbal or written assault. It's not a private disagreement; it's more like a public invitation to ridicule someone (online comments, oy vey). We see it in multiple forms: tweets, Facebook posts, essays, articles, blog entries, radio verbiage, memes, and YouTube videos. After Raven's comments, my Facebook newsfeed was filled with nasty and disapproving status updates that mostly added up to a single "Oh, hell no."

Take-downs are pervasive; look out for them.

Kendrick Lamar says the wrong thing? Take him down. Phylicia Rashad? Some random person in your Facebook newsfeed? Take them too. Effectively, take-downs say, "Shut up, you're wrong, and I never want to hear from you again." Oprah Winfrey could sniff the take-downs to come when Raven made the defiant statement on her show, her immediate response being, "Oh, girl, don't set the Twitter on fire!"

Take-downs get us hype; they gather energy in the same fashion as a seventh-grade cafeteria fight. They happen quickly, draw a crowd, and no one remembers it the next week.

What I'm interested in here is revisiting how people responded to Raven's controversial statements. I'm not so much interested in Raven as I am in the ways in which we interact with each other when we disagree, the silence we engender, and the complexity that we glide away from. For me, the intense coverage and subsequent backlash Raven's statements provoked said something about this ahistorical take-down-driven culture we live in. (Although much of the backlash came from within the African American community, I say "we" because I think take-downs are pervasive in American culture at large.) What take-downs fail to reveal are the nuances—the long-spanning connections we have with each other and with those who preceded us.

Raven was not the first black woman artist to publicly express her desire not to be categorized. Indeed, she is in excellent company with women like Zora Neale Hurston and Nina Simone. These women made folks—black and white—ill at ease with their independent and sometimes unpopular antics. The take-down most certainly isn't a new phenomenon. Zora and Nina had their share of haters as well. I've continued to think about the Raven drama in part because I think the conversation left out a legacy of black women who rejected labels. There are so many ways of thinking about this. And even as I brace myself for a potential take-down, I demand a safe space for these ideas to exist.

Today, Zora Neale Hurston and Nina Simone are considered to be among those at the vanguard of American art. These women are very different from each other, and they are very different from Raven. Let me be clear: I have not set out to convince you that Raven-Symoné's artistry is in any way parallel to the iconic and soulful Nina Simone or the brilliant Zora Neale Hurston. But I do wish to highlight a connection between these women who were criticized by their audience and their peers yet said what was on their mind anyway.

Nina Simone refused to adhere to the confines of category, racial or otherwise, and it drove people nuts. In her 1992 autobiography, *I Put a Spell on You*, she wrote, "It's always been my aim to stay outside any category. That's my freedom." Like hell it was. And Zora was on a similar wavelength. In the 1928 essay "How It Feels to Be Colored Me," she wrote, "At certain times I have no race, I am me." Sound like Raven? Zora continued to say:

> But in the main, I feel like a brown bag of miscellany propped against a wall. Against a wall in company with other bags, white, red, and yellow. Pour out the contents, and there is discovered a jumble of small things priceless and worthless.

Zora's "brown bag of miscellany" seems to align with Raven's comments on being a melting pot below:

> I don't label myself. What I really mean by that is I'm an American ... I have darker skin. I have a nice, interesting grade of hair. I connect with Caucasian. I connect with Asian. I connect with black.... I connect with each culture.... Aren't we all (a melting pot)? Isn't that what America's supposed to be?

When I read Zora's loose racial and ethnic identification for the first time in the ninth grade, I thought it was for the birds. If Twitter was around then, I might have tweeted about it. *How could she, at any time, ignore or not feel her blackness in racist America?* I thought. Since then, I've had a lot more time to think about Zora. Now I see that subversion comes in as many different forms as there are people.

I continue to ask myself the larger question of why we get so ruffled by those who decide to challenge the road laid out for them. It seems to me that one of the reasons is connected to our desire to categorize and contain as a mode of control. It's the sort of strength-in-sameness logic. If someone breaks the pattern by disidentifying, there is a threat to power and control. But we really must ask ourselves this: Are the Ravens of the world really the problem, anyway? Are they at the root of racism and inequality in America? I think not.

Perhaps what's threatening to some about Raven's expression of freedom is that it pushes us to look deeper at the black activist script and at our attachment to race. In fact, it disrupts the script entirely. Black female subversion is not of a singular aesthetic; acts of subversion in general do not fit a one-size model. But it's the tradition; it's a rich and informative history that's there to remind us to cool it and make space in the room for multiple voices, other ways of being. When folks respond to Raven's rejection of labels with jokes of ridicule, we enter the ugly territory of the take-down. We don't have to agree, but at the very least, we must recognize that there are a variety of ways to engage the struggle.

Take-downs are an easy way out of the unglamorous and unpopular work of thoughtful disagreement. Absorbed in the flurry of the moment, they refuse to look backward or forward. They don't challenge us to be better humans, and they certainly don't foster a culture of love, sisterhood, or reflection. I don't have all the answers; maybe I'll change my mind on Raven. Maybe I won't. But I do know that I am sending out a call. As women, sisters, feminists, womynists, humanists, whatever label you want to claim (if any at all), I insist that we revisit the spaces where we disagree when the flames have lost their sparks. Let's do away with the here-and-now attitude of hotness that has infiltrated our culture. It's played out. We can decide to be thoughtful and loving instead by thinking deeply before we tweet, post, or do whatever it is that we do online. We can talk to each other in our written discourse and not just at each other. We can enter into disagreeing discourse with an ethic of empathy. It's romantic, but worth a try.

A Pre Narrative Manifesto:
kari edwards's Trans Poetics

Trace Peterson, December 2016, revised 2022[1]

I VIVIDLY REMEMBER when kari edwards first appeared on the experimental poetry scene in the early 2000s. She was broadcasting a strong signal on important literary listservs, appearing in prominent reading series, and publishing everywhere, all of which was unusual considering that there had not been a visibly "out" trans woman poet publishing in English in the US before, and considering that she resisted making her poetry "about" being transgender in any overt narratively autobiographical way. As a pre-transition trans woman poet just out of my MFA program, who had been writing about my gender experiences since 2000, it was a revelation for me to encounter such an impressive trans role model on the poetry scene. I had previously thought I was alone and had been trying to articulate my poetics without any sort of visible tradition. I sought out kari as a mentor in 2003, and we corresponded and later met up in Brooklyn when she visited New York. Though we argued on some points and our poetics ended up being different, she influenced my writing in ways I am still just beginning to understand. As a major ancestor for trans poetry, edwards deserves a tribute to what her poetry was attempting to accomplish on its own terms.

kari edwards's poetry is a Pre Narrative manifesto: it disrupts narratives that would otherwise objectify or freeze the self in place. Her writing seeks trans liberation on the level of linguistic form by jamming the frequencies of all pre-commodified narrative—even the LGBTQ narratives propagated by corporate media sources—in the interest of imagining how a writing subject who is surveilled and hypervisible could take control of decisions about her own representation. Pre Narrative does this by introducing little bits of narrative and then quickly abandoning each one, through fragmentation, repetition, and exploding traditional uses of grammar. edwards created this aesthetic as a trans woman writer at a moment—the late 1990s through the early 2000s—when there were few, if any, visible trans poets, trans women poets, or trans women writers publishing anything besides prose memoir.

It begins with a metaphor about salad bars and gender. In "Table Top Gender" from edwards's first book *POST / (PINK)*, published in 2000, two people eating at a restaurant are having a conversation that begins, "Life is a salad bar." They're thinking about how the options available in the restaurant, "big-o salad bar," are consumer choices with a dimension of personal meaning. But soon the subject underneath the discussion is revealed—a meditation on the history of trans medicine:

> could we go back to the salad bar thing?
>
> no!! the question is why did storm troopers tap danced oblivion across the first clinic that performed sex changes?[2]

This passage refers to the Nazis' burning of the library of early sexologist Magnus Hirschfeld, who pioneered certain aspects of trans medicine. What gender clinics that were censored by Nazis might have in common with salad bars turns out to be the act of choosing—someone can choose aspects of their gender or sex just like they can select dishes from the salad bar and make them into a new combination:

> someone with a plate full ... you know from the salad bar ...
> a full course in vegetarian transexual delights – the next
> person in line wants heterosexual spam, processed cheese
> on white bread
>
> but that could be war.[3]

edwards identifies a dilemma here, that consumer choice can enable either transsexuality or heteronormativity, depending on the situation. Seen only through the lens of choice, it's potentially difficult to distinguish the choice of a trans gender from the choice of a cis gender or politics that would reinforce societal norms. The fact that there clearly is a difference, given existing prejudices and social inequalities, results in the ominous realization "But that could be war."

This dilemma edwards notices about the relationship between capitalism and individual expressions of identity inspires her poetics. In an interview from 2002 discussing *a day in the life of p.*, she shows how

this awareness turned her away from memoir as a genre and toward
something she felt was less confining:

> I think it was trying to write the experience of being trans and not
> necessarily fitting into any sort of signifying economy, without going
> "I'm trans..." It's sort of like losing language. Being trans, I've been
> doubly signified as medical, trans as history, trans means this, trans
> means that, so I was trying to not be that, but not be anything.[4]

edwards imagines the strategic move of "losing language" and the
move to "not be anything" as poetics antidotes to feeling trapped by
the limitations of narrative under capitalism and cis-heteropatriarchy.
From her perspective, if one avoids or delays telling a story about
oneself, one doesn't have to be an objectified thing:

> We live in a binary system, I mean it's like good/bad/right/wrong, and
> our choices would pretty much be diagnosable or man or woman or
> straight or queer or... you know, there's always this binary approach
> to it. And nouns sort of freeze things too, so once you're "it," what-
> ever "it" is, so whether it's trans, male, dog, or rock, you're frozen
> there. And it's like, living to me is more like a verb, but I don't have
> the verb that does it. It's not a noun anymore, it's more like verbing.[5]

The first comparison edwards makes here is that writing is like living
(with stakes that are equally high). The second is that identifying as
a noun would be like getting "frozen there" within the capitalist or
cis-heteropatriarchal binary system. Assuming the claims of both simi-
les are true, for a trans writer to exist, one needs to write while dodging
the forces that commodify identity; one needs to employ strategies of
"verbing" or "losing language" as resistance to being frozen as a noun.

edwards develops the Pre Narrative aesthetic by wrestling with
conventions of New Narrative, the experimental writing movement that understood queer desire as "founded in the commodity,"
as Robert Glück put it. Glück's question "What kind of representation least deforms its subject?" in his thinking about gay and lesbian
writers resonated in some ways with edwards's instinctive concerns.[6]
But edwards was equally influenced by other movements, such as
Beat poetics and the polemics of Language poetry. These influences,
combined with her transness and her newness to the scene, gave her
a bit of a different perspective on what linguistic strategies could be
most politically effective. Initially accepted by New Narrative writers

such as Kevin Killian and Camille Roy when she sought them out upon arriving in San Francisco in mid-2001, edwards proceeded to write *through* New Narrative on her way into something else. "Pre Narrative" is a phrase that I've coined, in the spirit of edwards's aesthetic, to describe that something else.

edwards's poetic novel / prose lyric essay *a day in the life of p.* (2002) solves for the problem of cis-heteropatriarchal capitalist objectification by imagining a speaker with multiple names, presumably a trans person going through various fraught transition-related experiences. edwards opens this book with a montage of the various personas that make up the main character "p.," who "in some zones is referred to as sometimes, something, whatever – or both." The multiple names here, most of them words for liminal or conditional things, allow a way for the trans subject to participate in a narrative of the self without getting trapped as a single object. These names also take on the quality of third-person gender pronouns, and throughout the text they flicker back and forth between name and pronoun as a form of linguistic trans liberation.

The salad bar metaphor reemerges in a later scene from *a day in the life of p.* to show that capitalism appears to offer choice while actually trapping the self. While being interrogated by the police, the character "whatever" confesses:

> so the commander in chief asked rank and dildo preference. whatever responded with a desirable affirmation and was one step further to the next step –
>
> > dinner at the kreplach buffet, where kreplach were boiled, steamed, broiled, sized and shaped to stick your fingers in and suck the insides out. where they had kreplach beyond the traditional palate, kreplach in bandito sauce, french crème ooh-lala, kreplach, kreplach and crecy and kreplach vacuum sealed. all of which came with canned apple sauce and tubed sour cream.[7]

At the moment of confession here, the narrative dissolves suddenly and the reader is plunged into a series of buffet options in which there is really no option. Everything comes down to "kreplach" prepared in different ways, just as everything comes down to being a "trapped" individual multiply signified by capitalism ("trans means this, trans means that"). The kreplach device offers a chance to escape; the narrator leaps out of the narrative dilemma to get perspective on it, allowing the character to avoid being harmed by a scene of confession to the authorities.

This is what Pre Narrative does as a poetics: it gives us a bird's-eye view of various options, an outsider's perspective that keeps a critical, political, and personal distance without "buying into" any of the choices and therefore becoming an object. This outsider perspective appears again in *succubus in my pocket*, edwards's second poetic novel (completed in 2004, published posthumously in 2015). If *a day in the life of p.* was concerned with how to tell a trans narrative that could be liberated from objectification, *succubus in my pocket* is its shadow, imagining the intersection of transgender and narrative as dystopian. Identity configurations get weirder in *succubus* as the narrator, named "honey with an 'h,'" imagines genitalia as rearrangeable or customizable in a manner not unlike the salad bar or the kreplach buffet:

> And it is not just genitalia to consider, there are all sort of combinations . . . I mean one could have breasts and a dick, two dicks and a one breast, or a hundred breasts to feed the multitudes with. . . . All this would be simple, a body part here or a body part there, changing at will or not at will. Sometimes the machine is put on random and in the morning I could wake up and take one part off and put another on before I walked out the door. I could add voice modulation from betty boop to the honorable arnold sheepherder, with an ever increasing progression of change. Body parts could move in and out and on and off of my body before my voice modulation could possibly catch up. . . . I could breakthrough this gender thing, truly let it go, there would be no limits.[8]

The options in this passage seem ambivalent: both potentially good and bad, like gender itself. We could read their proliferation as "verbing" that might truly allow one to "breakthrough this gender thing." Or we could read this passage as having an undertow or nihilism that prevents us from actually adopting any of the options. It seems likely that bewilderment is part of the intended effect, that this speaker is comparing gender fluidity with information overload. But most importantly, the Pre Narrative distance is maintained—each of these body options represents a little fragment that might have turned into a narrative but doesn't.

In her final two books, *obedience* (2005) and *Bharat jiva* (published posthumously in 2009), edwards arrives at the Pre Narrative aesthetic in its fully developed form, and it happens when she returns to writing poems after her two poetic novels. She jumps from a bit of a narrative perspective to another bit of a narrative perspective, challenging the reader to do the work to connect the moments into a larger whole. The following section from *obedience* demonstrates these principles of interruption:

> Maybe one day, during a point in time, without a particular point in time, without a reference, a point in time without a point, without a reference, without a connection, when someone or anyone being someone, processes a confluence of points and lines, designating nothing, processing in a process, proceeding in a connection, between a connection and an operation, and an operation and a process, connecting the process and operation to a future, between, voluntary actions and tangential beings, being one of many, doing an extended process, extending endlessly into an oncoming process, into the whole of matter at the beginning of the process, beginning with an ending and ending with a beginning . . .[9]

This crazy quilt of dependent clauses creates the effect of a bubbling surface, as if to embody the experience of a consciousness surfing on waves of language. There is something hypnotizing or mesmerizing in the way it somehow accomplishes being about nothing by being about everything. If someone were speaking this, you might say they were performing a type of meditation or acting out a confused monologue about trying to figure out what to order from the salad bar, but the comedy of the initial figure has fallen away. All that seems to be left of the salad bar motif is the urgency of being unable to choose and being overwhelmed by choice, and as the pathos of this feeling drives the syntactical fireworks of the passage, it dissolves into something else, like a kind of a bravado or glory or even dialectical joy at being in the midst of an infinite process. It's as if everything is blurred and we can't quite make out any scene. Our brain has to construct a scene from these weird fragments and present participles, which causes us to think in new ways.

Pre Narrative is the aspect of kari's work that I most love and admire, the one that I think holds the most possibilities for trans liberation. When I heard her read that section from *obedience* in person at a reading in Brooklyn in 2005, I had the vivid realization that something about that poem made everything about my own future as a trans woman poet more possible. And I hope kari's writing does the same for others still to come.

Reproductive Agency in Sylvia Plath's
Three Women

Marisa Crawford, October 2016

SYLVIA PLATH IS best remembered for her groundbreaking Confessional poetry and her novel *The Bell Jar*, but one important aspect of her writing that often doesn't get enough attention is its complex depiction of motherhood and reproductive agency. Looking back at Plath's 1962 play in verse, *Three Women: A Poem for Three Voices*, one of her lesser-known works, it's striking how well this piece speaks to our current political climate around reproductive rights—to Trump's ridiculous claims about late-term abortion, to his promise to appoint anti-choice justices to the Supreme Court who would "automatically" overturn *Roe v. Wade*, and to the widescale Republican war on reproductive rights. It's incredible, and terrifying, that we're still having this conversation. Right-wing anti-choicers could learn a lot from Plath's play, which takes place in a maternity ward and depicts—through a series of three monologues—three women's very different experiences with pregnancy. The "First Voice" is a married woman who's excitedly welcoming her new baby; the "Second Voice," a secretary who experiences a miscarriage; the "Third Voice," a student who places her child for adoption. Plath's play can be read as a meditation on the complexity of women's feelings—and those of all people who are able to become pregnant—about pregnancy, why reproductive options are right and necessary, and why cis men, the government, and other structures of power really have no right to say anything about it.

Each of the play's monologues holds equal weight within the piece, and the title, *Three Women*, conveys an equalizing recognition of all three perspectives on motherhood as valid, natural experiences. Two of Plath's speakers have deep feelings of love for their unborn children—First Voice excitedly anticipates her son's arrival ("I cannot help smiling at what it is I know. / Leaves and petals attend me. I am ready.") and Second Voice feels shattered by the loss of her pregnancy

("I am dying as I sit. I lose a dimension."). Third Voice, on the other hand, expresses feeling trapped and traumatized by her unwanted pregnancy: "I wasn't ready. The white clouds rearing / Aside were dragging me in four directions."

It's of course notable that abortion is absent from Plath's play, which was written over a decade before *Roe v. Wade*. Reading it, you can distinctly feel that abortion is not a viable, safe, legal option for addressing an unwanted pregnancy. Third Voice describes her pregnancy forming and continuing in spite of her not being ready to give birth to a child (it's also notable that the false dichotomy of being "ready" versus "not ready" to carry a pregnancy to term is influenced by respectability politics around reproduction; the logic suggests that everyone should want to have a child at some point, even if it's not right now). Plath hints at the possibility of abortion when Third Voice expresses regrets, saying that she should have "murdered" that which now "murders" her.

I see Plath's use of "murder" here as a bold and clear affirmation that abortion is not "murder" at all, as anti-choicers often claim—or if abortion is "murder," then the clearly metaphorical "murder" of the self committed by bringing an unwanted pregnancy to term is equally deserving of that judgment. It's not that both options are equally bad, though; instead Plath's Third Voice very clearly articulates that abortion would have been the better option for her. Perhaps because this option wasn't safely, legally available to her—and perhaps because abortion felt like a risky topic for Plath to write about directly—there's a sense in the play that Third Voice finds difficulty in choosing adoption. Upon parting with her newborn baby, she is at once relieved to keep her own independence and perhaps slightly haunted by her decision. She describes the tactile feeling of removing herself from her child's grip yet notes that the child looks peaceful as she leaves and compares herself to a ship setting sail.

Unlike the simplified narratives demonizing women who choose abortion that Trump and other anti-choicers promote, Plath's play in verse carefully maps out the conflicting, multilayered feelings of a person who chooses to not keep their baby, in this case by placing their child for adoption. This narrative also serves as an important critique of the anti-choice movement's supposed support of adoption as a solution for all unwanted pregnancies: Plath's Third Voice shows how physically and emotionally difficult such a decision can be. By placing Third Voice's perspective of choosing not to be a mother alongside the more traditionally accepted role of mother as selfless nurturer, Plath validates both points of view.

Three Women beautifully captures the complexity of choosing not to be a parent and equally gives rich dimension to the experience of choosing motherhood. First Voice embraces her role as a new mother, showing an instant love for her newborn son: "What did my fingers do before they held him? / What did my heart do, with its love?" At the same time, the play makes space for her to also experience ambivalence and doubt around her new role, noting feelings of loneliness, sorrow, and fear around her limitations as a caregiver that she can't quite escape. Rather than simply creating an either/or dichotomy between women who choose to be mothers and women who do not, Plath's play complicates and expands our understanding of both perspectives.

In sharp contrast to Plath's careful depictions of complex women characters with multilayered needs and emotions, the male figures in *Three Women* are often described by the female speakers as "flat." This flatness brings even more definition to the play's multidimensional female voices. Second Voice describes her miscarriage while at work in an office, surrounded by male coworkers who walk around her as she sits in high heels. More than just one-dimensional characters, perhaps in distinctly nonpregnant bodies, these male figures are *flattening*—they have a destructive effect on the world around them. They represent not just individual men but systems of patriarchal power that attempt to reduce—to *bulldoze*—women's dimensionality.

The "important men" in this poem can't understand first-person experiences of pregnancy as multifaceted and containing ambiguities and contradictions. They're scared, and "jealous," as the poem puts it, of women's true emotions and desires, and so they try to flatten out what they can't understand. Looking at *Three Women* in the context of today's anti-choice rhetoric and policies, there's a clear parallel between people in power favoring abstractions over the lived experiences of women and other people capable of getting pregnant, and working to restrict women's varied, layered, and ever-evolving sources of power.

Plath's work often challenged conventional mothering narratives by claiming space for women's complicated, sometimes difficult feelings around motherhood. The three voices in Plath's *Three Women* can be read as three separate people or as three different perspectives that have all been experienced by one woman at different points in her life.

In either reading, *Three Women* reflects a variety of complex, multilay-ered experiences around pregnancy and motherhood. Today, looking back on the play over half a century later, it serves as a poignant illus-tration of the many factors and feelings that inform our reproductive choices, and of all that's at stake as our government creates more and more barriers to accessing our right to reproductive justice.

The Tell-Tale Sign of Living[1]: Blackness and Sensuality in Ntozake Shange's *nappy edges*

Mariahadessa Ekere Tallie, October 2022

"The revolution ain't comin til we love each othah."
—Ntozake Shange writing under her
birth name, Paulette Williams[2]

I HAVE LONG believed the work of poet, performer, novelist, playwright, and scholar Ntozake Shange is a treasure chest overflowing with lessons on Black women's liberation. Works like Shange's 1985 novel *Betsey Brown* complicate common narratives about the process of integration in the United States. Her culinary memoir *If I Can Cook/You Know God Can* (1998) places us in the kitchen, cooking up the diaspora while considering the ways history, freedom, and collectivity spice the foods we eat as much as cumin, scotch bonnet peppers, or ginger do. But lemme tell you something—when Shange writes about love, sex, and sensuality, I believe she is giving us the keys to the universe.

Shange is best known for her genre-defying choreopoem *For Colored Girls Who Have Considered Suicide When the Rainbow is Enuf* (1976), which, as E. Patrick Johnson writes, "pushed not only the form and content of traditional theatre practice, but it also stretched the black body politic by moving from margin to center the voice of the black woman."[3] Through *For Colored Girls*, Shange's legacy as a writer who examines and dares speak the wounds and sexual trauma of Black women was cemented. However, Shange's work spans almost five decades. Her novels, poetry, cookbook, nonfiction, and performances also deserve critical attention in order to comprehend the fullness of Shange's vision.

Ntozake Shange's work was ahead of its time as a Black feminist project which encourages us to develop vocabularies for pleasure. What do I mean by Black feminist? In my own life, Black feminism is a way of being, a method of analysis, and the clay of creation. It's a self-love philosophy aimed at ending oppressive systems through various forms of activism; it is nonseparatist, liberatory, and based in the lived experiences of Black women. Black feminism is a path paved by our mothers, our grandmothers, and those way-back women who envisioned us and chose to survive.[4] Historically, much of Black feminist theory has necessarily sought to render visible the sexual traumas that Black women encountered during enslavement and colonization. Books like *The Black Woman*, edited by Toni Cade Bambara; *But Some of Us Are Brave*, edited by Akasha Hull, Patricia Bell-Scott, and Barbara Smith; and *Black Feminist Thought* by Patricia Hill Collins contain early Black feminist theorizations. Scholarship on pleasure was not work that Black women in the academy could freely embark on without serious consequences to their careers during the 1970s and 1980s; their commitments to Black feminist theory already placed them under scrutiny. But there has long been an abundance of art on sex and pleasure, and Ntozake Shange's work is part of this lineage, with her consistent insistence that "some love is due you."[5] Contemporary theorists such as Joan Morgan, Brittney Cooper, LaMonda Horton-Stallings, Jennifer C. Nash, and Mireille Miller-Young are among those theorists doing work on Black women and pleasure. Shange cleared space for this theorizing with a Black feminist philosophy that deemed love and pleasure as critical components of Black healing and liberation.

Hortense Spillers asserts that the ability to consent to or ward off another's touch is a mark of citizenship, belonging, and bodiedness.[6] Shange transforms the status of Black women from flesh (unprotected by due process of law, unfree) to body (free citizenry) through her description of welcome touch. The touch described in her poem "hands & holding," for example, is a generative one likened to the way plants get nourishment. It strengthens and steadies, encourages one to reach up, blossom, and bear fruit:

> hands & holding
> tongues & clits
> go well together
> the way
> the sun kisses the ocean at dawn[7]

The innocent first line gives way to the explicit pleasures of the next two lines. The casual tone conveys the naturalness and the beauty of sex. The narrator renders lovemaking a sunrise and suggests exalting in the tenderness and salt of bodies at play.

In African American poetry there is a long-standing tradition of writing blues poems. Langston Hughes, Sterling Brown, and Sonia Sanchez are among the poets who exemplify this tradition. While Shange did not write poetry in the traditional twelve-bar refrain blues form, her work contains the blues. Angela Davis writes, "Naming issues that pose a threat to the physical or psychological well-being of the individual is a central function of the blues."[8] In her 1978 poetry collection *nappy edges*, Shange names many of the oppressions that African American women face. She discusses domestic violence in "with no immediate cause" and the sexual exploitation of Black women in "expiriese girl wanted." She details the links between poverty and violence in "i had five nose rings." Shange's work consistently bears witness to the terrors Black women face in their daily lives, and in this way her work aligns with Davis's articulations of a blues aesthetic. But Shange's texts embody blues in another often-overlooked way: her depictions of sex also place her very much in line with the tradition of blues women. As Davis writes, "The blues woman had no qualms about announcing female desire. Their songs express women's intentions to get their loving."[9] The blues was post-Emancipation music, and Davis explains that the ability to choose a partner, whether for life, for the night, or somewhere in between, was a new freedom for newly emancipated people. Black blues women sang a free song, they hummed tunes of wholeness, and the sonics of women singing the blues became the sound of women finally in charge of their own destinies. The influence of the blues created space for Shange to write Black women and girls as whole, which meant writing unabashedly about our desires. Shange links our sensuality and our sexual health to our overall health.

What's sensuality and love got to do with it? Love and sexual pleasure create what Saidiya Hartman terms "elsewhere" and "otherwise" when she writes, "What you wanted but couldn't name, the resolute, stubborn desire for an elsewhere and an otherwise that had yet to emerge clearly, a notion of the possible whose outlines were fuzzy and amorphous, exerted a force no less powerful and tenacious."[10] In Shange's work, sensuality, sexual pleasure, and love allow feelings of wholeness, well-being, and abundance otherwise off-limits to those of us on intimate terms with precarity.

> in the night/ochun's candles
> make ether glow waves
> thru the hairs of yr stomach[11]

In the Afro-Cuban tradition Santeria, Ochun is the sweet things in life: joy, love, community, harmony, and sexual pleasure. By placing Ochun in this poem, and many other works, Shange invites women of African descent globally to engage with a precolonial framework of sensuality. Ochun energy is of critical importance to Shange, and in an interview with Derrick Gilbert published in 1998, Shange said, "We have to understand that, for a people, the perpetuation of love and family is essential . . . there is power in love and coupling, and often those who are most victimized by some sort of oppression don't fully realize this power."[12]

In her poem "where the mississippi meets the amazon," Shange illustrates the power of love; she reimagines geographies of Black resistance and couples them with intimate moments to create a vivid portrait of Black sensuality where utopia is possible. By uniting these two major rivers, Shange engages the African diaspora and envisions freedom. The poem begins:

> you fill me up so much
> when you touch me
> i can't stay here
> i haveta go to my space[13]

Perhaps the speaker's lover fills her with talk, dreams, visions, feelings, inspiration, and thoughts. Perhaps the narrator is being filled by the lover's body. Or all of it. Their touching is an invitation to explore alternate geographies and histories of Africa and African descendants. She invokes a dream-altering love, which allows the speaker "to see the ferry from trois islets to rio" even though she has not left her home in the United States.

> you send me packin/for anywhere/i've never known
> where we never not exist
> in my country we are/always
> you know how you kiss me
> just like that[14]

Shange writes a love that shifts physical geographies beyond oppressive ones that dictate (or end) our lives. This love creates space where we are allowed to be and where we are empowered to love. This love and lovemaking bring Black citizenship to bear.

where the mississippi meets the amazon
neruda still tangoes in santiago at dawn
where i live
jean-jacques dessalines is continually re elected[15]

Shange's expressions of love and lovemaking remake time and revise
geopolitical history. Jean-Jacques Dessalines—the leader of the Haitian
revolution—is not assassinated. In this utopic space, Dessalines lives
and ushers Haiti toward its own independence, free from the shadows
of colonialism. In "where the mississippi meets the amazon," loving
and lovemaking are worldmaking actions that upend spatial tempo-
ral realities and secure Black futurity.

I celebrate the many healings Shange performed every time she
wrote a Black woman whole, lovable, and sensual. Shange was ahead
of her time with her daring mélange of Black arts sensibilities, experimental poetics, and sensuous womanism. Her body of work remains
current and capacious enough to steer Black women toward explora-
tions of the importance of self-love and sexual pleasure. The stakes
are high. With alarming statistics of HIV infection and STIs for Black
women and girls, and the overturning of *Roe v. Wade*, these are critical
times for us to discover and develop languages that help us embrace
healthy sexual practices and partners. Hortense Spillers writes, "Black
women are the beached whales of the sexual universe, unvoiced,
misseen, not doing, awaiting their verb. Their sexual experiences are
depicted, but not often by them, and if and when by the subject herself,
often in the guise of vocal music, often in the self-contained accent
and sheer romance of the blues."[16] By depicting sex that alters geog-
raphy, evokes utopia, and creates space for Black futurity, Ntozake
Shange's work stands firmly in the tradition of working-class blues
women and counters the erasure of Black female sensuality from
discourses on sexuality. Shange's poetry performs a healing by claiming wholeness for Black women through its depiction of us as lovable
sexual beings. Through Shange's work Black women are given numerous tools to uncover our "verb."

YASSS and NAWW: bell hooks and Laverne Cox at The New School

Morgan Parker, October 2014

BELL HOOKS IS not a fan of *Orange Is the New Black*. But she, like everyone else, loves her some Laverne Cox. The two sat down for a conversation as part of hooks's 2014 residency at The New School, poised on either side of a coffee table like a Black feminist yin and yang: Laverne's long blond weave and red bottoms, bell's uniquely braided short hair and flat sandals. They agreed and didn't agree. They acknowledged their varied histories and perspectives. They talked identity and love. They talked labels and risk. They did and didn't cater to the patriarchal gaze.

Here are some moments when I shouted YASSS and NAWW during their talk.

YASSS: "Janet [Mock] said to me, 'You speak so eloquently about race, yet you so rarely talk about it publicly.' And . . . it was a read," Laverne said, admitting her fears about being political in the public sphere. I love that her friend was able to call her out on making her feminism more inclusive and acknowledging how oppressive systems overlap and intersect.

YASSS: Talking up her documentary project *Laverne Cox Presents: The T Word*, Laverne said, "I think it's courageous for transgender folks to just step out of their houses as themselves and live their truth." YES. I love the word "courage." I love the agency given in this statement, the protest. I love the universality of leaving the house as a revolutionary act. As bell said later in their talk, "Decolonization is a constant vigilance in our culture." At the heart of their discourse was the mutual recognition of struggle, of the very serious effort it takes to remain awake under an "imperialist white supremacist capitalist patriarchy." Laverne noted that decolonization is a *practice*, something active and continual.

NAWW: "I wish we could get rid of labels . . ."

YASSS: ". . . and we could all be queer."

Mixed feelings here because of how cute it was watching bell hooks
call for universal queerness and how detrimental it can be to buy
into myths of sameness and postraciality.

NAWW: "All those other tired-ass Black women who are just repro-
ducing stereotypes." Okay. She ain't wrong, and we ain't all angelic
in our vigilance, but I would have expected more love and care in
bell hooks's language than "tired-ass."

NAWW: "One of the issues I think that many people have with trans
women," bell said, "is the sense of a traditional femininity . . . that
many feminists feel like we're trying to get away from." To which
Laverne responded, "A lot of trans women do not embrace this kind
of femininity. My choice is about what I find aesthetically pleasing
. . . and this is where I feel empowered and comfortable." I give a
general YASSS to this conversation. I was happy they were discussing the different aesthetics of feminism and that Laverne pointed
out the variety of ways trans women choose to present, the variety
of politics they have. Likewise, it felt important for bell to quickly
remind Cox that she was, in fact, appealing to a patriarchal gaze
with her traditionally feminine presentation. But then Laverne said,
"I've constructed myself in a way that I don't want to disappear. I
think so often there is an erasure of certain bodies and identities,
and I have never been interested in being invisible." The conversation flattened as bell called for criticism and Laverne stroked her
hair lovingly. And I felt disappointed they didn't prod one another
more on the subject, which I find complex and worth exploring
further: How do we dismantle patriarchy and traditional, sexist
expectations of women when we are also fighting to remain visible
where we've been erased? Or, in the case of many women of color,
both trans and cisgender, to reclaim agency over our bodies in the
face of objectification? This dilemma, of course, is also at the heart
of bell hooks's disapproval of Beyoncé.

YASSS: I'm pretty broke, so I was absolutely there for bell hooks on
finances (financial activism?), on rallying against the oppression of

capitalism while also understanding money as a tool for facilitating freedom. Then she said this, and I just about got up from my seat: "I wanna say to every Black woman in this room, 'Girl, go get your money straight.'" bell keeps it real, and the really real is: whether we like it or not, we live within a capitalist structure wherein well-being is facilitated by financial independence. As a friend said to me after the talk, "How am I supposed to march if I gotta go to work to pay the rent?" That's really real. It's something I've had to continually "check my privilege" on—while I was in school, or at poetry readings, or spending lazy Saturday afternoons debating Audre Lorde with friends. While feminist theory and wide-eyed activism may be at the center of many of our hearts, it's important to marry politics with practicality. As a Black woman, financial literacy has always been an inaccessible privilege in my mind—something murky and hazy and not for me. I really appreciated the reminder that financial empowerment is a road to freedom. That maybe in order to make change, you gotta make paper.

YASSS: "Whiteness is a construct. Nobody is as white as they think they are," Laverne said of privilege, which is an intriguing though watery point. bell responded, "Some constructs allow for greater well-being than others." *Church hands.* This exchange perfectly encapsulates the twenty-first-century "postracial" complex. While we know that race—whiteness, Blackness, otherness, and the spectrums of privilege therein—was constructed as a means of oppression, it's impossible to call for race neutrality in a society where, for example, Black boys are dying for reasons that white boys aren't and women are paid less than men. We can't ignore that opportunity is selective, that historically and presently (not to go all Hegelian master-slave dialectic on y'all), some people do the oppressing and some people are born into oppression. And we can't fight what we don't acknowledge.

Sex Permeates Everything:
The Poetry of Lola Ridge

Terese Svoboda, February 2016

LONG BEFORE THE dawn of sexting and frank depictions of women's sexuality in TV shows like *Broad City*, the candlelit tea rooms of 1920s Greenwich Village boomed with women's sex talk. World War I had just ended, as had the terrible flu epidemic. Both were short, and their casualties enormous. What else for the survivors to do but fuck, or at least talk about it? According to Foucault, poetry at the start of the seventeenth century was the only sex talk there was until two centuries later, when sex scientists like Havelock Ellis began a murmur that turned into the roar of the sex-positive 1920s. When women writers rediscovered sex in the 1920s, poetry was what the wild girls wrote. Bookstores couldn't keep women's work in stock, with poems like Mina Loy's "Songs to Joannes"[1] flying off the shelves.

During this era, literary soirees broke out all across town—late-night wild parties with Prohibition "tea" and drugs of any kind (most were legal), where poets burned candles at both ends. Bisexual Edna St. Vincent Millay dropped her robe at the bedside of one of her patrons, and the poor woman never got over the shock. If the parties went too late, Millay was supposed to have said, "Well, tired little boy, if it's too far to your place, you might spend the night with me, only one flight down . . ."[2] But she wasn't the only one out late. Even virginal Marianne Moore often read her first poems of the night at 2 a.m.[3]

Moore was reading at a party thrown by the anarchist poet Lola Ridge, who was known to host the best soirees of all. Raised during New Zealand's wild era of drunken, sexually exploitative, and promiscuous gold miners, Ridge began writing about sex in code, the way the Victorians used flowers to secretly convey the erotic. The unpublished stanza from her poem "The Bush" (no kidding!) reads:

> The rival sunbeams their fingers thrust
> Amid her guarded & most secret sweets;

They steal & nestle on her swelling bust,
And view unhidden all her chaste retreats.[4]

After extricating herself from New Zealand, Ridge spent four years
living among North Sydney's bohemians who promoted "wine, women,
and song," and where radical freethinker William Chidley delivered
speeches about sex in a toga. The body was important to Ridge. She
modeled—probably in the nude—at art school and later, after she
arrived in New York City in 1908.

The first thing Ridge did upon emigrating was take ten years off
her age, which gave her more time, sexually and socially. After all,
nobody was checking her passport—nobody had passports. By October
of that year, Ridge was working for Emma Goldman, the century's most
famous anarchist. Sexual freedom was at the top of the list of anar-
chy's demands. Goldman lectured all over the country about sex and
birth control—it wasn't just political ideas that brought on the cops.
She also wrote very explicit love notes to her raunchy lover Ben Reit-
man and practiced "varietism"—a chaste-sounding term that meant
three- and foursomes, gay, straight, all preferences.

Through Goldman, Ridge was named organizer of the anarchist
Ferrer Center in the Village. The center's sexual openness attracted
the money of Alden Freeman, the gay heir to the Standard Oil fortune.
Under Ridge's aegis, Margaret Sanger spoke on the titillating topic of
birth control at the center. Theodore Schroeder, founder of the Free
Speech League, talked so often about the obscenity of religion that
reporter Lincoln Steffens commented, "I believe in Free Speech for
everybody except Schroeder,"[5] and writer-historian Will Durant spoke
on sex psychology. According to him, Ferrer Center audiences were
"delighted to hear that almost every symbol in religious history, from
the serpent of paradise to the steeples of churches in nearby Fifth
Avenue, had a phallic origin."[6] Appointed instructor for the Ferrer
Center's school, Durant promptly married his fifteen-year-old student.

"Sex permeates everything," Lola Ridge wrote in her 1909 notebook. She quit the center and went traveling across the country in
1912 with David Lawson, a much younger man. They had been living
together in the Village, where, according to one critic of the time,
"love without marriage was seen as infinitely superior to conventional
partnerships."[7] Ridge already had a husband—he had threatened to
murder her if she took their son to America. Under an assumed name,
she smuggled the eight-year-old boy to San Francisco but deposited

him very quickly in a Los Angeles orphanage en route to New York. The son, released at age fourteen, lived with Ridge and Lawson for three years while they were traveling but was then left behind in a Detroit school, and she never saw him again. Ridge was a "New Woman" and did not let the errors of her sexual past impede her present. After Goldman was deported under the Immigration Act of 1918 despite being twice married to an American—and all the addresses of her friends and associates were confiscated, Ridge must have had second thoughts about her marital status. She married Lawson, making her a US citizen—and a bigamist.

By 1918 Ridge was one of six editors of Margaret Sanger's new *Birth Control Review*. The magazine ran articles like Maude Durand Edgren's "Regeneration through Sex," which posed the question, "What is there between the deep sea of celibacy and the devil of sex gluttony?" Lower Manhattan was then notorious for licentiousness: the Tenderloin district supported some two thousand brothels, and judging from the number of abortions at the turn of the century on the Lower East Side (about a hundred thousand), everyone in the Jewish ghetto was having sex. Ridge's editorial position on the *Birth Control Review* coincided with the publication of her very popular first book, *The Ghetto and Other Poems*. In these poems, she praised women's sex:

> Nude glory of the moon!
> That leaps like an athlete on the bosoms of the young girls
> stripped of their linens; stroking their breasts that are smooth
> and cool as mother-of-pearl
> Till the nipples tingle and burn as
> those little lips plucked at them.
> They shudder and go faint.[8]

and S&M in "Brooklyn Bridge":

> Pythoness body—arching
> Over the night like an ecstasy—
> I feel your coils tightening ...
> And the world's lessening breath.[9]

Ridge hooked together sex and gender in a groundbreaking speech she gave in Chicago called "Women and the Creative Will." This speech outlined how sexually constructed gender roles hinder female development—ten years before Virginia Woolf wrote *A Room of One's Own*. "Genius," wrote Ridge, echoing her 1909 notebook, "is a quality of the spirit rather than of the brain, and spirit is as much permeated with sex as the flesh." Funded to turn the essay into a book, she worked on it for the next ten years but gave it up when her publisher told her she would have no audience for it.

The title poem of Ridge's 1920 book, *Sun-Up and Other Poems*, features a bad girl who beats her doll, bites her nurse, wonders "if God has spoiled Jimmie" after he exposes himself to her, and intimates that an imaginary friend is her bisexual half-being, suppressed by her mother.

> [Jude] is fading now . . .
> He is just lines . . . like a drawing . . .
>
> You can see mama in between.
> When she moves
> She rubs some of him out.[10]

Ridge owned Freud's *Group Psychology and the Analysis of the Ego*, published a year after *Sun-Up*, but his *The Interpretation of Dreams* had been translated in 1913, so she certainly could have known about his theories. The poem "Secrets" begins in dream: "Secrets / infesting my half-sleep . . . / did you enter my wound from another wound / brushing mine in a crowd . . ."[11] "After Storm" ends with "Silence / builds her wall / about a dream impaled."[12] In the aubade "Wild Duck," the speaker sings "a hot sweet song to the super-stars," then says a casual goodbye to her lover—"'Twas a great night . . ."[13] In "Time-Stone," the moon breaks a date with the city, "playing virgin after all her encounters,"[14] and in "Train Window" there are whispering small-town churchgoers—"how many codes for a wireless whisper"[15]—just before, of course, "Scandal," and then "Electricity":

> Out of the charged phalluses
> Of iron leaping
> Female and male,
> Complete, indivisible, one,
> Fused into light.[16]

"In Harness" details what must have been a well-known perk of the rag trade: orgasms in the sweatshop. Foremen were told to listen for

runaway sewing machines because women climaxed frequently using
the treadle for so many hours.

> The girl with adenoids
> rocks on her hams. . . .
> Her feet beat a wild tattoo—
> head flung back and pelvis lifting to the white body of the sun.[17]

Soon after *Sun-Up* was published, the soon-to-be novelist Evelyn
Scott wrote in an admiring note to Ridge, "One thing I am sure of
always is my love for you—your man size courage and woman size
understanding and your complex bi-sexual brain."[18] Scott had just
arrived in New York after near starvation in South America, where she
had run off with a married man twenty years her senior and returned
with a new baby. She sent Ridge a present after their first meeting, and
Ridge answered with a mash note: "Your action is the greater gift, that
I would not return if I could but shall keep always like a flower . . ." It
was love at first sight, and their ensuing twenty-year correspondence
is replete with endearments like "Lola I never think of you but with
the taste of metal in my mouth as if the gods were moulding you with
fire." Did they have an affair? Women of the time often sounded on
paper as if the heights of passion were being scaled. Perhaps they were.

Ridge's reputation for poetic sexual forthrightness was the subject
of a parody by fellow poet Margaret Widdemer in *A Tree with a Bird
in It: A Symposium of Contemporary American Poets on Being Shown a
Pear-Tree on Which Sat a Grackle.* Widdemer makes fun of Ridge's (and
many other poets') glorification of the city but emphasizes Ridge's
real interest in sex:

> Here are trees and birds and clouds
> And picturesquely neat children across the way
> on the grass
> Not doing anything
> Improper . . .
> (Poor little fools, I mustn't blame them for that
> Perhaps they never
> Knew How . . . .)
>
> But oh, God, take me to the nearest trolley line!
> This is a country landscape—
> I can't stand it!

God, take me away—
There is no Sex here
And no Smell![19]

Ridge's sexual nature is almost repressed by politics in her third book, *Red Flag*, published in 1927. "Russian Women" subtly suggests bisexuality: "You swing of necessity into male rhythms / that at once become female rhythms."[20] In "Moscow Bells 1917," the bells ring:

Loose
over the caught air that trembles like love-flesh
Songs of all wild boys who ride forth
to love and death . . .[21]

In "After the Recital," dedicated to Roland Hayes, an internationally famous Black tenor, there is the suggestion of (illegal) interracial sex:

Who cared . . . amid the suave-shoed, white-skinned day
That scanned his body . . . if beneath her fires
Yet throbbing like five wounds, unhealed, he lay
Back turned . . .[22]

Ridge's fourth book, the hastily written *Firehead*, is a retelling of the Crucifixion, mostly from Mary's point of view. Jesus is the great seducer, and all endure "the searing fire of that glance."[23] Among *Firehead*'s "tirelessly extended metaphors," writes critic Julia Lisella, lies "an anachronistic poetess-like lyric style in the service of clearly un-lady-like material,"[24] with lines like "Let thy trumpeting mountains urinate upon her their scalding lavas."[25] Even Christ does not escape eroticization. After it seems he has raped his mother, he begs to return to her: "Thou wound of time that gangrenes now, thou mud of ages, / open and take back thy son."[26]

"Nice is the one adjective in the world that is laughable applied to any single thing I have ever written," Ridge writes two years later.[27] Yet such is the strength of her work that the radical preacher John Haynes Holmes, founding member of both the NAACP and ACLU, invited her to read at his church on Park Avenue that year.

Ridge's last book, *Dance of Fire*, contains no overtly sexual material but was published just as she was beginning an affair with a Mexican man during her travels on a Guggenheim Fellowship when she was

sixty-two. Left in Ridge's correspondence around the time of this liai-
son was a slip of gold-orange paper with a note written in her hand:

> that has nothing to do with the emotional attractions of one being
> for another in which while it lasts anyhow—dignity is pretty gener-
> ally forced to abdicate—and most every other attribute of the ego
> that is likely to obstruct that very exclusive jealous and single
> urge . . .[28]

It might not have been her first affair. There is a letter from a "Stan" five
years earlier that's very suggestive of a brief relationship. Addressed to
"Darling" and signed "all my love," the letter is replete with compliments, as well as the timid assertion that he "dare to talk to you as an
equal." Adultery was all the rage. Millay rendezvoused with a young
man with her husband's consent, and Ridge's friend Eda Lou Walton
had affairs with Margaret Mead's husband and brother—and many
others. For years, Ridge had hoped that her husband would take a
lover, complaining that if he gave her money, he wouldn't be able
to afford a girlfriend. She even tried to act as a matchmaker, but he
refused to be involved with anyone else. After her affair in Mexico, she
was marooned penniless in California, and Ridge's husband offered to
take her back. She died a few years later in an apartment they shared
in Brooklyn.

Her husband bequeathed Ridge's library to Bryn Mawr College, writing his name inside four of her eight books on phallic worship, two
of them heavily illustrated. *Ophiolatreia* begins, "O, the worship of
the serpent, next to the adoration of the phallus, is one of the most
remarkable, and, on first sight, unaccountable forms of religion the
world has ever known." Ridge notes of the author of *Sex Symbolism
in Religion* that "This man is too biased and undeveloped." *Phallicism
in Ancient Worship* features pictures of pillars and columns, and *The
Story of Phallicism* devotes many pages to Roman prostitution. Ridge's
statements on bisexual creativity are affirmed in *Sex and Sex Worship*,
published a year after her speech in Chicago. It cites Philo, a Jewish
philosopher contemporaneous with Jesus who believed that Adam was
an androgynous being "in the likeness of God," and Plato, who saw
male and female as sexual halves.

As Lola Ridge put it in a 1935 interview, "I write about something
that I feel intensely. How can you help writing about something you
feel intensely?" Her writing spanned highly political topics such as
executions, labor leaders, race riots, and lynchings, but sex was central

to Ridge—celebrated but not separate from her anarchist politics. Her work has been historically neglected partially because Ridge was too radical, in life and in work—which begs the question: Is her sexually charged work still too hot, even for today?

Anonymous Was a Riot Grrrl:
On Virginia Woolf and Nineties Feminism

Eleanor C. Whitney, April 2023

IN SIXTH GRADE, I decided that I was going to be a feminist. It was 1993. I was stubborn, independent, and loud. I was enraged by the fact that society treated girls as weaker, dumber, and less important than boys. Somehow I missed feminist-infused teen magazines like *Sassy* and even the historically important *Ms*. But I did find Virginia Woolf.

I spent my summers in middle school and early high school venturing to the public library and reading *To the Lighthouse*, *The Waves*, "The Death of the Moth," and, quintessentially, *A Room of One's Own*. In the summer between middle and high school I attended a horseback- riding camp in rural Vermont and dragged my borrowed hardcover copy of *To the Lighthouse* along with me. On a free afternoon I sat in the dappled sun, leaning against the scratchy bark of a willow tree by a small, still pond, reading Woolf and feeling like I was accessing something profound. I let her language wash over me even when I couldn't fully grasp its meaning. I was struck by her determination to put her voice into the world as a free spirit pushing against the bourgeois ideals she was raised on. As I read her work, I searched for a road map for being a feminist, a writer, and a person who mattered to the world. I was intrigued by her intimate relationships with women as I tried to name my own queer sexuality. I treated my ability to work through her dense, difficult texts like a feminist badge of honor.

When, later in high school, I discovered Riot Grrrl music and zines thanks to the local Portland, Maine, record shop and an issue of *Spin* magazine, it felt like a lifeline and a way to channel my feminist anger. Riot Grrrl was the feminist template I had been looking for. Its urgency and insistence that girls' voices and experiences mattered now spoke to my soul. The queer and feminist themes that had been subtle or implied in Woolf were made explicit in grrrls' zines and music.

Emboldened by their energy and punk attitude, I ditched my emotionally manipulative first boyfriend, came out as queer, cofounded a teenage feminist activist group, and started a band and zine, which I mailed to other Riot Grrrl pen pals. The idea of self-publishing, of making our own culture and controlling the means of production, felt empowering and punk. As I came into my own as a self-appointed revolutionary and third wave feminist, I thought I was leaving Woolf's rarefied literary world behind and moved on to more contemporary, intersectional authors and activists.

But the phrase "Anonymous was a woman" seemed to follow me everywhere. It adorned purple bumper stickers stuck to Volvo station wagons that passed me on the highway as I learned to drive, the teal T-shirts of my mother's artist friends, a faded mug on my English teacher's desk while I argued with male classmates that the reason there weren't more "great" women writers was because of structural forces of oppression (the central argument, of course, of *A Room of One's Own*).

I didn't pick up Virginia Woolf again until the winter of 2023, when I reread *A Room of One's Own* while researching a longer writing project exploring feminist notions of home. As I read, I felt like I had stepped back into not only the 1920s but the 1990s. I hadn't realized that "Anonymous was a woman," a slogan that felt so ubiquitous in 1990s feminism, had been lifted directly from Woolf. Why, I wondered, did Woolf, and *A Room of One's Own* in particular, have such a direct impact on feminist ideas and ideals in the 1990s, nearly seventy years after its publication?

The 1990s were partially defined by "culture wars," debates in Congress and popular culture about who was allowed to hold power, have a voice, and be recognized as being part of "American" culture. Congress argued over arts funding and institutional recognition, and representative Robert K. Dornan famously referred to Judy Chicago's groundbreaking feminist art installation *The Dinner Party* as "ceramic 3-D pornography." Around the country, ballot measures sought to either expand or restrict abortion access and rights for the LGBTQ community, which brought debates about gender roles, sexuality, and identity to the forefront. Overall, as formerly marginalized groups demanded political power and cultural recognition, it set off a conservative moral panic about the erosion of "American" values—a political reality that feels all too resonant today in 2023 with the erosion of reproductive, LGBTQ, and trans rights.

A Room of One's Own speaks to these tensions. Woolf's writing directly took on how power functioned systematically and structurally to elevate some voices, namely men's, and shut out others. *A Room of One's Own* is concerned with issues of access to the means of cultural production and with whose needs and ideas get taken seriously—who gets credited and lauded in history books and who gets lost, forgotten, actively suppressed, and filed away as "anonymous." Woolf's essay is a critique of how patriarchal culture defines whose story is deemed worth telling, which, by extension, defines whose life is worth living. Woolf scrutinized how systems of education and religion and cultural institutions like libraries, museums, and publishing worked together to discount and exclude women. She explores how systems of structural power impact who gets cultural capital, recognition, and political power. In 2023 struggles over who is allowed to participate, or even exist, in American culture have roared again to the forefront with "Don't Say Gay" bills, abortion and gender-affirming care bans, and the erasure of Black history from textbooks. Woolf's writing is a reminder that these issues are not new and of how much is at stake.

Riot Grrrl was Woolf's critique updated for the 1990s. Riot Grrrls didn't ask for equality; they demanded space and created a scene of their own. They seized the means of punk cultural production, making their own zines—much like Woolf, who formed Hogarth Press and published her and friends' first works by hand—organizing meetings to discuss topics deemed taboo in the mainstream like sexual assault and fatphobia, forming in-your-face bands, and demanding "Girls to the front!" to create safe spaces for girls at punk shows. The question I so desperately wanted to find the answer to as a teenager was how to build a creative, uncompromising feminist life. This is a question central to Riot Grrrl but also to Woolf's work. Bikini Kill, my nineties feminist heroes, even has a nod to Virginia Woolf in their song "Bloody Ice Cream," which interrogates cultural narratives around women writers and suicide, and how a new generation of feminist writers can amplify their voices and fight against erasure.

It's been twenty-five years since I published my first zine and nearly thirty years since I started reading Woolf. Yet the questions that first drew me to Woolf, and then to Riot Grrrl, have stayed with me: What does an intersectional, feminist life look like? How do I assert myself as a writer? Am I looking for legitimacy and validation inside an existing system, or do I want to tear it down and build a new one with equity and inclusion at its core? How do I push against systemic power and oppression, which are intent on erasing oppositional voices, while also recognizing my own role in perpetuating it? The writers, artists, and movements that came before can't provide complete answers but have provided me with ideas to investigate, explore, and critique. There is no road map or template for perfect action, but there are legacies of struggle that I'm proud to carry forward.

Living and Shaping Literary Legacies

The Limits of Representation

Christopher Soto, October 2015

BACKGROUND ON THIS essay: It was written while experiencing intense violence & disassociation. I was looking at the literary community talk about diversity while I was fearing death. I felt like the literary community forgot about me because I wasn't producing work. I was angry about all the talks of diversity & inclusion because they felt so middle-class to me. I consider myself part of the literary community & was wondering why none of the literary activists were outreaching hands of support to help me get better, to help me survive & to continue producing. Helping a transfemme latin@ poet that you know survive & continue to produce work feels like activism & community to me. I felt so alone, disappointed & disinterested in those conversations about diversity.

WHILE COCURATING THE reading series for *Nepantla: A Journal Dedicated to Queer Poets of Color //*
people said shit like, "The event needs more women, the event doesn't have any Latinos." And people NEVER said shit to me like, "Why aren't there more youth represented? Why aren't disabled queer people of color more represented? How do you center incarcerated QPOC? There aren't enough trans/gender-nonconforming poets in the reading."
  ... Thus, I am wondering, who is worthy of being represented and who is not?
  ... I am worrying that we look at race and cisgender folx // then forget about all the other nuances of our identities.
  ... I am worrying that we profit on the disenfranchisement of the most underrepresented members of our communities while asking for our inclusion. We ask to be published in the name of literary diversity, to represent the trans community, but then we forget about the trans girls who don't have access to the MFA or know any contemporary poets or have money to afford submission fees for journals.

I am not interested in retroactively adding another woman to the reading lineup. I am not interested in adding another Latino. Just cuz folks want more representation of _____.

That feels HELLA TOKENIZING to me, to ask someone to join a lineup because of their identity markers & not cuz I'm down for them/ their work... I'm not down for that retroactive bullshit, but I am down for conscious organizers who strive for "inclusion." I am down for attempts at diversity while acknowledging its limitations and working to undo various systems of oppression simultaneously.

DIVERSITY IS NOT LIBERATION FOR INCARCERATED QUEERS!

In curating events & publications I try to have a diverse array of folx represented // but I'm not particularly interested in (attempting to) have an exact representation of race and gender in my journal.

Cuz that's not possible. We don't have enough pages to represent everyone. We are too complex as people. &&&&

REPRESENTATION IS NOT LIBERATION.

Representation is meant to fail us. Representation is barely a starting point.

WHAT ARE WE REALLY ASKING FOR WHEN WE ASK FOR REPRESENTATION??

Is it about your individual inclusion? Or about an obliteration of the power structures which create various exclusions? Or ...

REPRESENTATION DOESN'T MEAN SHIT IF WE DON'T HAVE AN ANALYSIS OF STRUCTURAL OPPRESSIONS (I.E., THE POLICE ARE INHERENTLY RACIST, NO MATTER HOW MANY BROWN/BLACK COPS YOU HIRE).

I.E.

THE JOURNAL I CURATE CAN STILL BE CLASSIST, ELITIST, EXCLUSIONARY, OPPRESSIVE (even if I only publish brown faggots) ... Especially if I don't consider _____.

incarcerated poets.

working-class poets.

undocumented poets.

Aside from race and gender representation, what inclusion do I want?

What does representation actually mean?

On the Road with Sister Spit

Virgie Tovar, March 2017

I'VE ALWAYS UNDERSTOOD the allure of the road. A chance to play at something else, something bigger, get swallowed up, get away.

My childhood was filled with curly lipped churchgoers who spoke in tongues, an aunt with curious hands, a stultifying fatphobia that ripped my tongue out of my mouth, and an unstable mother who liked meth houses.

I survived this through the pathological pursuit of achievement, a rabid dick-hunger that activated an ancient understanding of pussy as barter, and the most meticulously crafted isolation—a rococo house with no doorknobs. I built a road out of my past, one trophy, one fuck, one stifled meltdown at a time. Roads—metaphorical and literal—are precious to me, representing motion, change, and the promise of a novelty that touches me and awakens my heart.

I'm about to hit the (literal) road with seven other writers and artists for the Sister Spit Twentieth Anniversary Tour. Started in 1997 by Michelle Tea and Sini Anderson, Sister Spit was a brazen response to the dude-saturated open mic scene of 1990s San Francisco. The tour is legendary for having started as an all-girl lineup traveling the country by road and bringing provocative observations about the strange world that had built itself around them—stories of sex and love and survival and the million ways a country can disappoint you.

I remember the first time I got into the tour van—we just call it "The Van"—in 2014, seven years after the tour's "Next Generation" revival in 2007. I was an angry, fat, suspicious, horny, narcissistic, confused burgeoning thinker, newly published, who wore very tight gold clothes that I had cut up and down to optimize cleavage and thigh cellulite exposure. Most of my stories were about my ravenous lust for donuts and dick and a boredom so epic that language could hardly bear it.

A year later I sat down with Michelle at her little round kitchen table to talk about the Sister Spit Tour. I had inherited the position of tour manager, and I was scared of fucking up and of disappointing her. She told me stories about the road and what it meant for a bunch of feral girl poets to navigate an America that was hostile to their existence.

She told me what it was like to own the stage, the highways, to tell a different story than the one we grow up with—where women act only as cautionary tales, where road travel always ends in murder or sexual assault. Where only men can travel freely, without a care, sleeves rolled up, doors unlocked, sun in their face, resting in the joyous aloofness of a barely articulated impenetrability unfairly won.

Sister Spit was different. Tough girls—almost all dykes—took care of each other, talked back, cursed and swore, showed their asses, pedaled chapbooks, shared cigarettes and stories and the worst parts of their lives that had made them the best writers, the best friends.

"The Van" is something real but also something mythical, like a metaphor brought to life by strange poets, artsy queers, and memoirists who elevate oversharing to an art form with their skill and finesse.

Reminiscences about snorting NyQuil in the mornings pair with tales about that time someone blew glitter out of their asshole into a kiddie pool filled with lube.

We drive all day, passing the terrain of the United States of America—at turns stunning and then all too quickly barren and inhospitable. A zoetrope of cascading waterfalls, shitty gas stations, two-hundred-year-old redwoods, tumbleweed-ridden farms, snow-topped mountains, and truck stops that house vending machines filled with Ben Wa ball–studded condoms.

We stay at haunted hotels adjacent to murder forests, and sometimes penthouse suites in Las Vegas where we get our own personal butler named Steve. We know the country, and yes, even the West Coast was filled with piece-of-shit bigots before Trump was elected; we stopped in racist counties where old white men on motorcycles told one of our tourmates to go back where she came from while she was playing in puddles outside a coffee shop run by gay witches.

Life on tour mirrors the life of an artist and the versatility that gives us access to many worlds, no matter how debased, no matter how opulent. The shocking turn of events making each experience new, like jumping into a cold pool after you've been in a hot one. Blood moving inside like it remembered that it was keeping something alive.

On the eve of Sister Spit's twentieth anniversary, I am amazed and moved and humbled to tears by the will and love and urgency that has kept this tour alive. Each new tourmate becomes part of a family, and not just in the cute ways. In the hard ways too. The tour offers an intimate education in the road, the country, one another.

The Van offers the kind of intimacy that renders a person defenseless, the kind that offers me the prospect of softening or continuing to retreat. As terrifying as that offer is, that's what I love about the road. You can't predict how it will open you up and change you. Each new journey is an invitation to come as you are, fear and all, and to be moved by something bigger than you.

We Out (T)here: Afrofuturism in the Age of Non-Indictments

Morgan Parker, January 2015

I'VE BEEN THINKING a lot about the future. What will I do, who will I be, how will I love, will everything be okay. I've been thinking about the planet and how it is not doing very well. I am thinking about marches and earthquakes and the Book of Revelation. I am thinking a lot about death. I am starting to understand I'm not welcome. In my ear I hear Sun Ra whisper, "Space is the place." In my other ear I hear Kanye say, "We wasn't supposed to make it past twenty-five." This is what Black American women are wondering: *What's up to us?*

I can't read another goddamn news article. I don't want any new hashtags or reasons to protest; I just want all my friends on a beach, their brown skin smiling with relief. I want us to feel safe and light and regular and unchained. There is no indictment again. And maybe that is the point. Maybe Black Americans were never supposed to be welcome. Maybe we were never meant to unchain ourselves from our ugly beginning on this continent. I wear the past. I drink it, even, and sleep in it and kiss it.

The lesson I am supposed to be learning from the people who brought us here in the first place is I will be obsolete. At the Museum of Contemporary African Diasporan Art (MoCADA), where I give tours as the education director, someone says it's funny, they never see Black people in sci-fi movies. At the museum I tell students the paintings were made last year, and they address contemporary social justice issues. I tell them what "contemporary" means. They still say they think the paintings are about slavery. Because Black people are from the past.

Black people are from the future, I keep saying. And Jesus fucking Christ do I need to mean it. I am tired of talking about Selma, about Ferguson, about the present and past. I am tired of understanding I am not welcome. My friends and I house-hunt in Brazil, in Canada. I am ready to talk about the future.

Afrofuturism, despite its recent resurgence as art exhibition theme and pop music aesthetic, is not new. None of us wonder why now. It comes when we need it most, when we need to remember that even if the earth fails to be fertile for our blooming, other options await us in the sky. Why do we so innately understand the magic of Octavia Butler's books, why are we entranced by Janelle Monáe's music video for "Q.U.E.E.N," why does THEESatisfaction's *EarthEE* album cover look like something we've seen before, in a dream?

In Wanuri Kahiu's gorgeous sci-fi film *Pumzi*, exhibited in MoCADA's 2014 *a/wake in the water: Meditations on Disaster* exhibition, the earth is ruined by ecological war. A few survivors trudge through life in a sterile spaceship. Its only hope for reinvention is a small sprouting seed in the hands of a Black woman.

I like control a lot. I like making things up. I'm constantly battling a society that doesn't want me to have any control, any say over what happens to my body or my story. Engaging with Afrofuturism is giving myself permission. It is no coincidence that some of the most exciting Afrofuturists are women. In that it is an assertion of self, of the persistence of self, of the survival of self, futurism is inherently feminist. It envisions a world, it creates space, it welcomes. As Black women, maybe we have given up on the present. We see that we are not welcome, we see that we are not in control, so we time travel. Our future existence is wish fulfillment.

Reading through *SPOOK: Issue Four*, which explores Afrofuturism through the lenses of young Black writers and visual artists, I see a deep mistrust of and mourning for the present, as well as a desire for escape. I see a complex understanding of time and space. I see a taking of the reins. Most importantly, I see excitement. Black excitement. Black assurance. Not only do our lives matter, they will remain. Like it or not. And it is that audacity, that self-confidence, that freedom to dream that I find most healing about Afrofuturism. It assumes a mysticism. As if we, as a people, have already lived in space, were born in space, and can access another world just by closing our eyes and daring to imagine it.

Bad or Boring: Doing Without Ethics in Poetry

Caolan Madden, March 2015

HI GUYS. I've noticed something about the word "boring."
I noticed it most recently in discussions about Kenneth Goldsmith's performance of his version of the St. Louis County autopsy report for Michael Brown. Many people responded with outrage to Goldsmith's appropriation and objectification of Brown's body (Rin Johnson's "On Hearing a White Man Co-opt the Body of Michael Brown" for Hyperallergic and Amy King's VIDA piece asking "Is Colonialist Poetry Easy?," among others); many of them saw his performance as symptomatic not only of an individual poet's bad taste or careless sense of entitlement but of the inherently white-supremacist values of avant-garde poetry specifically and the American literary world in general (values that Cathy Park Hong brilliantly exposes in "Delusions of Whiteness in the Avant-Garde" and that the Mongrel Coalition Against Gringpo continues to critique and rage against and lampoon). Goldsmith's performance, many of these critiques point out, is a logical extension of a position he outlined in a 2009 interview in *Jacket*:

> I really have trouble with *poethics*. In fact, I think one of the most beautiful, free, and expansive ideas about art is that it ... doesn't have to partake in an ethical discourse ... it can take an unethical stance and test what it means to be that without having to endure the consequences of real-world investigations. I find this to be enormously powerful ...[1]

The word, or the concept, of *boring* seems to come in when people want to preserve this anti-ethical practice but disavow the specific performance Goldsmith gave. I think that's happening in a response from the publishers of Spork Press, which celebrates Goldsmith's "right to fail" as an artist but notes that "personally I find the autopsy piece (offensive,) facile, and more specifically, boring."

I've noticed this logic before, in similar contexts, in discussions of writing or visual art or performances that appear to celebrate or propagate or enact violence: Let's not try to discourage artists from producing hurtful or unethical work, because that might lead to self-censorship, to art that takes no risks, asks no uncomfortable questions. Let's not reject this work on ethical grounds. But let's reject it because it's boring. "Boring" becomes a feint to avoid ethical judgment, to pretend your only rubric is aesthetic, to uphold your avant-garde commitment to innovation, to preserve the fantasy that art is the one space in the world that is free from ethics.

What a relief, I always think. It's just *boring*. I wasn't there at the reading, but Goldsmith's reading of the autopsy sounds boring. And, as both King and Johnson have said, lazy. Could it be that the exercise of privilege, of colonization, of exploitation is *always* boring? Because it's so ubiquitous? Because we're so over it? Because oppression is built not only on dead bodies but on dead metaphors? Because of the banality of evil? Remember when Krystal Languell wrote for VIDA about a Male Poet who read for too long, and all the poems in his crown of sonnets were about a girl seeing "her father's cock," and the women's bodies in the poems were exoticized and objectified? And I was kind of like, "Gross, but this doesn't really seem worthy of a Misogyny Alert, Krystal, this is pretty typical Male Poet stuff, *yawn*." And then I figured out that *that's* why we need a misogyny alert, because the misogyny was so common that it was normal—it was boring. Maybe we *can* reconcile "boring" and "evil"; maybe ethical and aesthetic systems tend to intersect at the point where we can point to "boring" and also be pointing at "evil." We should remember, though, that this is superimposition, not identity. We should remember that sometimes evil is new and exciting, or can feel that way. Evil systems—or systems that perpetuate evil—produce beautiful art. By which I mean religion, imperialism, feudalism, capitalism, globalism. Don't they? Can I bring myself to invoke *The Birth of a Nation* or *Olympia*? (You can invoke Godwin's law now, or maybe you already did when I made a reference to *Eichmann in Jerusalem*.) We can see what is innovative and thrilling in these films. We can debate whether formal innovation can be separated from content that replicates state oppression, whether they should be taught as historical warnings or aesthetic triumphs, but if we saw them when they came out, or see them now, should we have tried to suppress our anger?

BUT ALSO WHAT about how I kind of like boring stuff, how I think there's a value to being bored? (See *Twilight*, the bureaucracy scenes in *Fifty Shades of Grey*, *Jeanne Dielman*, marathon readings of Gertrude Stein, long car rides, reviews of the fondue chain restaurant The Melting Pot written by science grad students.) Or if (some) conceptual poetry wants to be boring, how useful is it to dismiss an individual example as boring? Or what about Gamergate and not feeding trolls, ignoring them because they're boring, but what if you're too scared to be bored? Obviously a poem can't physically hurt someone; maybe the correct response to everything but physical violence is boredom. Goldsmith himself seemed to feel physically threatened, not bored, by the fantasy of violence—or the fantasy of a fantasy of violence—in the language of a tweet by poet Cassandra Gillig: "I want 2 organize large bene-fit reading . . . 100000 poets strong 4 the death of kenneth goldsmith we wld take donations of weapons not $." Twitter suspended Gillig's account, perhaps because her tweet wasn't as boring as the countless rape and death threats that women, particularly queer women and women of color, get on Twitter every day from accounts that remain active. Boring!

One version of the *boring* argument goes like this: If we focus on ethics, if we "police" each other, writers might stop taking risks. (To be "policed" in the real world, especially for people of color, is to be subject to surveillance and violence. We've been using this word a lot on the internet—"tone policing," "attention policing"—usually to indi-cate when someone with power is trying to silence someone with less power. But slowly "police" seems to be becoming a synonym for "crit-icize," or maybe "angrily criticize," even if that criticism is directed at power.) Poets with privilege will stay in their ivory towers, too fright-ened to engage with issues of race or class or sexuality (see Cathy Park Hong's terrifying explication in "Delusions of Whiteness" of the way in which critic Marjorie Perloff uses "racially encoded oppositions" to figure white intellectuals as besieged or conquered—"policed"?—by "nameless hordes" of "indistinguishable minority writers"[2]). If, however, we focus on aesthetics, or specifically on *boring*-ness, writ-ers will keep trying until they produce something worth reading.

Is that why I, as a white woman, am reluctant to write about race? Because I don't want to be "policed"? Maybe a little. My own silence about race is probably one part complacency, one part discomfort, one part fear, one part respect. I'm trying to make that silence a listen-ing silence, then hopefully an amplifying voice. Is it worth the risk, ethically or aesthetically, for me to replace another person's voice or body?

(Am I doing that now? *So, shut up, then.* Somebody is policing me, in my head. That might be okay, actually. Look, I'm still typing.)

What would the reward be for taking that risk? Maybe I can make a poem that is a (beautiful) body you would love to see, but its making does violence to someone else's (beautiful) body. Is that ethics? Maybe I can make a poem that is also a beautiful killing machine, its ignition studded with pearls. Maybe I could turn into a poet-supervillain, the best one, my cloak aswirl with velvet and surprise. Do you stop me for aesthetic reasons? *Yes*, you say, boy-critic hating *this* purple-velvet prose. Refusing to imagine my optative brilliance, the sci-fi future in which my evil poetry is worth your attention.

Is that the fantasy, for some of us? Supervillain?

But also: Yes, if you stop the supervillain's lovely machine, that *is* an aesthetic act, right? Because no machine is as beautiful as a real person. That's another way to reconcile boring and evil: your poem is more boring than the real person it effaces.

It gets complicated. Who's getting effaced and why: those questions matter, of course. There's no bright line. But the fact that there's no bright line separating art from life means that your aesthetics has an ethics. I'm sure it does. To put it in terms white broets can understand: when you stand against capitalism, bourgeois domesticity, Official Verse Culture, when you say "burn down the museums!," those are ethical stands. The question is not whether you make ethical judgments about poetry. The question is who does your ethics protect, and against what, and how far.

OR IS IT not a question of whether that ethics exists but whether it matters in the larger scheme of things? In a blog post about Goldsmith, the poet Ron Silliman told us all to "lighten up a little, folks. Take a deep breath. Some tone deaf poet is not your enemy any more than *Charlie Hebdo* was anybody's enemy."[3] Silliman's point is that the forces of late capitalism are so powerful and terrifying and impossible to fight, and that the planet is so doomed, that squabbles about poems on the internet are kinda meaningless, and, like, I get it, I'm in total despair about how doomed the planet is, let's all give up on all of this and wade into a swamp, I'm *serious*. Is there a swamp big enough for all of us. But also: here's more rhetoric casting Goldsmith as boring ("some tone deaf poet") and us as boring if we get worked up about him. Or is he so boring after all? In one deft twist, Goldsmith and *Charlie Hebdo* both get elevated to the role of Holy Equal-Opportunity Trickster: nobody's enemies, but the joke's on you if you get upset! Or rather: if you get upset, you're not only boring, you might be a terrorist.

No, but seriously, will someone make me a chart plotting the aesthetic and ethical value of the following: #thedress, breastfeeding, a poem, a novel, *Unbreakable Kimmy Schmidt*, a climate march, coffee cups at a climate march, *Serial*, the Mongrel Coalition Against Gringpo, AAA videogame titles, ethics in gaming journalism, *Charlie Hebdo*, polar ice caps, an ice-bucket challenge, capitalism, a Christmas tree, a rape joke, a "death threat" made by a woman poet against a male poet, a death threat, a doxing threat, a bomb threat, *The Norton Anthology*, the Oscars, *The New American Poetry*, disposable diapers, *Weird Sister*, *Against Expression*, Michael Brown's life, a police officer's feeling of safety, a swamp, Plato, the Bible, a father's cock, cloth diapers, risk-taking, silence, Sheryl Sandberg, hunger, human trafficking, human rights, poverty, our water supply, manspreading, dignity, private property, the Second Amendment, the First Amendment, censorship, silence, violence, ethics, aesthetics, boredom.

We're going to have to get a really brilliant, blameless creative genius to make this chart. But when we finish the chart, it will all be clear. We can spend our working hours advocating against the number-one ethical problem until it's solved. We can spend our leisure hours in guilt-free enjoyment of only the funniest, most exciting aesthetic objects and ignore the rest. Our blood pressure will be so low, except for these brief spikes of pleasure! We will all get along so well! No one will police anyone. No one will be even the least bit bored.

Yi-Fen Chou and the Man Who Wore Her

Soleil Ho, September 2015

I WANT TO mourn Yi-Fen Chou, the Chinese American woman poet who doesn't exist. Her recent achievement, notable for the fact that she is not real, is snagging one of the seventy-five highly competitive slots in *The Best American Poetry 2015*. Ingeniously, she was formulated as the Stepford edition of the modern writer of color: a version of us who is white in all but name, who will never know the pain of having her name "bungled or half-bungled" by a well-meaning literary editor MCing her reading, who will never find any reason to celebrate spotting another Asian woman writer from across the vast AWP Bookfair complex, who will never be inconvenient or angry or vocal. Instead of being a real person—which is always so messy, so loaded with the things that make good poetry!—she is a mask, her name peeled off by someone who probably can't pronounce it at all.

In his bio/confession, the man who wears Yi-Fen like a pair of boxer briefs writes, "There is a very short answer for my use of a nom de plume: after a poem of mine has been rejected a multitude of times under my real name, I put Yi-Fen's name on it and send it out again. As a strategy of placing poems this has been quite successful for me."

So Yi-Fen, how does it feel to have a name that is so carefully calculated in its foreignness? To be chosen for the slight spiciness you add to your bearer's tongue, the dash of Sriracha in his turkey sandwich? Your Chineseness is deliberate in its weaponization. (Set phasers to submit!) We know there's a reason why you weren't allowed to choose for yourself an Americanized nickname like Eve or Elaine, like so many of us do in order to lubricate social interaction in the West. You had to stay visibly Other so you could remain a racialized fetish-object; the more assimilated you seem at first glance, the less reason he would have to use you to garnish his work.

(An aside: How many of us Asian women writers have been mistaken for each other at literary events? Raise your hand if you didn't point out the mistake just to save the dignity of the other person/thrust yourself into denial over this event occurring at all! Raise your other hand if you made a beeline for the wine right after!)

I suppose it could be that easy to wear one of us like a mask, as long as all the tedious aspects of our identities and politics were stripped away. Cut out the background, the body, the pain, and the pleasure that all come with being human and you have the perfect cipher. Yi-Fen's captor has achieved the ultimate in separating the political from the personal, which happens to be the poetic endgame that he professed in a letter to *Poetry* in 2010. In reducing a racialized identity to a mere alias, he seems to be making a subtextual argument for racial color-blindness: we are all humans under our cultural baggage, right? But if that were true, why would he even think to use Yi-Fen to bolster his career? How cynical can you get?

Yi-Fen's appearance and unmasking in the 2015 edition of *Best American Poetry* purportedly puts the lie to the curatorial model that champions diversity: a not-very-good poem was ostensibly published because its writer appeared to be Chinese. The esteemed editor of this year's edition, Sherman Alexie, says as much in his defense of her inclusion: "In paying more initial attention to Yi-Fen Chou's poem, I was also practicing a form of nepotism. I am a brown-skinned poet who gave a better chance to another supposed brown-skinned poet because of our brownness." And maybe this new "brown nepotism" *is* a system that could be taken advantage of for ill-gotten gains— by disingenuous white people. I don't buy the argument that being transparent about trying to tip the scales ever so slightly toward racial and gender justice in publishing is at all equivalent to the systemic and unquestioned white-male affirmative action that rules the literary world and modern literature education to this day. I don't buy the completely self-deprecating argument that our writing is only as good as our skill at branding ourselves.

But within all of this outrage, I still end up feeling the most sorry for Yi-Fen. What I want to know the most is this: What kind of poetry would she write if she were real and not just a white man's fantasy?

What to Eat When You're an Asian American Writer and the *New Yorker* Is Racist and Scarlett Johansson Is Asian

Hossannah Asuncion, April 2016

While Catching Up via Twitter on the Latest Inkling That the *New Yorker* Might Not Have Enough Asian American or Other Editors of Color to Say, *Um, No*.[1]
Bittermelon and beef with black bean sauce.[2]

When You're with Your Friends after Work and You've All Agreed to Cancel Your *New Yorker* Subscriptions and Instead Subscribe to the *New Republic* and/or the *Atlantic* Because, Respectively, Cathy Park Hong and Ta-Nehisi Coates.
Dan dan noodles, Sichuan pickled vegetables, steamed chicken with chili sauce, fried lamb with cumin, Chongqing diced chicken with chili peppercorn, tears in eyes, hot and spicy crispy prawns (in the shell), and Sichuan spicy ma po tofu.[3]

---

1. "We're in the Room, Calvin Trillin," *The Margins*, April 11, 2016, https://aaww. org/in-the-room-calvin-trillin/.

2. I didn't like bittermelon (or ampalaya or liáng guā) when I was growing up, but I look for it on menus because sometimes the appetite is rumbling and isolation. Bittermelon, when it is in the mouth, is no language other than what it speaks.

3. The quantity of dishes is correlated more to the emotions represented at the dining table than the number of people seated. The dishes are selected to sear and then numb mouths in intervals, much like the pace of conversation—when anyone gets past their learned diction, a burning bite takes the place of language before the Sichuan chili, as is its nature, anesthetizes the mouth to prepare it for further discussion.

When You Read the Comments.
Mashed avocado with milk and sugar.[4]

While Trading Texts and Animated GIFs with a
Friend Living and Writing in Another Country.
Palabok and lumpia.[5]

While Rereading Timothy Yu[6] Because Stuff Like
Mickey Rooney in *Breakfast at Tiffany's* Is Still
Around and Really?! Scarlett Johansson?[7] So,
Can You Please Pass the General Tso's . . .
. . . chop suey, crab rangoon, Mongolian beef, fried buns, and a fistful
of fortune cookies that say *Change.*[8]

---

4. This is thought, not eaten. A memory of it as sweet before it was savory. It cascades in and out at 3:00 a.m., trying to derail the language of others who translate as a kind of censorship. How many ways are there to say *This is not what you should feel*?

5. The next day everything, including the leftovers, is wilted.

6. Timothy Yu, "White Poets Want Chinese Culture Without Chinese People," *New Republic*, April 8, 2016, https://newrepublic.com/article/132537/white-poets-want-chinese-culture-without-chinese-people.

7. Carly Ledbetter, "Asian-American Actresses Speak Out Against 'Ghost in the Shell' Casting," HuffPost, April 20, 2016, https://www.huffpost.com/entry/asian-american-actresses-speak-out-against-scarlett-johanssons-ghost-in-the-shell-casting_n_5717a698e4b0018f9cbbd121.

8. Change?

On Being Unreasonable

Jennif(f)er Tamayo

CONCEIVED AND WRITTEN between the years of 2014 and 2015, these pieces reflect a critical shift in my creative practice and a desire for greater accountability from both my poetry community and myself.

Part 1: To Being Unreasonable in 2015

October 2015

in spring of 2014 you hear Alice Notley read for the first time in your life. because it's spring, you wear the wrong things and end up with a pile of cardigans and scarves piled at your feet and tucked into your armpits. you drink champagne because you were, at the time, in a depression. hours earlier, the day of the reading, you had seen Alice in front of a Popeye's in Bed-Stuy. you couldn't be sure but you were sure; *it was her. you felt it, and it was a strange thing to feel.* the day after the Notley reading, you find a brick wall near your apartment and write out in capital mint-colored letters the only thing you remember from her reading: "I DON'T HAVE A PLAN / I HAVE A VOICE." *you don't know why you do it but you do it.* this feels important.

a few weeks before the Alice Notley sighting, you go to a colleague's poetry reading at Unnameable Books. afterward they are going to the Copula reading at Wendy's Subway—they ask if you want to join. you want to and don't want to—*something feels off*—and ultimately walk home sulking. you don't know how to make friends and this has become a problem. you feel shy. or are you distrustful? people make you nervous and exhausted. especially poetry people—the possibility for false intimacy is high. to ease your anxiety, you tell yourself you would have just gotten drunk at Copula and would be hungover the next day. *you know what that space is like.* later in the night, you get a few texts telling you to come to Copula but you don't. the moon is full inside you like a knowing thing.

the next morning your friend Cori Copp writes on facebook that her friend was drugged at the Copula reading and did anyone have any information. you feel sick. you feel relief. you feel sick. too many months later, it comes to pass that at least three women were drugged. you feel sick forever.

that same spring, The Claudius App covertly self-publishes a piece by a male writer you had once considered a friend. the piece lampoons many in the poetry community, including some poets published on the same site. the piece is misogynist in a way that confuses you. you also notice the piece is strangely bereft of poets of color. as if poets of color are not worthy of being called out or lampooned. they are not even on the register. or is this the point, perhaps? this piece scares you. what is this "community" you are living in?

on another coast that summer, you see something violent at a poetry reading afterparty. a man friend purposefully shoves himself onto a woman friend. you see it, and because you are very sober, you really see it. the violence. you tell the male friend this was fucked up. you don't do it in your most severe voice, and you don't confront either of them the next day. you tell a friend who wasn't there. *this is as much as you do because you don't want to feel anything.* it's ugly; you want it swiftly behind you. you don't want to see it or think about it. you don't want to sit in the conflict that your friends are capable of violence. you are more comfortable doing nothing. weeks later, when the woman friend calls and asks you what you saw, you tell her the story, and in the telling, the shame rises to the surface. you feel yourself in the moment. you feel her pain. & your complicity. months later, you find out this same poetry party was hosted by a man accused of sexual assault.

on September 8, you announce on facebook: "A DECISION'S BEEN MADE: if your NYC reading event has more than 2 people in it and all of them are white, i'm not going." it gets a lot of likes but you basically stop attending most readings unless you are reading.

later that fall, you read several brave pieces about rape in literary communities and decide maybe it's time for you to be a little brave too. there are things you want to share. there are things you know other women want to share in the company of other women. on September 30 you post: "ENOUGH IS ENOUGH. cis and trans women poets of NYC, we are holding a community/consciousness-raising meeting at Berl's [Bookshop] on Oct. 26th—time TBD—to discuss the lack of safety in our poetry community and our actionable next steps. more details to come but please save the date and spread the word." the accounts of abuse, assault, and harassment you hear over the coming months become commonplace. *you feel* you've been, in some ways, looking the other way.

it's now winter of 2014: disappointment or outrage are no longer things you feel. sometimes you use the word "down" or "depressed." at other times, "demoralized"—or simply, "not okay." you like it when your friends default to asking if you are "not okay" because it's December, you live in New York, and no one is okay. Michael Brown. Eric Garner. Akai Gurley. and the others you can't name because they weren't newsworthy enough to make *your* register. where are the women's names? where are the Black women's names? you use the word "hellscape" at the start of emails to friends. you feel it.

a month or so ago, over dinner, a friend tells you that she and a few other women friends are strongly considering creating a countermovement that calls out your activism(s) for being violent and divisive. you have difficult conversations with the friend—you wonder how much discord your friendship can sustain. that same week, a male poet who you admire writes you saying, "I don't understand your strategy," regarding an informal boycott you started doing in the fall in response to the unsafe spaces that remained despite so much information coming to light. in a forwarded email, you see the words "reckless" and "patriarchal" as descriptors for *Enough Is Enough*, now the name for the series of meetings you helped coordinate.

it becomes clear to you and to others that you don't know what you are doing. that you don't have a plan. you don't have a plan because you don't know what you want.

IT'S FEBRUARY OF 2015—and it's time for a plan. I can't afford to rely on my voice only. I don't live in an Alice Notley poem. HERE'S MY SURVIVAL IN 2015:

- i will embrace not just disagreement but conflict, if necessary.

- i will embrace conflict; when i see something fucked, i will call out its fuckery in a respectably loud voice.

- i will embrace conflict; when i do something fucked and get called out, i will reflect on my fuckery.

- i will support efforts following the trajectory of articulated vitriol and pain without exception. this is a good place to start: THE MONGREL COALITION AGAINST GRINGPO.

- i will have challenging conversations i need to have with my family and friends; i love them.

- i will support the "necessary spaces" (often replete with strategic negativity, conflict, discord) that push these conversations forward—even when they make me uncomfortable, because this is not always about me and my feelings.

- i will be okay pausing friendships whose politics are not in line with this necessary, public rage that I've, in the past, worked to delicately negotiate.

- i will be okay working through problematic friendships, when i need to.

- i will be a better collaborator on efforts and extend beyond my immediate networks; i need to make new friends.

- i will "reach toward ancestry to betray whiteness" (thank you, Lucas de Lima, for this & so much more).

- i will no longer perform what Kameelah Janan Rasheed calls "emotional acrobatics" or unstrategic "affective labor." i can't do your work for you.

- i will, when invited to read, engage in dialogue with curators about what they want from the reading.

- i will organize counter-readings when I can't find readings to attend.

- i will read more carefully and respond to everything i read (thank you, Natalie Eilbert, for this idea).

- i will ask that you be transparent with yourself about your politics; you need a plan.

- i will continue to be politically aggressive with my poetry and performance; this is part of my plan.

- i will be a witch. i will follow my intuition, *what i feel to be right for me* (thank you, Becca Klaver, for this).

- i will be excessive, obnoxious, and annoying about my own survival.

- i will, in other words, not shut up even when i'm sick of my own voice.

- i will continue with my activism efforts when a group is twenty or when a group is three.

- i will be unreasonable. i will be so fucking unreasonable.

Part 2: 28 LESSONS LEARNED FROM A YEAR OF "BEING UNREASONABLE"; FOR BROWN AND BLACK POETS & OUR CHOSEN FAMILIES

a status report on my piece from earlier this year: "To Being Unreasonable in 2015"

LESSON #1: Embrace your hostility. Be angry. Be a stain. Be what others call a "negative" person. Create what Lucas de Lima calls a "zone of hostility so large it creates a forcefield of care for yourself and your kin." Pick every last fight. Learn the words "go fuck yourself." Wake up each morning and say, "Our mothers didn't bring us here to shut up." Those who do not want to hear your anger do not want to hear you at all. Those who wonder why you are *so negative all the time* don't realize how vocalizing this anger publicly and loudly might, in fact, be part of your survival.

LESSON #2: As a result of lesson #1, your inbox will become an unsafe space; don't check it in public or late at night or too early in the morning. Or at the bar. Or on the train. Or before work. Take special care

with emails from well-meaning white friends who have been confused by you: *Are you referring to me in that tweet from 2 weeks ago???* 2 p.m. is the best time to check email—far enough into the day that you can still make it through.

LESSON #3: Learn that your first English words, at the age of four, were HI! & PLEASE! & THANK YOU!—and that you were taught these words before you really knew what they meant. Learn that you performed them like a parrot to try to pass as American at an airport in Texas. Learn that from the moment you entered this country, you've been excelling at passing, so this heartbreak you are feeling now, this unlearning that feels like death, this feeling that you've been a phony your whole life is actually somewhat real, *because, who are you? who have you been?*

LESSON #4: You are a mestizx, a person with unchecked proximity to whiteness, yes. There are things that were taken from you that you are going to have to forcefully take back.

LESSON #5: For a moment, leave a room (. . . a press, a magazine, a reading event) that is mostly white—even if you have friends there. Leave the room. Has it changed without your brown body? Is it all white now? Notice how your body feels when it is away—and who it meets on the other side. Notice if you are simply replaced with another brown body. Notice how you change. Notice how the room looks different to you. Notice how you look different to you.

LESSON #6: Ask. For. Money. If a white colleague asks you to edit their magazine or submit an essay or run a contest, ask for money. Ask for money. Ask for money. Ask for money. NO MORE FREE LABOR toward a literary community that often replicates the free and cheap labor systems that made and sustain this country.

LESSON #7: You may feel like a failure when you read for a mostly white room. Notice when you cry and when you emote. Notice the work your body is doing to feel heard. Feel resentful. Feel complicity. Notice you'll go home with these poems, these experiences in your body. Worry that your white, straight peers will just go home feeling satisfied for feeling, even if for a moment, with you. Worry that they will take their own pain, their own suffering, and use it to erase yours. Worry that, on the path to empathy, they will forget you, remembering that one time they were really, really hurt.

LESSON #8: Worry endlessly about being a token. Stay up at night counting how many of your recent achievements in poetry-land are because you are a token. An "anchor token"—the special STAR TOKEN. THE KWEEN OF THE BROWNS who keeps other Black and brown poets from divesting from certain spaces.

LESSON #9: & worry endlessly about how you yourself may have supported systems of tokenism. Because of the limits of "diversity," see the same six poets of color (yourself included) get invited to read over and over and over again. You can name them and so can everyone else. This wasn't, of course, what you intended but it's what happened anyway. This was a misstep.

LESSON #10: & worry endlessly about how maybe it's also been your perspective that is a problem—your whitewashed gringpo eyes. It is not simply that *the* poetry community is mostly white; it is that *your* poetry community has been mostly white. Maybe for sensible reasons your poetry life has been wedded to whiteness; maybe it's time for separation. Maybe it's time to bite the hand that has fed you but refuses to protect you.

LESSON #11: If you have a white partner, get into fights on a weekly basis. Feel like your lover will never understand you—like, no matter what. Ever. Fight about everything. Fight about the podcast they show you featuring a Cambridge professor on the benefits of offensiveness; feel annoyed about the book they are reading on white supremacy; get into a yelling match about how "yes—they enact their privilege all the fucking time." Go to bed saying, "I want to love you forever," but deep inside feel like this part of yourself will drive you apart anyway because no amount of research or reading on their part will ever equate to the lives you and your ancestors have led. Realize *this* part of yourself can't be fully known by them. & worry they won't be able to catch up. This is unfair, but feel it anyway.

LESSON #12: Reminisce on all your white lovers and make a list of the moments they failed to love you right. How one lover took you to Indiana where you counted only one not-white person in their whole hometown—and how they laughed when a family friend asked if you had "been out in the sun for too long." How another lover told you that "growing up white and poor is probably just as bad as growing up being brown."

LESSON #13: When you find yourself (subtly?) defending a white friend's questionable actions to your colleagues of color—someone you may love despite real disagreement—interrogate that defense. You'll say things like *But that's not what they meant*, or *Well, that's not as bad as what so-and-so did*, and *I really care about them so this is hard for me.* Interrogate how your defens(iveness) makes your poc colleague feel in that moment. What is this erasure of suffering you are replicating?

LESSON #14: Have at least three friends who are attorneys. Inevitably, your big brown boca will get you in trouble. Your mother will text you saying, "Jenny, are you sure what you are doing is safe? I want no harm to come to you." You, of course, say yes—but you are not sure if you are being safe. You don't care if you are being safe.

LESSON #15: Realize, finally, that there are no safe spaces. Not with friends, or families, not your inbox or your journal. Reread diary passages you wrote as a younger person and feel sickened with yourself. Read a passage in your graduate school notebook where you say, "I don't like Anzaldúa—she is stuck in the past." Realize you are not a safe person. You were raised in America, and this makes you unsafe to yourself and others.

LESSON #16: Try your hardest to not fight publicly with poets of color— not because you don't disagree but because you refuse to compound your exhaustions. Your survivals will look different. Repeat: *Our survivals will look different.*

LESSON #17: Fight publicly with anyone you want. Be contradictory. Don't cohere.

LESSON #18: Fight.

LESSON #19: Give yourself a quota of white-minded poetry friends in whom you are willing to invest emotional labor. A good number is three. These are friends with whom you are willing to talk and argue and love and forgive through hardships. Give yourself a quota because you don't have all fucking day.

LESSON #20: You work at a nonprofit. Spend most workdays worrying about what you are participating in. Serve on the "Diversity Committee" and spend most of these meetings worried (even more) about what you are participating in, what white fantasy you are contributing to here.

LESSON #21: Realize you have enough energies to do it all. You have enough energy to hate the world and write your love poems. You have enough energy to sit in bed eating Pop-Tarts and watching Netflix. You have enough energy to edit this post for weeks. You have enough energy to go to the protest. You have enough energy to cry. To send a friend a sweet text message. To start a difficult conversation with a peer. You have the energy. You don't know how, but it's there.

LESSON #22: Feel pain and overcompensate your brownness because, as Amiri Baraka writes, you are "deeply mortified" by how long you have colluded with your oppressors.

LESSON #23: Build your legacy and build institutions. This is important because, as Baraka writes, you need to build institutions that won't erase or co-opt your efforts. Seek out presses with black and brown editors. Bring qtpoc voices to the front. Don't look back.

LESSON #24: You mix up your friend's pronoun during a reading. Remind yourself, every day, that you have so much self-work to do. Remind yourself to apologize for your mistakes—and to move on swiftly lest you get caught up in your own fragility.

LESSON #25: You want nothing more to do with a poetics of abjection. JENNIFER BARRRRFFFFF TAMAYO is over. You don't need or want any more mirrors; you don't need to be made "uncomfortable" by a poetry replicating others' suffering; you need a road map. A trajectory toward becoming the person who was taken from you. Write poems about all the things you want and desire and love. Write about hope. Write about pleasure. Write sci-fi short stories about ANDROID JENNIFER TAMAY00-0 swimming Lake Guatavita to meet Pachamama.

LESSON #26: Feel moderately resentful toward older generations of poets of color who tell you, sometimes lovingly and sometimes not, to *not fight so much*. To *just ignore the KGs or VPs of the world—to do your own thing*, to *stop giving them so much attention*. To *harden up a little bit—this is how it works. Look the other way. Your own work will speak for itself*, they say. In some ways, not all the ways, these mentors have failed you and your peers of color; what did they leave you with. What unjust systems are they letting stand with their silence, their gaze turned upward.

LESSON #27: Your most important work is at home with (chosen) family and friends. You can post on facebook and you can attend the protest rally and you can sign the petition, but the "uncomfortable conversations" you have with those you love are the ones with the most potential. Wonder how things would change if after the protest rally, white activists went home to have "difficult conversations" with their parents about anti-Blackness. Wonder how your own family of whiteish latinos has so much to learn about solidarity. How you do this without pain or confusion or discomfort or loss, you don't know.

LESSON #28: BE HOPEFUL. BE SO FUCKING HOPEFUL, because every week or so—despite all the reasons you have to stop publishing altogether—you hear a friend or colleague of color talk about their survival and their brilliance. You see poets of color betray whiteness and the "model minorities" who continue to preach ambivalence and nuance. No to your nuance in the face of black and brown pain! Let yourself consider a radical nonpositive non-rah-rah-hope—a hope so unreal it lives under your eyeballs. Consider it like a serious, worthy thing. A real possibility. Realize you can't say the word *hope* as it relates to the changes you are going through without feeling endlessly ridiculous for still giving a fuck.

Hope is not cool, you might think to yourself

Hope is not for poetry

Feel it anyway

Double, Double Pop Culture Trouble

The Zack Morris Cell Phone Aesthetic

Becca Klaver, April 2015

THE ZACK MORRIS Cell Phone Aesthetic—a poetic philosophy that Marisa Crawford and I recently invented and that nobody's
ever heard of—says: Yes! Go ahead and give in to the urge to put
those soon-to-be-outdated pop culture references and technologi-
cal devices into your poems, and don't you worry your pretty little
posterity-preoccupied head about it. The Zack Morris Cell Phone
Aesthetic is in the same family as the Lisa Frank Sticker, Hello Kitty
Lunchbox, Which Baby-Sitters Club Character Are You aesthetics
(which are part, but not all, of the Gurlesque aesthetic), but in lots of
ways it's the opposite. Because it's fun to put stickers and songs in
your poems—there's a pleasure in the nostalgia and in the flipping-off
of those who want to police the pop out of poetry (say it like "police
the *fuck* out of poetry"), but the Zack Morris Cell Phone Aesthetic has
to be slightly embarrassing. Like that feeling you get when you see
a giant cell phone or a boxy computer monitor on an old TV show.
Like, you're trying to pay attention to the story but you can't, because
god that thing is so big, uhhhhhhh . . . It is pure spectacle, that thing
that freezes narrative. But it wasn't distracting at the time: that was
just how life looked then. We don't have tons of examples of how life
looked for most of human history, so now that they've started to pile
up and life has started to look so different so fast, it's kind of morti-
fying. Like your mom did something humiliating but "culture" = your
mom. "Your mama's cell phone is so big . . ." To get this kind of feeling
into your poetry you're going to have to dig out not just the memo-
rable kitsch but also the toys you never told anyone you played with.
Your secret collections. Maybe that bag of troll dolls with their hair
cut off that you found in a closet at your mom's could count, but that
might be too cool. To achieve the Zack Morris Cell Phone Aesthetic,
you can't be a complicit consumer in a winky way; it has to be something you'd prefer to never tell. Is this just Confessionalism all over

again, but with more stuff? (And what would it mean to want it more
than wanting to stand in line outside the phone store to get the six,
seven, eight, nine, ten . . . ?) What it offers for nostalgists like you and
me is the reminder that the past isn't always cute but is definitely
full of space junk. And we play Kick the Can in the landfill of our own
obsolescence.

Black Grrrl Joy on the Thirtieth Anniversary of *Ferris Bueller*: LaSloane Peterson's Snow Day Off

Aja Leilam Love, August 2016

I ALWAYS SAW myself in John Hughes's films, even if he couldn't see me in them.

I don't say this lightly. Hughes's body of work is consistently characterized as the pithy zenith of coming-of-age movies, enduring due to his representation of real teenagers with typical problems. Yet people of color were either absent or horrifically stereotypically represented in his films. How American. In Hughes's iconic film about the joy of young white mischief, *Ferris Bueller's Day Off*, the only POC are:

1. Two garage hands who take the Ferrari for a joy ride, which is exactly what Ferris & Co. have done, but somehow the narrative holds them as more criminal.
2. The Asian chief of police (legit a rare and brief nonpejorative caricature—and he's a COP, which is like "oh hey, assimilate and

enforce the police state and you're cleared for representation kthxbye").
3. An entire cadre of black people who magically appear and do a "Thriller"-esque choreographed scene during the parade sequence.

Long Duk Dong in *Sixteen Candles* is the filmic heir to Mr. Yunioshi in *Breakfast at Tiffany's*. His name alone is a violence it hurt to type. That one in particular I find excruciating to watch. *Some Kind of Wonderful*, *Pretty in Pink*, *Ferris Bueller's Day Off*, and *The Breakfast Club*—all of these spoke to a Carrie growing up in the nineties, a decade after they were made. I was that Baby Dyke (#ijs) in *Some Kind of Wonderful*. I was that girl making her own clothes from what she found at the thrift shop in *Pretty in Pink* (and I maintain I could have made something *WAY* cuter than what Ringwald ends up with from what she had to work with). I was literally EVERY CHARACTER in *The Breakfast Club*. I was a jock and a nerd and a weirdo and (sometimes) a pretty girl and (always) an angsty rebel. But *Ferris Bueller's Day Off* was aspirational. *Ferris Bueller's Day Off* was a bunch of shit my black ass would have gotten arrested or killed for doing. *Ferris Bueller's Day Off* was FUN. If Ice Cube's "It Was a Good Day" had been a movie, maybe I'd have seen it and not had a need for Ferris. That said, it bears mentioning that I was a black girl being raised by a white mother, around white people. I saw *Ferris Bueller's Day Off* for the very first time on VHS with my cousins who were actual white teenagers. Not seeing myself, but finding some connection, some familiarity there, is a function of my intersectional privilege. That's right. In our America, it can be a privilege to even have access to a child's representational wish.

Which is one reason why generally I'm a "parallel structures" bish, i.e., I don't believe in asking white people for shit, least of all to be "included" in their movies—I'd rather we have a redistribution of resources and get to make our own, or even be left the fuck alone long enough to enjoy the amazing shit we make sans resources, without being locked up or shot at or micro-/macroaggressed. I hold that at the same time as I hold teenage Carrie's giant crush on the *FBDO* trifecta. On John Hughes's sense of story and angst and innocence. On that moment Cam's sick and disabled (I said it) self jumps up and down with angry anxiety behind the still and empty interior of his little basic car. On that moment Sloane and Ferris kiss in front of the

Chagall windows at the Art Institute. On that moment Jeanie (pre–nose job Jennifer Grey) does the dorkiest turn-'n'-squee move on the stairs at the police station after making out with a nameless leather motorcycle–jacketed Charlie Sheen. And especially on that carefree, fast-talking, irreverent life that Rosa Parks and Sandra Bland and Mya Hall and all the beat and dead black grrrls, who deigned to do a thing as irreverent as sit in the white section of the bus or fail to signal in the face of white impunity or exist as a transgender woman, were denied.

In 2016, thirty years after Ferris first captured the hearts of teenage white America, somebody offered to take me to Chicago for a *Ferris Bueller's Day Off* date. Teenage Carrie said YES. She got to have her day at the Art Institute with a handsome high school–boyfriend type

in a bomber jacket. She got to lean out into the Chicago sky from the top of Sears Tower and feel large and small at the same time, wondering what would happen when the season changed. She hashtagged her adventure #LaSloanePeterson's #SnowDayOff, a nod to the (oft racistly derided) brilliance of black baby-naming, Mia Sara's quiet glamour, and Chicago's March weather. We took pictures, and I made a video about the whole thing.

The day after #LaSloanePeterson's #SnowDayOff, I went down to 2337 West Monroe Street, on the West Side of Chicago—the place where Black Panther Fred Hampton was murdered in 1969 by the FBI as he lay sleeping next to his pregnant fiancée. I left flowers there, red ones for the black blood that continues to spill from state violence. Carnations for love and gerbera for joy and alstroemeria because it was the most bountifully blooming stem my broke black ass could afford. I lit a candle and left a page torn from a notebook on which I transcribed "Youngblood" by Assata Shakur.

2337 West Monroe is unoccupied and bears no marker. The neighbor saw me fussing at the gate and came to help. I scribbled these notes in the airport later:

> **Free Time**
> Dave left his
> next-door porch in
> a Obama/King pantheon tshirt
> in 35 degree weather
> to block biting wind from
> killing the light i lit
> at Fred Hampton's gate
> "i've been living here 50 years" he said
> & then, "i wish i had more free time."

Even though 1985 Black Chicago was living with this near-past legacy, Ferris and Sloane and Cam were not. To be black is to never get a day off. John Hughes never considered this. *Ferris Bueller's Day Off* is often called his "love letter to Chicago"—it follows that there was no love for Black Chicago or any other Chicago apart from the bucolic suburban/downtown urban white-flight universe of Ferris and his squad. So LaSloane's Day Off is a disruption. It's me saying that I'm going into that art museum and up to the tippy top of Chicago with Fred Hampton and his baby mama in my heart. It's saying I am gonna BLACK

JOY all over this bitch, John Hughes. Thanks/no thanks and may you rest in peace.

Grown As Fuck Carrie is talmbout: #BlackJoyOrDieTryin. This hashtag is absent hyperbole. It's Joy or Death out here for a Black Grrrl.

PS. Currently accepting offers to be taken to Kellerman's for Queer Black disruption of *Dirty Dancing*, to make offerings to the enslaved people who built that place.

Ten Images of Women Writing on Screen

Li Patron, March 2016
Illustrated by Forsyth Harmon

DURING A RECENT first-time viewing of *Romancing the Stone*,
I found myself transfixed by the opening scene: the protagonist is
alone in her workspace, deep in the throes of her writing process.
As I watched, I wondered—how many similar scenes of women writers at work had filmmakers captured, and what themes could I make
out across them? Would I spot my own writing habits at play in their
fictionalized ones? I set out to find more of these depictions in movies
and TV shows, pressing pause whenever I spotted a woman writer
mid-scribe. Behold these ten examples of women writers at work,
presented chronologically, spanning thirty years of TV and film.

Adventure novelist sobs while completing her manuscript in *Romancing the Stone* (1984). Visible writerly equipment: oversized plaid nightshirt with sound-canceling headphones, overturned Chinese takeout box, lit tapered candle, typewriter, can of Tab, an empty box of tissues, the silhouette of Texas on a corkboard. Not pictured: a cat named Romeo, tiny airplane-style liquor bottles, a Post-it Note reminding her to buy more tissues.

Mystery writer plots out her novel in *Murder, She Wrote* (1984). When she's not gone fishing, riding a bike, or slinking through her seaside town in a sleek trench with a determined look on her face, you can find this writer pecking at keys in her dark, musty den, delighting at her tale's twists and turns. In later seasons, she's shown in her sunnier kitchen studio, typing at furious speed, framed in neglected potholders, dishrags, and appliances.

In *Just One of the Guys* (1985), a teen journalist breaks from writing her prize-winning article on how "you can be cool even if you don't dress cool" to negotiate some critical high school affairs. Visible writerly equipment: shoulder-height stack of textbooks, Webster's English Dictionary, overhanging houseplant. Not pictured: fringed white-leather mini with totally sharp boots.

- DEAR DIARY, I WANT TO KILL.

Diarist bangs out an entry in *Heathers* (1988). Visible writerly equipment: monocle, silk robe, mesh inbox, letter organizer, white vessel with a cork in it, stuffed toys on a sill or in a fireplace, bookshelves. Not pictured: upper-crust parents.

In *Poetic Justice* (1993), a poet pens thoughtful curlicues in a leather-bound notebook propped against her steering column between shifts at an LA hair salon. Visible writerly equipment: car parts and a laminated pansy. Not pictured until later: Maya Angelou!

In *The Hours* (2002), a foremost modernist surrounds herself in fanned stacks of paper, everything dappled with light. Visible writerly equipment: a teacup, a half-smoked cigarette, sensible Mary Janes, a loosening braid. Partially pictured: her inalienable inner despair.

THE HUNTER AND THE
HUNTED...

In *The L Word* (2005), a writer aims to rid her short story, "Thus Spoke Sarah Schuster," of what her instructor deems "hubristic, overly precious puns." Visible writerly equipment: red Bic pen, legal pad, Peter Pan collar, black jumper. Not pictured: the doe-eyed visage enclosing her formidable brain.

I EXPECT YOU PEOPLE
TO DIG DEEPER!

In *Ugly Betty* (2008), a creative writing student recoils when her instructor admonishes her in front of the class. Visible writerly equipment: troll doll pencil topper, spiral-bound notebook, puffed sleeves. Not pictured: the know-it-all professor who raises his voice in an ALL-CAPS effort to make her find hers.

My mother never held my hand.

Memoirist pens her first-ever tortured account in *Violette* (2013). Visible writerly equipment: consistent color palette of red, blue, brown, green, and plaid; a perch of moss-covered stones; and disused buildings. Above her (not pictured): the waggling bare limbs of trees.

Jane turned to her writing to make things better,

Hopeful romance novelist mends a rift in her writing group by offering a cheerier critique in *Jane the Virgin* (2014). Visible writerly equipment: billowy nightshirt, gossamer curtains, colorful notecards, muted lighting, soulful aura. Previously pictured: Jane Seymour, workshop instructor extraordinaire.

IF WE TAKE these depictions as true, women writers are working at home in poor lighting in the off hours, wearing their choicest pajamas. They write publicly in classrooms, nature, and parked cars. They are sometimes struck with emotions that leave them with delighted, soulful, bereft, or beatific facial expressions. While there's plenty that's not pictured, this isn't too far off from my own experience as a woman writing in the world. How does it match up with yours?

How Girls See Girls: A Closer Look at
Pretty Little Liars before Its Final Season

Flannery Cashill, April 2017

THERE'S A LOT of gossip but a dearth of good scholarship about *Pretty Little Liars*, or, familiarly, *PLL*. Why is this? It's true, *PLL* is dumb. The show revolves around four or five girls, each a different shade of Disney princess, each from improbably wealthy families. The drama begins when queen bee Alison goes missing; a year after her funeral, her friends start receiving texts that threaten to expose them as liars, lesbians, precocious Lolita types, and/or former fat kids. Occasionally they get group texts like this one: "I'm still here bitches, and I know everything. —A."

Spoiler alert: this show gets so fucked up, I don't know how it was ever on television, let alone ABC Family. A, the anonymous author of these texts, will eventually break into their Chinese takeaway, fill it with dirt and worms, then text, "This is what live bait looks like." In a separate episode, A will extract the fortunes from their fortune cookies and replace them with a note of their own: "Liars and tigers and bitches, oh my!" A will sneak into their cafeteria and tamper with their Alpha-Bits, replacing all twenty-five other letters with *A*. (This episode is called "Touched by an A-ngel.") A will sabotage a memorial fashion show with heavy metal guitar and flame graphics, screaming over the PA, "THE BITCH IS DEAD!" In their final coup, A will build a dollhouse in the middle of nowhere, with facsimile replicas of the girls' rooms, then submit them to psychological battery. One will wake up covered in blood; another will get her hair cut short. A is that unpredictable.

Who is A? It doesn't matter. Like *Twin Peaks*, *Pretty Little Liars* is most enjoyable when it meanders, when the lead character gets lost in the woods or stuck in a stranger's cabin. The comparisons end there. *Twin Peaks* was sexy and cool; *Pretty Little Liars* is not. It's a flaming circus tent of tween vulgarity, a sweet-sixteen cake that's pink, black, and mostly fondant. Adam Lambert makes a cameo as himself. Every week is either Halloween or homecoming, and every dance is a masquerade ball. Actually every day is a masquerade: no one needs an occasion to wear fascinators in earnest or corsets as outerwear. If you find the Dresden Dolls cringeworthy, you'll find *Pretty Little Liars* disgusting. Trust me, I do.

I watched about two million episodes of this show, studying its politics, its motivations, and its ethics. Guess what: it doesn't have any. Rosewood is an extremely wealthy town, majority white, with a few racially ambiguous hotties, a lesbian bar, and an international airport. The weather always calls for layers and belted dresses. The girls aren't feminists, but they do solve crimes. They deal with gaslighting, manipulation, and slut shaming, but that doesn't stop them from waking up, curling every inch of their hair, and choosing a new outrageous outfit. The identity of A, once revealed, will shock viewers like me into searching for its implications, of which there are none. *PLL* is oblivious to conversations about identity, feminism, or intersectionality. There are no special episodes, no stereotypes except one: every single person might be a supervillain cyberstalker.

Pretty Little Liars has nothing to say about anything. It's dumb, yes, but how dumb? Novelist Charles Baxter came to class during my time in graduate school and rhapsodized about *Breaking Bad*, comparing it to *The Godfather*: "Americans like to see men pass a threshold, after which there is no going back." Fair enough. Maybe I like to watch teen girls drive cars off a cliff. If *Pretty Little Liars* is so dumb, why did I watch so much of it? The gold standard of this new golden era of television, it seems, is how far men can transgress, how long before they break out of their domestic routine to announce, "I am the one who knocks." The central premise of these shows is that people are corruptible, families are changing, and everyone has a price. If the greatness of a show is measured by how far it will go, may I nominate *Pretty Little Liars* for consideration? At one point, A breaks into the Magic 8 Ball biz, delivering four of them, custom made: "Kisses, A." *Pretty Little Liars* realized the narrative potential of cyberstalking years before *Black Mirror* did the same. It predicted doxing before smartphones were even a thing. *Pretty Little Liars* is not just tons of fun; it's prescient, if goofy.

This theory of threshold-crossing relies on a few other things Charles Baxter did not mention, including plausibility, middle-class ordinariness, and male fantasy. No matter how stupid a show might be, it will be taken seriously if a man can wonder what he would do better. *Pretty Little Liars* has no point of entry for male viewers. In my experience, it scares men away. The soft focus of early episodes quickly yields to something more critical: how girls see girls. What is Aria wearing? What the hell is Hanna thinking? What will Spencer do to maintain her GPA? And how many yellow tank tops were hurt in the making of this show?*

Pretty Little Liars spoils its female fans. For men, it offers little incentive. Few guys would project themselves onto the needy boyfriends that nag the main characters or the sociopathic losers that stalk them (one often turns out to be the other.) Fans of hard-boiled detective stories will be disappointed by the show's pizzazz. According to the New York Times, the viewership of Pretty Little Liars is 94 percent female. As far as I can tell, the show's producers couldn't care less. The Lana Del Rey song in the background lets me know that Pretty Little Liars cares first and foremost about me and my friends. I struggle to see what's so great about TV right now, but I've let go of my qualms with PLL. It's fun. It's fucked up. And, poor me, it's almost over.

*Credit to the Forever Young Adult forums for this joke.

Twin Freaks: Being Both Victim and Protector

Emily Brandt, November 2014

MY PARTNER AND I just finished watching *Twin Peaks*, and now my sleep's gone to shit/the Black Lodge. About a decade ago, I unknowingly watched the final episode, and so I knew that (spoiler alert even though this happened circa 1991) Agent Cooper would become Bob, and I had no interest in going back to the beginning to watch the unfolding of this tragic trick. But, frustrated with our dwindling Netflix queue, we decided to check out the first episode. Admittedly the opening credits sequence is pure sawmill mechanistic glory. But the first ten minutes of episode 1 left a bad taste in my mouth. It opens with a shot of a wispy-voiced Chinese-American woman applying makeup in the mirror with a look of seductive devastation. Five minutes later, we find the washed-up corpse of a blond homecoming queen, naked and presumably raped before her murder. These tired tropes again. So tired again.

And yet, by the end of the first episode I was hooked. My partner, Eric, was too. Anyone who's watched the show knows why: the camp, the sincerity, the doubling, the mystery, the set decoration, Audrey Horne creeping through motel walls, pretty much everything said by Agent Cooper. I'd watch Coop projected on our basement wall, glance over at Eric, whose profile looks like his, and wonder if my love, too, could get possessed by Murderer Bob.

TV series have a way of interrupting our lives. When *The X-Files* was on, my Sunday meals were planned around each episode, and my dreams consisted mostly of Mulder, Scully, aliens, bounty hunters, and those mutant brothers from the episode "Home"—you know, the one when Mulder tells Scully she'd make a really good mother. Incest remains a taboo directors love to investigate, and David Lynch used it to unnerve *Twin Peaks* viewers while taking a fairly annoying say-little stance when talking about the show. Maybe we shouldn't need an explanation for art. But. When my sleep gets interrupted by the vision of Leland Palmer staring in the mirror at Murderer Bob's face, someone's got some explaining to do.

Since I knew the show's final revelation before watching it, I thought for sure my emotions would stay nice and tidy throughout the twenty-nine episodes leading up to the finale. Not so. The first sight of Bob utterly unnerved me, and I had two full-fledged nervous breakdowns throughout the series. The first one was Bob-related, but I can't peg the moment. Must have blocked it out. Maybe it was that first sighting, when he was crawling around the Palmers' sitting-room carpet. The second was the horrible murder of Maddy by Leland/Bob. After that, Eric had to peel me off the floor and put me to bed, where I'd wake up from nightmares only to look over at Eric who would be looking like Agent Cooper, so then I'd have to worry that Eric was possessed by Bob and maybe if I looked at his reflection in the glass pane of the bedroom door I'd know for sure if that was the case, but I definitely was not about to start looking for reflections of Bob in my very own bedroom, so I'd better just close my eyes and think about ponies-in-the-daytime. In a fictitious world of doubles—Black Lodge/White Lodge, Laura/Maddy, Twin Peaks itself—Agent Cooper reminds us that there is no justice. If Coop is corruptible, susceptible to Bob, then no one can possibly be immune. Of course, at the time of his possession, Cooper was made weak by love and once again off his guard (as when Windom Earle killed his wife/Cooper's lover). Yet my night fear is that Eric will be possessed, not that I myself will become Bob and therefore be susceptible to murdering someone I love. As a woman viewer, I'm positioned as victim.

Now Eric was, of course, freaked by Bob too. But no peeling him off the floor was necessary. I don't chalk this up to the stoicism of men, because who would buy that? Bob only murdered through the bodies of men, and all of his victims were women. The cards are stacked against us girls, as they are in most horror cases and in real life. Men dominate the air, and they don't tend to make movies or TV shows about men being raped by men possessed by demons. So while Eric found the whole incest/possession/murder thing disturbing, I found it terrifying. The dynamic is similar to that which we see in responses to real-life acts of race-based or gender-based violence. There are those who feel "how horrible that that could happen," and those who feel "how horrible that that could happen to me." In this case of responding to fictionalized, though visceral, violence, Eric could conveniently be positioned as the one to offer comfort and strength to my weaker nerves. By the end of season 2, however, Eric woke up with his own nightmares of Windom Earle. Of course Earle was, at this point, enslaving and torturing Leo, the formerly terrifying male abuser now reduced to a groveling electric-collared lapdog. It took a white-man-as-victim to keep Eric up at night.

While David Lynch has little to say about his show, it doesn't take much to see the perception differences in women and men viewers, which seem to line up with my and Eric's varied viewing experiences. For instance, in Andrew Goodwin's not-worth-reading 1991 *Chicago Reader* article "On TV: What's Going On in Twin Peaks?," he asks, "Isn't the crypto-feminist critique of *Twin Peaks* for its image of violence against women (Laura, Madeleine, Shelley, Catherine, Josie, Audrey, Blackie—half the women in the show, it seems) a mistake? Aren't we no longer distanced from these women through intertextual joking, and instead required to feel?" Line up Goodwin's "requirement to feel" against Cynthia Arrieu-King's worth-reading assertion, published online in 2011 as part of Bitch Flicks' "Guest Writer Wednesday: A Review in Conversation of *Twin Peaks*," that the show "is nakedly pushing those emotional sexual violence id buttons to their unbearably absurd extremes." Doesn't seem that feeling was merely a "requirement" for Arrieu-King. Yes, it's much easier to coolly observe violence with dis/pleasure when you're not identifying with the victim.

While Eric's and my nightmares ended up syncing up in time, their intensities were still vastly disparate. I am a survivor of sexual violence, so my Bob terrors resonated way deeper than the hypothetical. The chances of Eric being lured into the woods by a psychopath who will electrocute him every time he doesn't comply are pretty slim. The context of each terror is different, and as we know, sexual violence is not confined to fictions and anomalies. That said, I did somewhat relish my role as big-strong-comforter when Eric woke in night sweats.

After we turned off the projector on the last episode, I had about a week to think about the relevance of coming so late to the *Twin Peaks* party—the show originally aired when I was a preteen. Then came the timely announcement, coinciding with Lynch's first major art exhibition at the Pennsylvania Academy of the Fine Arts, that nine more episodes of the show, making up a third season, would be aired in 2016. Laura Palmer's statement to Cooper in the final episode, "I'll see you again in twenty-five years," now made serious sense and left me nervously wondering what unanswered questions would get addressed in the next season, and whether we'd have to endure/relish in further acts of horror. And, how would Bob manifest without the terrible face of the late Frank Silva, set decorator of the millennium?

I was able to tune out some of the blatant misogyny and racism of *Twin Peaks* because the show was twenty-plus years out—riding the wake of the 1980s backlash against feminism. The trochaic "Who killed Laura Palmer?" may have been the catchy question of the year then, but I'm not sure such a trope would hold up so well now (though I may be being far too optimistic). One way Lynch saved himself then was by empowering Laura, albeit in her Black Lodge shadow-self form, to whisper the answer to the question of her own slaying directly into Cooper's intuitive ear. If Lynch maintains the original ethos of *Twin Peaks* in its third season, I don't think I could stomach it so (un) easily. I'm dying for women to come out of the diners and brothels and bedrooms and to stop creeping between walls and to get out into the world, not get killed, gamble at the casino, do some spelunking, ride their motorcycles all night long to blow off steam, and maybe get themselves possessed by some demons of their own.

My Guns N' Roses Death Wish

Neelanjana Banerjee, September 2018

ON THE FROSTY January day in 1992 when Guns N' Roses came to Dayton, Ohio, on their *Use Your Illusion* tour, I couldn't sit still in math class. My teacher was a twenty-something brunette who let us listen to music as we worked on our problem sets, and we would flip between the commercial pop station Z.93 and the independent alternative station 97X, discussing the merits of commercial rock versus the grunge bands coming out of Seattle that we were all starting to love. Guns N' Roses was playing at the almost brand-new arena, the Nutter Center, with Soundgarden opening, and I had convinced my parents that I *had* to go and that my older brother—home on winter break from his first year in college—could take me and some of my friends. I don't think my parents knew that GN'R had caused a riot at their show just six months earlier at Riverport Ampitheatre in St. Louis, or about their wild reputation, but I was ready to see some blood.

In math class, we were talking about the possibility of a similar scene at the concert, imagining all of us caught up in ripping the new arena—named after the grandfather of one of our rich classmates—apart seat by seat, visions of chaotic violence and being trampled to the tune of a band that I loved. It sounded heavenly. "If I die tonight, at the concert, it would be worth it," I announced, and my math teacher scoffed at me, telling me that it was a ridiculous thing to say. But I didn't care—and I recognize the night now as one of my first moments of courting and desiring danger. Nothing anyone said could take away my emerging feelings of self-loathing, my baby death wish.

I was a thirteen-year-old Brown girl: braces, already a 36C bra size, black Chucks covered in doodles, and I was deeply and blindly influenced almost entirely by white male artists. I read Jack Kerouac and had Aldous Huxley quotes that I didn't understand stenciled on the brown paper wrappings of my books. I had gone to see *Terminator 2* seven times in the theater that past summer. At that time, there was no one who looked like me in popular media, definitely not on MTV. At the core of me, there is still the terrible sensation of feeling so completely invisible in the world—the isolation and loneliness of not seeing yourself reflected back anywhere at a time when you are starving for any kind of attention or guidance. I was so often stewing in the rage that comes from feeling invisible. And then I'd be home alone watching MTV, and there was Guns N' Roses reflecting all that anger back at me. What else could I do but cheer on their callousness? Only now, from a distance of thirty years, can I identify the self-hate that was so deeply tied up in my desire for all things white, male, powerful, and rebellious.

That time in my life was marked by a feeling of searching, of trying so hard to figure out what kind of person I wanted to be. I already felt a pull to be an artist, but there was no one guiding me toward art or literature that seemed to have anything to do with me. So I looked for it in whatever was available, spending hours watching MTV or kneeling in the aisles of the B. Dalton bookstore in the mall, reading books by Henry Miller or William S. Burroughs. I played my brother's *Appetite for Destruction* cassette tape on my pink stereo, folding open the tape's insert to examine the Robert Williams image of a woman raped by a robot, which the album took its title from. This insert, the sex sounds on "Welcome to the Jungle," the heroin references on "Mr. Brownstone," scenes from *Naked Lunch*—all of these images of white male misogyny, violence, and excess conflated in my head to form the only model for rebellion I had access to.

That night at the concert, the whole arena was a bundle of anticipation as we waited for the lights to go down and the spectacle to begin. Soundgarden finally came on at 9:30 p.m., an hour and a half after the show was supposed to start. I'll always remember recognizing for the first time bassist Kim Thayil's South Asianness from a distance, a rare moment of seeing someone who looked like me reflected back in the pop culture I was consuming. We waited for hours in the brightly lit arena while rumors rippled through the crowd of almost entirely white drunken fans: "Axl's private jet was held up"; "Axl is refusing to come out." My brother and I climbed up to the lobby several times to call my parents on the payphone. When GN'R finally came out after midnight, the hours of waiting hadn't soured my excitement. Axl ran around in tiny spandex shorts, his contempt for us his primary motivator. He spoke of how his stepfather was from Dayton and he hated the place, hated going to the Air Force museum. "Fuck this town!" he spat at the crowd, and we cheered at his vitriol.

I think about that moment often: the power of that disrespect and how it seemed godlike to me. Coming from an immigrant family, I had been raised on ideals of being twice as well-behaved as everyone else, stemming from the idea that we were guests in this country, essentially visitors. Seeing this man, howling into a microphone and being bold enough to scorn a crowd of people who had been waiting hours, who had paid good money to see him, felt deeply pleasurable, like being spit on or slapped by a lover—which is not a feeling that I could comprehend then, but I cheered my heart out. I, too, hated my suburban town, and the Air Force museum that my family always took out-of-town guests to, forcing me along. I've read about Rose's complicated life in the Midwest, and his abusive relationship with his stepfather. How powerful it must have been to come back and channel that pain in a stadium of that size, and what an act of extreme privilege.

By the time we left the arena, there was freezing rain pelting down hard. My brother lost a contact lens somehow on the way to the car, and the drive home was frightening—silent except for that urgent beat of the windshield wipers and the gasps every time the car swerved. For a minute, I wondered if we really were going to die, and I'm not sure I wanted it any less.

This summer, Guns N' Roses released a thirtieth-anniversary reissue of *Appetite for Destruction* and a box-set edition you can buy for $1,000. Reflecting on the time that's passed since the original album's release, I listened to Guns N' Roses on a long car ride across Los Angeles, where I now live—and marveled at how, in my thirteen-year-old mind, LA and the Sunset Strip were tied up with this band, and how my life and home in East LA has nothing to do with any of that. I still knew all the words, but I got fatigued after a while and switched over to listening to KDAY, the local old-school hip-hop station that plays Ice Cube and Tupac every hour, music that became increasingly important to me as I got older.

When I look back on that Guns N' Roses concert, I don't feel anger or disgust about being there to witness such epic bad behavior, but only a deep sadness at how moments like this were braided into my adolescent feelings of self-hate. In my world at the time, so ruled by white supremacy, GN'R didn't stand out as particularly racist. Slash, the band's hard-partying guitar player, is biracial (his mother was Black)— which was more color than you could say for most other "heavy metal" bands at that time. Their infamous song "One in a Million"—which has been removed from the reissued album—includes anti-immigrant and homophobic lyrics. It wasn't a song that I listened to often, but its brashness read to me more about the power to say whatever you wanted. What feels better than being invisible? The idea that maybe I could be noticed for my difference.

The part of me that wanted to die at the Guns N' Roses concert in 1992 was the same part of me that wanted to court racism out of the side-eyes and backward comments and uncomfortable questions I had been raised on. Growing up an Indian American girl in Ohio in the 1980s and 1990s was a litany of microaggressions, but I had no language for that then. There was only Axl's howl as he opened that set with "Welcome to the Jungle," and I remember closing my eyes and feeling that sound vibrate in my chest—and at that time, it was everything.

Rejecting Forgiveness Culture: Women in Revenge Films

Rios de la Luz, May 2016

I HAVE AN affinity for revenge stories. Three of my favorite movies are revenge films. *Sympathy for Lady Vengeance, Lady Snow-blood*, and *Kill Bill: Vols. 1 & 2* have a special place in my heart. I love the ruthlessness that accompanies the main female characters in these films. I love the unapologetic politics of killing those who have wronged you in the past. I love the lack of forgiveness. These women have lost a part of their humanity and this is what is left. The anger. The rage. The power to delve into a dark part of themselves because this is what is necessary to get rid of the evil men. They will not be silenced.

So, here's the thing about silence: Silence sunk into the depths of my chest. It made my body heavy and lethargic. As a child and into my twenties, I carried my heavy bones and a heavy heart, promising myself I would let the earth swallow me whole if it wanted to. Silence sent me nightmares about shadow people numbing me into unheard screams. Silence made my traumas private. I carried these "secrets" because he told me to stay silent. He told me to stay quiet. *My mom would get mad at me. My family would be upset with me. It was our secret.* These are the things he repeated to me. In these moments of being threatened by a grown man, fear froze me. I thought of myself as someone who could stop time. Time stopped because I was so afraid, and time stopped because I could feel myself floating out of my body. I thought of myself as a ghost from another life warning me to try and stay alive, keep living, even after this man disappeared to Idaho. *Keep living and mourn for yourself as long as you have to.*

I write about my trauma because I am no longer afraid. I write about my trauma because I know I am not alone. I never deserved to carry that burden. I was very angry for a long time. I was angry with the fact that I felt responsible for his actions. I was angry that he was still alive. From a very young age, I understood humanity was very flawed and complex, but I only understood his existence as evil. He didn't deserve to love or be loved. Why did he get to experience warmth?

My family knows. My family knew. I heard a lot about forgiveness: *Forgive him. Forgive him. Forgive him.* I refuse. I still refuse. I will not forgive him. Forgiveness is not the last step in processing my trauma. I will play my favorite songs on the day he dies, and I will sing to the clouds. The birds will hear me and some of them will get scared, but others will know. They will carry the message in their wings: *another evil man is gone.*

So, here's the thing about catharsis: I started searching for outlets when I was eight. I found catharsis in songs. I loved hearing women scream at past lovers. (Thank you, Selena, Alanis, and Gwen.) I found catharsis in writing poetry. I found it in reading horror books and then writing my own horror booklets detailing every gore-filled moment of murder committed by a killer ghost or creature from outer space. Sometimes I daydreamed about finding the abusive man, and me being so strong, I could drag him by the hair and dump him into a grave deep enough to reach the core of the earth. He would never be seen again. I often thought about punching my tiny fists through his lungs or shoving him off a tall building. In these instances, I imagined him as a splat on the earth or deflating into himself before disappearing.

In my search for catharsis, movies provided me visual representations of something I thought about a lot as a child and a teenager. I wanted this abusive man dead. I wanted to find him and, through a megaphone, announce his sins and then rip his tongue out so he couldn't say any last words to anyone he ever loved.

Seeing Yuki in *Lady Snowblood* unapologetically intrude the spaces of those who thought their pasts had been forgiven brought me a sense of solidarity. Watching Beatrix Kiddo in *Kill Bill: Vols. 1 & 2* leap around gracefully with a sword in determination to find her ultimate enemy made my heart beat faster and faster with excitement. I wanted her to win, and I wanted her to show me there is redemption for us. In *Sympathy for Lady Vengeance*, seeing the fury in Lee Geum-ja's eyes as she plotted against the man who framed her gave me a sense of relief. My anger was not a weakness but a coping mechanism in processing what had happened to me.

Revenge is an extreme, but you have to understand what trauma does to those affected by it. I was seven when I was sexually abused for over a year. Part of my healing has come through a lot of mental exercises in telling myself I am composed of resilience, but not because of him. I would have turned out this way without the abuse in my history. I have breathing exercises, I run, I paint, I cry with no shame. I have my routines in helping me heal.

Sometimes it feels as though you have no control of your body, your brain becomes infested with thoughts of the perpetrators, their faces are imprinted into your memory. So, in your mind, you tear off one of their limbs, you watch them become dust, you see the fear in their eyes, and it is only in your imagination, so no one can tell you that you are hurting another human being.

Forgiveness works for some toward their path of healing, and this is great, but it has never worked for me.

For the women in these three particular films, revenge is loud. Victims are expected to be silent or to be the bigger person and absolve the perpetrators of their inhumane actions. In these films, blood splattering their faces and clothing is an accessory. The blood is evidence that the perpetrator is not forgiven, that they can rot in the ground, they can disappear so they cannot hurt anyone else. In these films, the women give off an overwhelming aura of calm. There is no anxiety or voice in the back of their heads telling them their mission is flawed. They are there to get rid of those who have wronged them, and this will give them peace in the middle of the night. Revenge gives them the ultimate ability to reject a culture of forgiveness.

I AM JENNY SCHECTER, PLEASE LOVE ME

Sam Cohen, October 2020

WHEN *THE L WORD* first aired, I was in the middle of coming out, but I didn't watch. I didn't know yet that TV could be good. I think the thing about TV that I never connected to was that the characters were always so consistent, so themselves. I could never be consistent; I didn't know how to respond to things, what to do with my face.

When I finally did watch, Jenny Schecter was the first TV character I witnessed moving through the world without a stable identity, engaged in the work of constructing a self. The surface similarities were compelling: Jenny was Jewish, also from one of the Midwest's Jewish enclaves, also newly in Los Angeles, trying to write fiction.

Jenny and I were prospective writers, and prospective lesbians, who came from communities that had formed us completely, under their safe gazes, communities that offered us a single, coherent model for who to be. In my and Jenny's Midwest of the eighties and nineties, it was community work, making the Jewish girl, keeping her in town, getting her married to a Jewish boy. Jenny and I had been very, very invested in, and we had to move far away in order to unmake ourselves, away from the eyes of those whom we'd disappoint for failing to return on those investments.

I always felt like an imposter as both a lesbian and a writer. I knew what I really was was a Jewish girl. There was one bad Jewish girl in the vegan restaurant where I worked. She had pink hair and piercings and was in a punk band. She was a rebel. But Jenny and I were not rebels; we just wanted to know our desires and follow them. We wanted selves.

Jenny allowed me to consider the possibility that a writer is a person in flux, a person who can't accept the way of being that's been handed to her, even if she doesn't have another one yet. And Jenny is working. She is typing late in the living room, waking with her cheek smashed into books. And she's fucking, which is part of her work too, her life and her writing smushing together in a constant desperate process of self-making.

I needed Jenny. I was always the kind of girl who could only evolve by twinning.

Joon Oluchi Lee, writing about Jenny Schecter in 2008, called Jenny a "Brando femme," meaning she was someone who just relaxed lazily into straight-seeming femininity rather than working on becoming anything else—and I deep read Jenny's season 2 doily dress in a way that, for me at the time, only a couple years after I came out, felt like it gave me permission to be a dyke: "Jenny's femininity is much like a doily: kinda whiny, her gaze in a perpetual, dreamy glaze, as if she wants to occupy a different timespace; kinda like a doll."

I started the process of coming out two years after graduating college—like Jenny, early enough not to feel my whole life was wasted in compulsory heterosexuality but still late enough to prompt a total epistemological crisis. I was a doily femme too—dollish with Peter Pan collars and very intense girlface and glazey eyes and fashion that suggested a desire to time-jump. I played with my hair and uptalked and got called words like ditz and wrote in my little notebook.

My friend Martabel taught me the acronym LAG, Lesbian After Graduation, as an empowering reversal of LUG, Lesbian Until Graduation, a slightly derogatory acronym for the girls willing to experiment when it doesn't count. LAGs have their own sets of issues, though—we're coming out when it *has to count*—it feels like we've missed the window for experimentation, for uncertainty, and there's a push to declare who we are while we're still in the process of figuring it out, following feeling in the dark, swimming high on oxytocin. We're earnest and committed to queer identity while we still have a straight girl's fear of naming and pursuing our desires, a straight person's archive of cultural references, and so we're catching up on movies screened on our first girlfriends' beds, listening to gifted playlists like homework.

There's this period as a LAG when you don't have queer friends yet and your straight friends think you're in a temporary fugue state. My straight friends would call and ask, "So are you still a lesbian?" *I'm queer*, I'd insist, feeling like that identity was capacious enough to hold whatever I was becoming, plus it allowed me to foreground politics and avoid discussing this want—scary, bodily, embarrassing, coming from some pulsing, slimy inside place. When friends visited me in my new gay life, they'd insist, "You don't *look* like a lesbian," and I'd see my dumb coquettish face and doily outfits and feel like maybe I wasn't. But Jenny made me feel okay about being a doll dyke, a doily femme, about having these movements, this voice of a haunted object-girl half broken by the patriarchy, who is claiming dyke identity anyway.

Jenny and I were not just LAGs but the kind of LAGs who didn't even take women's studies in college or meet any queer people until we moved to the big city. Jenny sees lesbian sex for the first time when she moves to LA—she peeps through the gate next door and Shane is there, fucking a random blond. It is as though, up until this moment of witness, queer people were mythological for Jenny.

I, too, had this moment of realizing queer people were real when I went to NYC and stayed in the bedroom of a lesbian. The lesbian was my friend's roommate who was out of town, but I slept in her room with its (seriously) lavender walls and pinup calendar and queer poetry books and *vibrated* with desire—not desire for the girl, whom I'd never seen, but for such a room of my own, for the possibility it represented for other ways of being, of loving. I stayed in New York and immediately moved into an apartment of lesbians. The first time I saw one of them make out with her girlfriend, I ran to my room and hyperventilated into my boyfriend's chest. This is embarrassing, but it's just to say that *I know*. I get how a single moment of seeing what could be otherwise, of seeing queerness from outside, as a deeply closeted person, can be totally upending. Lee Edelman wrote in *No Future: Queer Theory and the Death Drive*, "Queerness can never define an identity, it can only ever disturb one."

The lesbian sex Jenny witnesses disturbs her. She runs from her blond buckish fiancé, Tim, into the arms of Euro-vamp Marina, who seduces Jenny and then reveals that she has a wife, leaving Jenny in the world-smashing, identity-reconfiguring sex wake of her first lesbian experience all alone. Marina mocks Jenny's engagement ring, essentially stripping Jenny of her entire symbolic order. In her book *The Queer Child, or Growing Sideways in the Twentieth Century*, the queer theorist Kathryn Bond Stockton writes that coming out is always a kind of death and rebirth: the gay child is born at a "post-mortem" moment, "straight person dead, gay child now born . . . even, for example, at or after the age of twenty-five." Jenny, then, is a twenty-five-year-old walking fetus, plus a ghost.

Appropriately, Jenny leaves heterosexuality behind in the desert—that space of imagined nothingness, which is also imagined possibility, where symbols collapse or are hallucinogenically transformed. The teen girl who picks Jenny up as she hitchhikes back from her abandoned wedding informs Jenny that the one lesbian she knew "*totally died*." The consequences of slipping from straight meaning-making are potentially fatal. The thing is, we all know this.

Lesbian-death-as-punishment is a familiar plot, and pulling it out as a threat feels like an acknowledgment in season 1 that Jenny will be offered some kind of reversal of this plot, a lesbian survival story. It seems like *The L Word*'s audience, having recognized the promise implied in this early scene, would demand this.

But instead, Jenny witnesses a lesbian sex scene in her neighbor's pool within the first ten minutes of the entire *L Word* series and, basically, can't look away for six whole seasons—Jenny just keeps gazing at this WeHo pool sex scene and then she *DIES in this VERY SAME POOL* six years later.

Instead of being upset, the show's queer and feminist fan base celebrated Jenny's death. Lesbians marched at Pride in T-shirts that boasted *I KILLED JENNY*. In Daniel M. Lavery's "fixed" version of *The L Word* on *The Toast* (RIP), he kills off Jenny before the series begins. As *The L Word* rebooted, Showtime posted fan reactions to the new series, including one that reads, grimly, "As for Jenny Schecter I could care less if she's still face down in Bette and Tina's pool."

As a Jenny-twin, I can't really figure out why Jenny was so hated originally. It surprises me that Jenny, as a survivor of sexual assault, garners so little empathy from *The L Word*'s queer audience. I can't think of any other television character who we get to watch come to terms with sexual trauma and struggle with the formation of adult identity—especially queer adult identity—in its wake.

It doesn't surprise me that Jenny's Jewishness is missing from the conversation. The show kind of lazily hints at Jenny's inherited trauma—her sexual assault flashbacks are layered with Jewish music. Mia Kirshner is the granddaughter of Holocaust survivors—her father was born in a displaced persons' camp. I can't help reading inherited violence and displacement in Jenny's weird broken-doll voice and creepy stares. And a lot of what people dislike about Jenny is what people dislike about Jewish women. In her 2009 obituary for Jenny, my friend Gina Abelkop writes that Jenny embodies the "shrill hysteria, entitled arrogance, nagging, confused identity" that are stereotypical of Jewish women. But every time I start to think about the possibility of anti-Semitism as part of the cheering-on of Jenny's death, it feels like a snake eating its tail. *We didn't know she was Jewish*, my lesbian writing group tells me, workshopping a version of this essay, and I believe them, but I also start to think about the convenience of refusing to see the specificity of Jenny's Jewishness while hating the things about her that are coded Jewish. But then I start to feel like I'm being hysterical, nagging, confused. I feel like I'm probably overidentifying, and all I really want is for the lesbians to love and embrace *me*.

What I can say more confidently is that so many queer people claim to want new ways of being, new worlds, but then they can't handle the person losing their grip on the straight world, this person-in-flux, this person lost with desire, this person who has had her selfhood exploded open by queerness.

Two episodes into *The L Word* reboot, *Generation Q*, Bette's press manager asks Bette about the skeletons in her closet (because Bette is now *running for mayor*, which, *WHY, why can't we just have Bette as a hot dyke art professor?*), and Bette reveals the official cause of Jenny Schecter's death: "A friend of mine died by suicide on my property," she says coldly. It feels awful. As Mia Kirshner, who played Jenny, tweeted, "That's not the story that needs to be told about a survivor of sexual violence."

I feel almost hurt when Bette, Alice, and Shane get together and *never mention Jenny*. I feel actual hurt when Shane unveils the name of her new bar, and instead of naming it after the dead lesbian who was her roommate, her bestie, and, at one point, her lover, she names it Dana's, after the show's other dead lesbian, a fan favorite, but one with whom Shane never shared the same intimacy.

I want for *The L Word* to be the escapist lesbian fizzy candy it seems to be for everyone else, and it mostly is, but for me it's also always going to be in part about who killed Jenny and who is allowed to live in her stead. So far, the closest character to Jenny is Finley, who people keep calling the "new Shane," but who is much messier and needier than Shane ever was, who, like Jenny, can't handle her shit in LA and is heading back to a traumatizing religious family in the Midwest. And I wonder why the audience is so much more willing to embrace Finley than they were Jenny—is it because her dyke realness is not in question? Because Jesus is a more relatable god to have fuck you up? Because she's more butch, doesn't have haunted doll vibes?

I want to recall what, for me, is one of *The L Word*'s most moving scenes. In season 2, Jenny invites her friends to a strip club. They're uncomfortable and confused until a new stripper comes onstage: Yeshiva Girl. It's, of course, Jenny. To an absurd klezmer version of the *L Word* theme song, Jenny swaggers onstage in the dykiest outfit we've ever seen her in: a muscle tee, baggy jeans, hands in pockets. It's her coming-out moment—what femme doesn't have a period of trying really hard to look gay? Men shout and jeer hyperbolically, everywhere.

They look monstrous, more like the men in Jenny's short stories than like real men in a real strip club. We're entering Jenny's art.

As Jenny removes her clothes, she chants the Shabbos candle prayer silently, in her head, *Baruch atah Adonai* ... until she is standing naked, arms in a vee, both victorious and vulnerable.

The scene is juxtaposed with scenes of Bette watching her father die. Bette has serious problems, real-person problems. Jenny is not a real person, though. Her problem is that she needs to become a real person.

This performance is an attempt at that: she needs to throw herself into the gazing maw of a hungry male crowd and prove to herself she's still there, that she can resist their interpretation even as she embodies it. At the same time, the strip-club stage is maybe the last place on earth appropriate or even possible for a Jewish girl to be. Jenny's performance is unmaking the Jewish girl at the same time as it's creating a new identity possibility.

"What the fuck is she doing?" Shane asks.

And that's the thing. Jenny Schecter is inscrutable to everyone, including herself. When Jenny is asked if she is a lesbian, tears fill her eyes and she whispers, "I don't know." But even when she's onstage, trying to tell her new community who she is, they can't read her. And it's her inscrutability, maybe, that's the real cause of what people can't handle about Jenny—the fact that Jenny feels most real when she is wandering the desert, roaming the city with her belongings in a trash bag. I want to feel like queers would have a space for trash-Jenny, for doily-Jenny (after all, a doily is also just pretty trash). But instead she remains metaphorically desert-bound, or trash-roaming, until she grasps so hard at legibility, at consistency, that she becomes monstrous.

Performance, Identity, and Public Space

How to Not Tell a Rape Joke—
Adrienne Truscott's *Asking for It: A One-Lady Rape about Comedy Starring Her Pussy and Little Else!*

Cathy de la Cruz, November 2016

ASKING FOR IT: A One-Lady Rape about Comedy Starring Her Pussy and Little Else! is a performance that's very much about performance. It's a one-woman show where the performer runs out into the audience to steal sips of audience-member drinks, leaving lipstick trails on our cocktail glasses. The character that Adrienne Truscott portrays is a party girl who just wants to go out and have fun. Along the way, she encounters a bartender who wants to get her blackout drunk so that the men at his bar can have their way with her . . . again. When told from this character's perspective, the idea is horrifying. Then you start to realize how nonchalantly this "joke" could be told from a comic's mouth into a microphone. Truscott's anonymous character is the female butt of a misogynist joke manifested in the flesh. She's the embodiment of the woman whose body and misery are someone else's punch line. Truscott wants the audience to remember that the woman on the receiving end of a rape joke is in fact a real human being who, statistically, is out in the world being assaulted somewhere right now.

Truscott's award-winning show uses the comedian's painstaking research on rape jokes—and the straight cisgender male comics who make them—to create a barrage of rape culture that is both empowering and disconcerting. *Asking for It* forces its audience to confront the reality behind the rape joke. It seems to say, rape isn't pleasant, so why should making jokes about it be easy? This is the first comedic show I've seen where every awkward moment felt intentional and necessary.

Performing the show nude from the waist down, Truscott creates endless tension around what she is going to say or do next. Bursting onstage in a long blond wig, hot-pink bra, denim jacket, and nothing else except for platform heels, she proclaims, "I feel comfortable even if you don't." Truscott pushes the audience to consider what it means when someone says a woman was "asking" to be raped. At one point, her character lists garments and accessories that women are frequently told not to wear to avoid being sexually assaulted, and realizes that maybe the safest bet really is for her to go out naked. As Flavorwire's review of the show put it, "Truscott's nudity seemed less objectifying and more confrontational than a sexy outfit would have . . . She had all the power."

Truscott enacts a character who says she is "new" to comedy but tells her audience not to worry because she's been "watching the pros." On the stage surrounding her there are framed portraits of at least a dozen professional male comedians who have either been accused of rape (Bill Cosby), made rape jokes (Daniel Tosh), or are rape apologists (Kurt Metzger). It's a horrific idea to think that anyone of any gender would enter a field thinking this is who they are supposed to look up to and learn from, but that's part of the constant questioning that Truscott's humor and style are composed of.

Truscott's idea of breaking audience tension is to ask questions like "So, anyone here ever been raped before?" One woman in the audience yelled that she had been. Then Truscott reminded us that statistically speaking, there was likely to be a rapist in our presence. No one laughed. And that's just one of the sharp ways the show works, asking audiences what's funny and what's not—where is that line between humor and going too far? As someone interested in the comedic process, I found the show exciting on that level alone.

Other highlights of the show included Truscott's character role-playing with men in the audience—and watching the interactions take unexpected turns—strategically placed video projections, a rape whistle, and a final manifesto against rape culture set to a Flo Rida song that managed to not feel at all didactic. In a perfect world, this show wouldn't have to exist as there wouldn't be enough material for it, but in a perfect world a rape whistle wouldn't have to exist either. Since it does, Adrienne Truscott is here to remind us that rape is not funny, but breaking the silence about the absurdity of rape culture can be hilarious and poignant.

Soy Emo, Hemorragia: A Bilingual Guide to Bleeding Properly

Julián Delgado Lopera, September 2015

TO MY FIRST menarche party I brought strawberries and red paper plates found in the forgotten Valentine's corner at Walgreens. Everyone was instructed to bring some blood-themed food to commemorate eggs falling uninseminated out of our vaginas, so on the table were red brownies, cherry pie, lollipops, beet salad, red wine, red chips, salsa, tapatío, red rice, red chicken, etc.

The lead facilitator wore a red wig and a red shirt with MENSTRU-ATION IS BEAUTIFUL, Coca-Cola style, across the boobs. It was supposed to be evocative. We sat in a circle passing around DivaCups, small tampons, regular tampons, big tampons, homemade pads, Kotex pads, douches, and any other possible menstruation product. The girl who brought the homemade pads explained how wonderful they were, how the textile softly touched her pussy, how old-school, how anti-capitalist, how pro-femme, how her mama even sewed her one. How she washed them in hot water at night and boom you got your-self another pad without supporting the white-supremacist capitalist heteropatriarchy. Everyone nodded. It seemed all the "natural," home-made products were winning in this game. Tampons were shamed, DivaCups exalted. There is no way a piece of your mama's cloth is gonna resist the avalanche that comes out of this pussy, I thought. Give me my extra-large tampons back and blessed-art-thou Kotex and the Colombian equivalent, Nosotras. Muchas gracias, reinita, pero no. But did I say something? Of course not. I nodded like the others. I didn't want to seem pro-capitalist and anti-feminist. Didn't want all these radical feminists to think I wanted some plastic shit up my vagina that was making some white guy, who had no idea about pussy bleeding, enormously rich. I was twenty-one, trying to impress everyone with my radical politics, and loving everything about your vayayay, espe-cially your period, was at the core of those politics.

The MENSTRUATION IS BEAUTIFUL girl gave the group a brief synopsis of the ways in which patriarchy + capitalism had distorted women's understanding of their bodies and their periods. *Can't you see? They are profiting on your bleeding and on top of that you are hating yourself and hating the vagina. No more vagina hate!* She went on and on about how we were being exploited plus made to hate our bodies at the same time, how your vagina was supposed to smell, how Vagisil odor products are another way of sanitizing and regulating, etc. etc. etc. You all know what I'm talking about, and if you don't, then, mami, you should be doing some soul-searching (the patriarchy is stealing your $$!). It seemed like there was a right way of bleeding, a loving way, a way I had never practiced before. It seemed people's vaginas behaved differently than mine. I, for one, have never experienced the saturated joy women in Kotex commercials do as they run to the beach and back into their boyfriend's arms. My vagina doesn't want to be tamed. When she bleeds, she bleeds. And when she bleeds, homegirl just wants to shut herself and scream for a day or two, banging on the fucking uterine walls until I swallow enough Midol to kill a horse.

THEREFORE, Ms. MENSTRUATION IS BEAUTIFUL continued, *menstruation is beautiful, and we should love it and learn to love our bodies.* Amén, sister.

The menarche party + feminist group changed my life. I remember stealing DivaCups from Whole Foods, trying really hard to fold it correctly to fit my vagina like a glove, but I never got the hang of the DivaCup. Once I spilled it all over myself, but, recalling the wise words of the MENSTRUATION IS BEAUTIFUL girl, I suppressed my anger and frustration with love, like hippies do. Oh this blood is the way my body cleanses! Oh I can also make period art! Oh period blood is great for facials! Oh the womb! Oh yonic symbolism! Oh mama earth!

I tried so hard for menstruation to be beautiful. For a while after that group ended, I continued prophesying my unconditional love for The Period and lecturing any person who did not share this love, at times almost shaming them. You do love it, you are just taught to hate it. Say you love it, say you love it, carajo. Believe. Please. Believe.

I felt like saying anything remotely bad about my period made me anti-feminist. Every month I repeated my mantra: Oh I'm gonna faint right now these fucking cramps are killing me! But I am happy! Happy! I love my cramps! I love almost fainting! I love not knowing if I have to shit when I sit down on the toilet because the pain is so terrible!

But I am happy! Happy! Keep them coming! Oh how wonderful it is to love my period! Ay qué linda, qué buena, qué hermosa es la regla!

The truth is, for most people menstruation fucking sucks. SUCKS. Sometimes it feels exactly like this:

You may think to yourself, mi reina, why you writing a piece about bleeding? That's so, like, 1965 second wave feminism. Because I live in a world where I still have to deal with stupid jokes from cis men (*I don't trust an animal that bleeds for three days and doesn't die*—and I don't trust an asshole who has had the same joke repertoire since third grade. Get it together, homie). Because we still have to murmur when asking for a tampon, because at work people suggest you keep your business to yourself, because we shush and hush about bleeding like we're plotting some coup d'état. Because we shame people constantly about their periods. And because I want to hate my period and know my period and understand my fucking bleeding in all its complexity, its magic and its fuckedupness. And I don't want any misogyny while I'm hating my period, okay? I wanna throw shade at myself in peace. I don't want any *yeah, it sure sucks to bleed*. Because one day that inferior bleeding person may slap you, madrefucker—or maybe we *are* plotting a coup d'état. Who knows. You feel me? Do you agree? If you agree keep reading, if you don't agree keep reading.

Recently I found a BuzzFeed article on new period panties, which really are a joke because who bleeds that little? No one I know. But that's beside the point. The best part of the article is the comments section where many people openly discuss how much they bleed (yes, in quantities. Like buckets and liters), how many tampons a day they use and how often (my favorite part), what methods they use (a huge DivaCup contingent), and how horrible it is that we don't get a real menstruation talk (amén). People were really into it. I was really into it. The more each person shared, the more other people felt comfortable in sharing. I couldn't believe some people bled that much or used that many tampons, because here I sat thinking I was The Bleeding Queen. This corner of the internet, a freaking BuzzFeed article with real bleeding measurements.

I love period talk. I love bitching about it with my friends. I used to love when my mom, my sister, and I lived together and were synced and we just yelled, screamed, and banged the walls asking for more tampons, asking for relief. We connected via our menstrual madness. The house transformed into a cave of hot water bottles, Buscapina Fem, and spinach soup. There's something liberating in allowing yourself to be mad for a day or two, because I certainly don't give a crap about a lot of things: I don't care how I look, I don't care if I'm pleasing you, I don't care if cis men are comfortable, I certainly don't care if an old person needs to sit on the bus, I don't care if shit is due. The pain is fucking real and you're in my way.

My period allows me—who am I kidding, my period *obligates* me— to take a break from the compulsory productivity of capitalism. She's going na-*ha*, mami, Ima be banging all night long so you don't do shit for a few hours. My vagina is inherently radical. I hate her and love her for that. I DO NOT have to pretend that menstruation is beautiful, the misogynists can go play beer pong and fuck a donkey.

HERE'S THE REAL T of menstruation:
1. Te duelen las tetas como si fueras una niña pre-púber de once años. // *Your tits hurt like you're a preadolescent eleven-year-old girl.*
2. Te da una ansiedad horrible y te quieres comer el mundo entero. // *You get a horrible anxiety and you wanna eat everything in sight.*
3. Granos. Lavar calzón a media noche. // *Pimples. Waking up in the middle of the night to wash your underwear.*
4. Sentir que la cuca se te va a caer. // *Feeling like your pussy is gonna fall off.*
5. Coágulos. Cuchillazos en el útero. // *Blood clots. Feeling like your uterus is being stabbed.*
6. La pálida. // *Fainting.*
7. Diarreita menstrual. // ***(alguien que ayude con la traducción.)
8. Estar en un lugar público y saber que te está bajando y no hay baño y no hay nada que hacer y te vas a manchar. // *Being in a public place knowing it's slowly leaking and there's no restroom and there's nothing you can do about it.*
9. Andar con el Kit de Regla en la maleta. // *Having a Period Kit in your bag at all times.*

A few tips to help with your pussy bleeding:
1. **My grandma's caspiruleta recipe for cramps** (I'm giving you part of my matriarchal soul): hot milk, one egg, nutmeg, vanilla extract, cinnamon. Blend and drink.
2. **The best way to not stain your underwear** at night is to put a piece of toilet paper right along your buttcrack (did you know that?

Try it). I always put toilet paper in my buttcrack now and it's magic. It's the difference between waking up in the middle of the night to wash my underwear half-asleep or just changing my pad. Voilà.

3. **Shout** is excellent to remove period stains. Keep it close.
4. **Masturbate** For Cramps!
5. **If you have jury duty**, you can call and say you have food poisoning. I tried it, it works.
6. **If you have to work**, you can call and say you have food poisoning. I tried it, it works.
7. **Hot** liquids. Hot water bottle. Hot shower.
8. **Fetal** position on the floor.
9. **Sex**.

Explaining the Mansplaining Statue Picture That Took Over the Internet

Cathy de la Cruz, May 2015

I'VE LOVED MY last six months of interviewing feminist comedians and creative types for my monthly *Weird Sister* "Funny Feminism" column, but I recently started to feel like I needed to take a break from the traditional profile or interview style I had grown accustomed to. I was wondering when I would feel inclined to just write exactly how I felt about feminism and comedy. Lucky for me, fate gave me this opportunity when an image I posted on Twitter went viral over the last few days.

As I type this, my original tweet has been reposted and liked 1,948 times, and feminist-journalist-superstar Ann Friedman's almost-immediate repost of my tweet has been shared and liked 6,678 times. In the last twenty-four hours, the *New York Times* via *Women in the World*, the *Huffington Post*, HelloGiggles, the *Daily Dot*, Boing Boing, *Bustle*, Someecards, and the *Daily Edge* have all published pieces on the phenomena of this tweet I called "Mansplaining: The Statue." The Writing Centre at Saint Mary's University in Nova Scotia turned the tweet's image into a meme. The tweet has been translated and reposted in various languages. People have started posting photos of themselves with the statues. Art critic Jerry Saltz appropriated the tweet as his own joke on Twitter, which was then reposted by writer Rebecca Solnit, whose essay (and later book by the same name) "Men Explain Things to Me" is often cited as the inspiration for the term "mansplaining."

Last week was probably the busiest week that I've had in months, and it wasn't until Friday, when I was barely able to crawl home from work completely exhausted, that I was able to take a look at the mansplaining statue photograph that my friend Ash had sent to a mutual friend and me midweek. I sat on my couch alone, eating a slice of pizza, and I quickly devoured the image the way I devoured my food. In one gulp around 5 p.m., I posted the image to my Instagram account, which is "protected" and therefore only accessible to a limited audience.

Cathy de la Cruz
@SadDiego   +& Follow

A friend spotted this in Texas: #Mansplaining
The Statue.

RETWEETS   FAVORITES
898   972

3:16 PM - 22 May 2015

The first comment on the photo came from a female filmmaker friend of mine who simply said, "Ugh." She wasn't laughing over my "Mansplaining: The Statue" image as it perhaps hit too close to home. Filmmaking is a field where I have experienced mansplaining hard, and I'm sure she has too. The rest of the comments were abbreviations indicating various types of laughter.

I took my next gulp via Facebook around 5:30 p.m. through another "protected" post. This time, writer Ann Friedman shared my posting, and I decided to make the image and caption public so our nonmutual friends could actually see it.

My final gulp was via Twitter around 6 p.m.—my only public social media outlet, which I've wavered back and forth on regarding its privacy settings throughout the years. Within a couple of hours, the tweet went viral thanks to Friedman's reposting.

By 7 p.m., I was texting Ash to let her know that hundreds of people had seen her photo. At 8:30 p.m., I was telling her that she had inadvertently "broken the internet." At 11 p.m., I told her "this was insane." Her only response was laughter.

On Monday, I let Ash know her image was a meme and she laughed again. On Tuesday, I let Ash know that *New York Magazine*'s Jerry Saltz had claimed the image as his own and that "things were officially out of hand." Her response was more laughter, followed by, "Saltz, you devil."

It was at this point that someone from the media wanted to interview Ash and me about the tweet going viral. Ash, who, if you haven't guessed, isn't on any social media sites, was surprised, but said she definitely wanted to participate in being interviewed.

The *New York Times*–associated *Women in the World* interviewer did not tell us that he would also be interviewing the male artist who created what we dubbed "Mansplaining: The Statue." Oh, the questions I would have liked to pass along to the artist had I known there was a chance to do so via his phone interview. It feels worth mentioning that Ash and I were interviewed via email.

I also think it's worth noting that in this piece, the writer essentially mansplains the image of the statue for readers. He describes the image as "a man with his leg propped up on a bench while talking to a woman seated with her legs crossed at the other end of the bench and an open book resting on her lap." I might at least describe this as an image of a woman, say, reading or a woman taking a break from reading or even a woman being interrupted while reading.

One item that didn't make it into the piece, which seems relevant, is that Ash and I met while both attending the high school operated by the University of the Incarnate Word, where the statue resides. In the interview, I half-joked about the possibility of fallout from our former school.

In the interview, I said, "I actually text messaged it [the image] to a friend before I posted it on Twitter—a friend who's both a feminist and standup comic, and she joked that she wanted the image to go viral," which feels different to me than, "Like any good comic, she tested the material first. de la Cruz texted the photo to a friend and fellow feminist and standup comedian who approved and said she wanted to see the photo go viral." The experience was a lot more natural than the piece suggests.

I have been tweeting since Twitter first existed. I have over 11,000 tweets, most of which are my attempts at being funny, but I've received little indication that what I'm saying is making anyone laugh. Whenever I'm performing on stage, I get the most laughs from the unscripted moments—the moments when I'm not even sure exactly what just happened so I probably won't be able to replicate it again. Similarly to my experiences onstage, I don't really know why this particular tweet, why this particular joke, was so funny at this particular moment. I didn't think I was being any funnier than usual, but I guess that's the magic of good humor: timing.

REGARDING THE SCULPTURE in question carrying any sexist undertones or symbolism—it doesn't take a sociologist to know that body language can say just as much as words do. Body language can reinforce gender roles and stereotypes and can assert dominance just as much as passivity. Likewise, artistic composition carries forth those same principles, whether they are conscious or unconscious in the artist/author's intent.

When asked if I was "cool" with Jerry Saltz "not crediting" Ash or me in his tweet, my response was, "I'm cool with it because I assumed he was making a joke about male entitlement." I also said that I felt very lucky Ann Friedman retweeted my original tweet. It's clear Friedman is so supportive of other female writers, particularly of other funny feminist writers. Her post and Saltz's post say a lot about the culture of male and female critics on the internet.

My implication here is that one gives credit and the other takes. While I realize that this is in fact a generalization I am making about gender and criticism, Friedman's and Saltz's approaches highlighted something I do believe is a problem with the linking of criticism, gender, ownership, and validity. As a filmmaker and lover of cinema, I am always checking in with myself in regard to whether I love something because I actually love it or because a history's worth of male film critics have told me the work is worth loving.

THE MOST EXCITING element of this tweet going viral remains that it highlights the importance of women's conversations with each other. Essentially, this tweet was a text message shared between a couple of longtime friends. The fact that the world wanted to jump in on the cultural joke and have a larger dialogue with each other about gender, art, feminism, public space, body language, humor, and more feels like a total gift I am thankful for.

In Defense of Sorrow:
The Sad Girl Internet Aesthetic

Emily Gaynor, September 2015

"BEING A WOMAN is the saddest thing," I said in a recent therapy session. I felt overwhelmed by daily experiences that are felt by many women, like: having a body that is treated as public property, legal and professional injustices, the price of tampons, article after article preaching *how not to get raped, how to make him fall in love with you (in only seven easy steps! Step one: change everything about yourself)*, a constant fear of attack, seeing little to no representation of oneself in movies and television, online hate. The list goes on.

These things make me angry. They make me want to shout and protest, but I also feel saddened by them. Usually, I keep those feelings hidden. Sadness is often viewed, socially, as a passing emotion that can and should be overcome, an unproductive state that should be actively avoided.

Today, young female artists, part of an emerging "sad girls" trend, are using the internet as the outlet for performing their heartache, sorrow, and despair, creating complex work online that deals with the double binds women today face.

The traditional patriarchal narrative portrays women as weak creatures in need of male support. This role is complicated by the fact that women must try not to seem too needy. Women are supposed to be givers, nourishing others before themselves. It seems that there's a narrow spectrum of emotions women are allowed to express. We can experience unhappiness, as long as it can be cured by a man, shopping, or chocolate; we can be sad, but never sorrowful. Thus there exists a gap between the emotions we experience and how much can be revealed. As a result, sadness often gets stored away and, like shitting or masturbating, isn't really a part of our cultural conversation.

On the other hand, contemporary feminism is often associated with the idea of the strong woman who rejects vulnerability in the fight for parity. Perhaps this equation of empowered womanhood with hard-shelled strength stems from feminism's legacy of protesting, among other radical forms of resistance. This depiction of superhuman strength, while seemingly empowering, is not a complete reflection of the female experience. Vulnerability becomes conflated with weakness, resulting in women feeling guilt for not being strong *enough*, for having needs that we cannot take care of alone. I recently had a conversation with a friend about whether we were "feminist enough" because we occasionally prefer to play a subordinate role in our relationships. If I'm not enacting the brash, outspoken feminist, I fear that I'll be perceived as a regressive 1950s housewife holding the symbolic martini of servitude for my husband.

There is, admittedly, a vast space in between these two caricatures of ultraweak and superstrong womanhood. The "sad girl" movement online explores the complicated territory in between these archetypal boxes. Neither leaves much room for the vulnerability that many "sad girls" are now using as source material for their work. We have a window into the lives of the "sad girls" in this growing movement through their online presences, where they frequently post poetry, videos, and collages.

Artists like Molly Soda, diesunshine, miseryclit, and sosadtoday are regular contributors on NewHive, a platform for creating multimedia experiences with minimal distractions. NewHive offers artists creative control with simple tools enabling them to break genre barriers in the creation of deeply felt, confessional works. They create pseudonyms and anonymous personas to explore personalities beyond their everyday identities. The internet becomes a communal space in which they can perform all the sadness they experience, without the consequences of expressing it IRL.

The "sad girl" aesthetic varies in style and tone but can generally be defined as a celebration of the burdens of womanhood, an exposition of everyday anguish, a shimmery jumble of daddy issues and internet-age references, a subversion of both traditional feminine and feminist narratives, and a blurring of the divide between public and private lives. Much of the work of "sad girls" deals with yearning, loneliness, and emotional hunger. This aesthetic represents a new kind of courage in which young women expose the everyday anguishes of womanhood in a deeply intimate and self-consciously ironic way. These women—though commonly referred to as "girls"—make use of stereotypical femininity and slumber party girliness, often incorporating hot pink, animated GIFs, and sparkly text into their work.

The artist creepyennui often uses these ultragirlie tropes to commu-
nicate messages about internalized instructions regarding sadness.
daily routines shows bubbly pink text layered over a GIF of the artist
wiping tears away from her face. The endless repetition of the GIF
rebels against the idea that sadness must be a brief activity despite the
instruction, reminiscent of a mother's advice gone awry, to "keep ur
breakdowns short 'n' sweet!" The title, *daily routines*, classifies weep-
ing as quotidian an activity as checking Facebook or washing one's
face. The irony in the perkiness of the pink text reveals the unrealis-
tic expectation that sadness should be moved past quickly. There is
no acceptable space in which to have an indulgent sob—only a quick,
shameful cry. By even giving directions on how to have a breakdown,
the piece comments on the implicit message that there is a "correct"
way to be sad.

Humor rooted in the failure to achieve unattainable expectations of
womanhood is often an intrinsic part of the work associated with the
"sad girl" aesthetic, exemplified in pieces such as "SO SAD TODAY" and
"the way things are" by Molly Soda. These works embody an extreme
femininity, becoming a glittering monument to the failure of attempting to be the perfect girl and ultimately mocking the notion that there
is such thing as "the perfect girl."

sosadtoday, the anonymous internet persona of perpetual misery
(who was recently revealed to be the poet Melissa Broder), uses clas-
sical and religious references throughout her NewHives, giving her
sadness a biblical and infinite weight. She enacts a feminine position
of weakness so crippling she is no longer a functional human but a
yearning machine. By doing so she reveals the destructive power of
this cultural ideal while simultaneously personifying it in what seems
like a cathartic way. Further, because sosadtoday's identity is anonymous, we are able to project personal experiences onto the work, which
becomes a source of catharsis for the viewer as well.

To read the "sad girl" as passive would be a mistake, for this new
miserable girl is actually disrupting conventional ideas of womanhood.
Her work considers the desire for dependency that can feel taboo for
some feminists. Her work buzzes with eternal misery, battling the idea
that sadness is to be overcome quickly and quietly. Performing sadness
is a self-indulgent practice, and that's part of what makes it radical.
The act of using public space instead of a private diary to work through
and document this emotional content is a bold resistance against those
who have attempted to silence women's voices. Being sad is one of the

most rebellious things a woman can do right now. Sadness is challenging. A woman who needs instead of gives is threatening.

The voices of these "sad girl" artists are contributing to a cultural
shift, one that values the complexities and hardships of womanhood.
They are opening up a space in which exploring sadness is part of a
healthy dialogue. By bringing these emotions into an art context, this
work proclaims that sadness not only is acceptable but also contains
an inherent beauty.

We Were There: Black Women Artists for Black Lives Matter at the New Museum

Hossannah Asuncion, September 2016

Black Women Artists for Black Lives Matter
Thursday, September 1, 2016
The New Museum, New York City

AT 6 P.M. THERE was a line coming out of the New Museum that went down Bowery and Stanton, nearly meeting Chrystie. We were here to see the one-night pop-up event *Black Women Artists for Black Lives Matter* (BWAforBLM). As part of her residency, artist Simone Leigh invited BWAforBLM, a collective she organized this past July, for an evening of solidarity.

We were all in line waiting to see Black women artists. We were essentially waiting *for* them. Through September 18, Leigh is exhibiting *The Waiting Room*, a statement on and response to what institutions do to the female Black body. She honors Esmin Elizabeth Green, who died after lingering for twenty-four hours in a hospital waiting room.

"Obedience is one of the main threats to black women's health; it was a survival mechanism that Green waited twenty-four hours before collapsing," says Leigh. "What happened to Green is an example of the lack of empathy people have towards the pain of black women."

For her exhibit, Leigh centralizes the care of the body and asserts disobedience as a form of self-determination. There are stations for healing and time for healers.

Waiting or not waiting is a form of privileged choosing. I saw the waiting of us, the diverse formation of folks standing in line, as a kind of belated honor to Black women artists. As I stood with friends, young people of color who work in museums, there was a patience in the statement our collective waiting body said to institutions of art that evening: *We value Black women, the bodies and spaces they inhabit, and the art they create. Give them your time, space, and attention.*

The artists were dressed in red, floating figures of the ether. An atmosphere resulting from artmaking as an act of resilience. It wasn't just exhibit; it was moment. For some of us, it was being part of one. For others, like me, who are not Black, it was being witness to one. This was not what it usually felt like in the New Museum or most spaces like museums. This was here because of Black Women Artists—what they brought with them, what they made within the evening, and what they shared.

Participation in and with institutions often comes with the covenant of propriety. The evening gave a glimpse of possibilities—what an experience could be if institutions shared space with artists instead of allowing artists in.

Black Women Artists for Black Lives Matter
includes the following artists:

Simone Leigh, Elia Alba, Omololu Refilwe Babatunde, Firelei Báez, Chloë Bass, Suhaly Bautista-Carolina, Laylah Amatullah Barrayn, Aisha Tandiwe Bell, Joeonna Bellorado-Samuels, Michelle Bishop, Tokumbo Bodunde, Janice Bond, Alicia Boone-Jean-Noel, Charlotte Brathwaite, Sheila Pree Bright, LaKela Brown, Tracy Brown, Rashida Bumbray, Crystal Z. Campbell, Alexis Caputo, Tanisha Christie, Andrea Chung, Elvira Clayton, Pamela Council, Aimee Meredith Cox, Vivian Crockett, Una-Kariim A. Cross, Stephanie A. Cunningham, Tamara Davidson, Joy Davis, Sonia Louise Davis, Danielle Dean, Lisa Dent, Abigail Deville, LaTasha N. Nevada Diggs, DJ Tara (Tara Duvivier), Abby Dobson, Kimberly Drew, Dominique Duroseau, Minkie English, Nona Faustine, Catherine Feliz, Yance Ford, Carolyn Lieba Francois-Lazard, Tia-Simone Gardner, Ja'Tovia M. Gary, Ebony Noelle Golden, Kearra Amaya Gopee, Stephanie Graham, Adjua Gargi Nzinga Greaves, Kaitlyn Greenidge, Deana Haggag, Carrie Hawks, Robyn Hillman-Harrigan, Kenyatta A.C. Hinkle, Lehna Huie, Rujeko Hockley, Kemi Ilesanmi, Ariel Jackson, Tomashi Jackson, Ashley James, Shani Jamila, E. Jane, Fabiola Jean-Louis, Steffani Jemison, Jacqueline Johnson, Natasha Johnson, Ladi'Sasha Jones, Jay Katelansky, Daniella Rose King, Nsenga Knight, Ya La'Ford, Geraldine Leibot, Toya A. Lillard, Stephanie Lindquist, Jodie Lyn-Kee-Chow, Anina Major, Helen Marie, Brittany Marrow, Nomaduma Rosa Masilela, Tiona McClodden, Paloma McGregor, Glendalys Medina, Nina Angela Mercer, Helina Metaferia, Joiri Minaya, Jasmine Mitchell, Elissa Blount Moorhead, Nontsikelelo Mutiti, Shervone Neckles, Jennifer Harrison Newman, Mendi Obadike, Lorraine

O'Grady, Adenike Olanrewaju, Sherley C. Olopherne, Jennifer Harrison Packer, Sondra Perry, Shani Peters, Julia Phillips, Ada Pinkston, Sharbreon Plummer, Mary Pryor, Kameelah Janan Rasheed, Amber Robles-Gordon, Shellyne Rodriguez, Karen Rose, Clarivel Ruiz, Annie Seaton, Karen Seneferu, Derica Shields, Alexandria Smith, Tiffany Smith, Mikhaile Solomon, Kara Springer, Mary A. Valverde, Sam Vernon, Shannon Wallace, Camille Wanliss, Anastasia Warren, Patrice Renee Washington, Fatimah White, Nafis White, Ayesha Williams, Saya Woolfalk, Lachell Workman, and Akeema-Zane.

Weird Sisters in Conversation

Chronology Doesn't Always Feel Good:
An Interview with Eileen Myles

Cathy de la Cruz, October 2015

IN 2013 I interviewed Eileen Myles over the phone. Our discussion was focused on their two-books-published-as-one, *Snowflake* and *different streets* (Wave Books, 2012). When Eileen released two books, *I Must Be Living Twice* and *Chelsea Girls*, on the same date in 2015, it seemed fitting to finally release this interview into the world.

Cathy de la Cruz: These questions are all about *Snowflake* and *different streets*.

Eileen Myles: I love this new twist in our relationship.

CD: I know ... It's so weird, but it's kind of hilarious. In my mind, you are this book right now and you're not my friend, Eileen. I mean that in the best way possible. Did you intend these books to be read as one or as two separate books? Does one book rely on the other? I read reviews where some people said, regarding the middle, that they felt like they were able to take a breath before they moved on to the next one. And some readers saw it as these two times in your life being permanently fused together in this way. If you could talk about that, that would be great.

EM: Well, you know, I just thought I wanted something to be really organic. When I saw one book coming—the way a book is, it's sort of like you're writing along and suddenly you realize it's approximating that amount of things that makes a book, and there's also some other thing which is asking what are the patterns or the meanings of this book. So I definitely knew that one book was ending or it was kind of full. And as you know, I had left California and moved back to New York and was puzzled how it was going to work with my writing because I was going to physically be a poet in New York and it's a different occupation, so when I began to write again in New York, I felt a little lost because I felt like I was writing in an open California way, but I was in New York, so I was feeling a greater emptiness rather than a greater spaciousness. Then this thing happened in my life where I fell in love with somebody, and it sort of sped up and started to have its own patterns, and when it came time to make books from both of these things, I really didn't want them to be separate volumes. It really was a lot of thinking about how one is a poet in certain spaces and how one is a poet of certain experiences and how certain experiences like falling in love really change the shape or space of your writing. There's a poetry convention where books have sections and of course I've done that in books of poetry in various ways, but it always seems sort of lame because it's in the same body, and we're like, "Here's a section," and now, "Here's something different and I don't know what it is," but it's still in the same place. I wanted to keep the flow of each book and not put some kind of lovely furniture between the two. I really wanted them to kind of screw into each other in this way. The way I put it, you've probably read this a lot, is that I wanted the two to fuck each other in a way. It really was because the connection was so intense and so literal. I felt like I was living one life that went through to the other one.

CD: Do you feel like it matters which side people read first?

EM: No. The thing that's so funny about putting a book together, and that's really different from making a film, is that you know that people are going to open it up and read it any fucking way they want. Particularly with a book of poetry—it's really hard to control that experience. The thing why it's actually a funny practice to be a poet is that you're still kind of operating in this sort of ideal of "If my reader sat down and read this book in a certain order . . ." The more I think about it, I don't care which side of the book they read first. And I kind of don't care how anybody reads it, period.

CD: Can you talk a little bit about organizing each book? Is it chronological in any way? If certain things are autobiographical, are they organized by the way that things transpired or in the order that you wrote them? Can you talk a little bit about the organization of each side?

EM: The thing about chronology that's great is that it's always the thing you can fall back on. There's something diaristic about putting a bunch of poems together. There's a way in which you know that this was early and that this was during this time and this was during this period. So there's always chronology to fall back on, but the thing about chronology is that it doesn't always feel good. You do these three things that really have a sequential meaning, but then if you really went to the next place sequentially, it would just feel flat and wouldn't be fun and it wouldn't change shape. It's sort of like, there's lots of cheating, and it's sort of acting as if you're telling a story, except that in the process, you're telling a lot of lies even in terms of one side of the book and the other. There are things in *different streets* that actually I wrote in *Snowflake*, but I just thought they were more interesting on the other side. There were even a few poems in both books that weren't written in that period of time at all. But they were poems that I never knew what to do with. It's sort of like making a house and how you might move through the rooms and how you might spend your time. You suddenly see that this painting would look good over this couch here, and you're solving problems and it's really fun. And it's also about content. There was all this stuff about computers and technology, particularly in the first book, so that made me think about how those things fit in our lives and how they can be disruptive. Sometimes it's like picking up a phone or remembering there is a phone or something like that. You change the subject all the time on the phone call.

CD: Did your publisher get excited or concerned over the idea of two books together as one?

EM: I think their first impulse was to talk me out of it. I think they thought that it might seem sort of cheap and gimmicky, and they were concerned people wouldn't take the book very seriously because it was sort of a kid-book idea or a funny idea. So I think there was that kind of concern, but you can't worry about people taking your work seriously or not. It's just like format in the art world or film: something is always getting challenged. Why shouldn't a book be a technology? That was part of the argument of the book itself: the book is a technology, so we get to fuck with that. I wanted to do something that was unconventional in the poetry world and kind of a little silly, even.

CD: Can you talk a little about the cover art? It's minimal and so amazing. I'm such a fan of it.

EM: Well, Xylor Jane is an amazing artist. She's into all these compulsive mechanisms. She's like a mathematical genius. She's very much an artist in the raw who's become discovered by the art world in a nice way in recent years. She was always someone who slept in her studio, radically punk and edgy and stuff. Somebody's work I'd seen coming up for a while and had been really excited about because it seems to be about light and time and strange spirituality and all that. But also, part of the thing with cover art is that you're always trying to deal with some strange limitation the publisher throws you. The last time I did a book with these guys, they were like, "Color is okay, but no images," and so I found a guy from UCSD who was a designer, and he came up with a design that sort of secretly did have pictures in it, but not right in your face. I could use the color green and the kind of paper matter. This time, they didn't allow color either. All they wanted the covers to be was font, so I thought, "How can I subvert that?" What artist do I know who does really interesting stuff with fonts? And I had seen some amazing fonts that Xylor had made, so I just went to her and presented her with the struggle, and she came up with a handful of solutions. Those were two of them.

CD: Has anything funny come up in terms of how the book gets cataloged in libraries or found in search engines because they're two books as one?

EM: Not that I know of. There probably has been, but I don't know about it. The thing that's funny about a book is that a lot of the life of it, you don't even know. You don't know where it's going. I think it's perfectly possible that people could own the book and not know for a while that it's two books. When I give it to somebody, I always have to flip it over, and for a while, they don't even know what I'm doing. I think the most innovative thing you could do is to get lost and rediscover it in some kind of funny way.

CD: I have a story about that. I didn't realize there's a poem in *different streets* that says, "For Cathy," and I'm assuming it's for me, but maybe it's not, and I didn't see that until recently and I've had this book for a while.

EM: And I can't even remember which poem it is.

CD: It's "Nervous Entertainment."

EM: Oh, of course. Yeah, yeah.

CD: But I read this book the night that you gave it to me at a reading. I didn't see that dedication, which is crazy. So yeah, I definitely rediscovered something recently.

EM: To me, you're in the book in a bigger way, which is a poem about recording in a car and music by a young person. You know the one?

CD: Oh, I know the one. I heard you read that at REDCAT a long time ago, and I thought, "Oh, I think that might be a reference to me and those mix CDs I made Eileen," but I didn't want to say anything because that just felt so presumptuous, and then you came up to me afterwards and said, "Hey, that poem was for you." And I was just like, "Yes. I had a feeling."

EM: I referred to you as the only person I knew.

CD: Yes.

EM: In a San Diego way of knowing.

CD: That was really great. Thank you.

EM: You're welcome.

CD: Starting with *Snowflake*, and maybe you already answered this when you were talking about chronological order, but why did you start with "Transitions"?

EM: Well, you know, a couple of things. One is that a long poem is always a great way to start a book. It's sort of like you just—the person opens the book and they start to read and they just keep going. The first poem sort of sets the tone. And I felt like *Snowflake*, the thing of the snowflake, the whole moment of that book was completely about transitions. You know, like literally in your life— you know something's about to change and you don't know what or how, but you know that that's happening and you see it everywhere, and snowflakes are these beautiful items of permanence that are so complete, and then they're so impermanent. And the timeline of so many people I know who were transitioning gender-wise. *Snowflake*, for me, just felt like the whole book seemed to be about all of that: about gender transitioning, about aging. I felt like it was the first book I wrote where I thought, I'm really thinking about aging a lot here, and also aging in a time of all this new technology, so it had some weird sci-fi feeling of aging in a world where you can be copying your existence and even potentially saving your life while you're dying. The first poem was about Rocco because Rocco was transitioning, but also just about the kind of odd thing of being in my life and seeing my dog die or feeling like my dog was about to die and being in this sci-fi world where you're picking up your phone, but it's doing the wrong thing and it's taking pictures and you're copying and saving and losing it all at once, and it seems like such a mega-transition—so that's why it's right there. It's like a fade of the whole book in one poem.

CD: The word "snowflake" comes up in that first poem, but then the actual "Snowflake" poem is the seventh poem between "Writing" and "#1 (With Music)." I wonder what your thoughts are about naming the book *Snowflake* and having the title poem placed where it is.

EM: It's kind of something I think about in novels or when I read other people's novels, but it's like when you read the title of a novel, there's always some way in which you're thinking, "At some point, I'll see what this title means." When it comes up, you're like, "Okay, what am I feeling at this moment, because that's part of what they wanted me to feel." The title is sort of like the name of the space. And you're moving through the space in this kind of unknowing way. To have a book of poems have a title, and for there to be a poem that has that title, sort of suggests that it's a title-poem, but it isn't necessarily. The word "snowflake" is inside a poem and outside a poem. It's weird how titles kind of operate to close a poem off, and yet the words just point to the book in this funny way. I have outside poems, between poems. All this is to say that I didn't know it was number seven, but I moved that poem around a bunch when I was putting it together to figure out both where I wanted it to do something and where I wanted it to not make too big of a splash.

CD: Talking about titles a little more, you have a poem called "The Importance of Being Iceland," which is also the name of your 2009 book. I was wondering if that is a regular occurrence for you—to have poems named after other pieces of your work?

EM: It was just really smug because I think when I was writing, that poem had a different title earlier and it was sort of untitled for a while, and then when I realized I just sort of had this title hanging around that was going to be another book, it was really fun to kind of brand my own poem with the title, and weirdly, I thought it was kind of a great title because it felt a little bit invisible because it had already been used, so it felt like kind of a thrifted title and it was really fun. "These are my books and these are my titles and I can kind of do anything I want." Earlier when you were asking me about the way you read a book, do I want people to read it this way or that way—part of what I was thinking about was how there are movies that people watch on TV, and they've stayed up all night and watched whatever was on TV and certain movies you saw again and again, and so that meant you could enter those movies at all different points, so certainly if you own a TV show or a movie, you just know it so well that you can just pop into the movie at any point. Something I really want for my work is a feeling of the opposite of precious. It will all be fused together in some way, and it will make a real place—like a home.

CD: You end the *Snowflake* side with a poem called "Choke," and I was wondering if you could talk a little bit about that. When I read that title, the word seemed so intense, and I can't help but think of *Snowflake* as the California side and *different streets* as the New York side, so leaving the California side on that note with a poem called "Choke," I was just curious about it. Also that poem ends with a few lines in italics, and I was wondering about those lines. I was wondering if those were your lines or if you were quoting someone else.

EM: Yeah, the lines are from a song that my father used to sing, and it's probably a song that the guys of the World War II generation sang a lot. Maybe my father sang it in childhood. It was like [*Eileen sings*]:

> *when the weather's too hot for comfort*
> *& we can't have ice cream cones*
> *it ain't no sin*
> *to take off your skin*
> *& dance around in your bones*

And you kind of sing the end of it like a pirate song, sort of like a real low man's note. It always seemed really creepy; it always seemed like dancing skeletons and something that was really hideous that you'd see in a cartoon, but it was really great and funny because it was so dark. It's weird: "It ain't no sin to take off your skin and dance around in your bones." I think choking in the context of that poem seems to be about failure. And there's just a way that everybody who's human just sort of fails because we're not god and we just die. So, everything just sort of ends with this colossal failure which is death. I felt like that poem was thinking about choking in the way that I had fucked things up, and I had this feeling that had to be sort of laughable or regrettable or punk in its way, so I kind of thought of it as sort of a dancing skeleton punk song at the end of it.

CD: That's great. And also, you sing really well. You should totally sing more.

EM: Thank you.

CD: Maybe that is your next big move.

EM: I'm ready, I'm ready.

It's Kinda Creepy Because I Am:
An Interview with Myriam Gurba

Gina Abelkop, March 2016

WHEN I READ Myriam Gurba's *Painting Their Portraits in Winter*, I got that special book-soulmate feeling that the best books give you, a sense that someone really GETS you and the universe. Because I can never love anything without going full fangirl, I knew I had to reach out to Myriam for an interview, which—lucky you!—you get to read below.

Gina Abelkop: My first question has to be about one of my favorite things about your writing: your sense of humor. It's silly, smart, biting, and joyful even in stories and poems that are emotionally taut. How and on what teeth was this sense of humor cut? Who are some of your favorite humorists, and what is it that you love about their humor and/or work?

Myriam Gurba: My sense of humor was primarily sculpted by the sickest people I know: HELLO MOM AND DAD. My dad likes to joke about the horrific, like free-range children and customer service, and by example, he taught me that these are the things you are supposed to laugh about. My mom is different. She's more elf than human. She doesn't say funny things; she says things funny. For example, she'll tell a story about getting into a car accident, but she'll refer to her car as her mystique since she actually drives a Mercury Mystique, and her story will take on this exciting, Daliesque quality because imagine a normal conversation about a car accident, but replace the word "car" with "mystique." My parents, however, aren't into queef jokes. In fact, I'm not even sure they could name a queef, though I'm certain they're familiar with the sound. In high school, I was socially attracted to girls who got accused of being unfeminine since they were funny and gross, and so they shaped me too. Boys accused me of not being feminine and of having too big of lips. My favorite funny people are people I know. My boyfriend makes me giggle. When I have low blood sugar and am surrounded by whites, everything gets hilarious. I appreciate humor that is gross, goofy, self-conscious, and above all, humiliating. As far as publicly funny people go, I like Carol Burnett, Gilda Radner, Cardi B, Kristen Wiig pretending to be Björk, Peter Sellers, Cheech Marin, Chris Rock, and angry teenagers.

GA: You're the author of two full-length books, *Dahlia Season* and *Painting Their Portraits in Winter*, in addition to numerous chapbooks and zines. In what ways did your storytelling shift between your first two books, and what purpose do you find your chapbooks/zines serving as they stand between these larger collections?

MG: When I wrote *Dahlia Season*, I wanted to write a story with a certain kind of protagonist. So in that sense, it's purely character driven. Character was the only thing that mattered to me. I hadn't read a book about a middle-class NOC (nerd of color) steeped in being goth, and I wanted to read about this girl, and so I DIYed her. I feel like *Painting Their Portraits in Winter* is an extension of that because much of that sensibility remains, but the writing in *Painting* is more mature and, form-wise, much weirder. Like, I hope it would be Desiree's, the main character in *Dahlia Season*, favorite book. Or at least a book she'd finish or keep on the toilet tank. My first chapbook, *Wish You Were Me*, is filled with experiments. Maybe they're poems. I wrote many of the pieces with the intent of writing unpublishably about subjects that are stupid and worthless. Like bad-tasting vaginas. It was my earnest attempt at being as shitty and offsides as possible on purpose. You really discover a lot about yourself when you do that, and I recommend we all experiment with being shitty. I self-publish a lot of stuff too because it keeps me busy, and if I'm not busy, I'm not busy.

GA: "Petra Páramo" is one of my favorite stories from *Painting Their Portraits in Winter*; how did you conceive of this ghost girl? (When I imagine her as I'm reading, I see the girl in your author portrait on the back of the book, which I imagine is you as painted by your abuelita.)

MG: I came up with her because I wanted to write a feminist response to the 1955 novel *Pedro Páramo*, which is told from the point of view of ghosts, one in particular, and of course he's a dude. I love the ghost-as-narrator trope and love movies and books where that's the case, and again, female narrators are a minority and dead female narrators are an even smaller minority. Once I came up with the idea of an amnesiac ghost of color telling a story, it just felt like I

Self-portrait from *MEriam* by Myriam Gurba.

was playing as I wrote about her. I put her in a make-believe/real forest and then let her show me what her journey would be as she left. Would she find her way to reality? Her story is very much not a hero's journey but a dead heroine's journey. The structure differs markedly.

That's really cool that you imagine that painting on the book cover as the ghost. That's a portrait of me at age fiveish, which my abuelita did paint. It's kinda creepy because I am.

GA: If you could have your work distributed in any format, what would it be? Imagine a Franken-format if it doesn't yet exist!

MG: I think my ideal format would involve an ambush. I'm not necessarily sure how that would manifest concretely, but I'm leaning toward some type of candid-camera scenario that would embarrass my audience.

GA: You have a selection of your self-portraits, titled *MEriam*, up at the Museum of Latin American Art's *Who Are You?* exhibit in Long Beach, California. These portraits, which you call "digital colonialism," remind me of your work in that they combine this tender, human earnestness and sharp critique with raucous humor. How did you begin making these portraits, and how have they changed over time? How do you pick which scenes/images in which to insert yourself? In what ways do you see your texts and these images interacting or playing off one another, if at all?

MG: I AM SUSCEPTIBLE TO YOUR FLATTERY.

I started making these images when my friend's mother died and I was helping out with funeral-related business and other things. The images were meant as a distraction from all the sadness, but I quickly got addicted to making them and the phrase "Who else can I become?" started frenziedly popping into my head all the time. Suddenly I could be all these things I couldn't be before because of my body. Having a body can be such a downer, but art lets me escape from it. I do have an awful relationship with my body. I'd love to not have one. I'd love to be so many other things other than a human body. I'd rather be mayonnaise than flesh. Many of the images that I chose for this "project" are formative cultural icons. For example, in high school, I watched a lot of trashy talk shows since they were among the queerest things on TV, so I'll transform myself into talk show host Sally Jessy Raphael and act inquisitive. I also really like becoming dead people but with a slightly surprised look on my face. I have a picture of myself as Sharon Tate where I

Self-portrait from *MEriam* by Myriam Gurba.

look very concerned because, you know. Also I have one of me as Scarlett O'Hara, and I've got a *who, me? But I'm Mexican* look.

GA: One of your projects is composed of a series of letters to Gertrude Stein. What is your interest in Stein in this context? In what ways is she (or the idea of her) or her work generative for you?

MG: Well, the bitch is problematic and I'm drawn to the problematic. I started writing the Stein letters as my marriage was crumbling the way a croissant falls apart when you dunk it in hot coffee and FORGET ABOUT IT.

I can get really shy about my feelings, so instead of telling a living human being about them, I was like, maybe I should tell Gertrude Stein. Which is fun because I kind of don't even like her. She was so stuck up, but that's kind of what I also find attractive about her. I am drawn to/repulsed by snobs. Also there's something hard about her writing but it's also unfettered, and I like forcing myself to interact with and grapple with hard language.

Her syntax is a trip. It's so simple, but she finds a way to make it hard. That, to me, seems like the essence of queering. To take something that might otherwise be really simple, and make it HARD AF. Lol.

So, I started writing all these little missives to Gertrude Stein, and the thing is, she listens. She has to. She's dead. And I was like, oh my god, she's such a good FRIEND. And then I just got really into writing them because she's like god. Gertrude is always there.

I wrote a creative meta-analysis of the process of writing to Gertrude. It largely takes place at Hooters.

GA: Who are some of your favorite contemporary artists and writers, and what is it that you find moving or engaging about their work?

MG: I'm super into art and writing by queers, women, and people of color. I kind of think white dudes need to just retire from making culture for a while so that reality can be rehabilitated. That said, who is rehabilitating culture through their art and writing in a way that needs to be talked about and then talked about more? Maggie Nelson's writing is the shit. Full of body and unique visions of love and family making. Not afraid to look at sadness, shit, and buttholes. Wendy Ortiz's writing is killer and important, and she reinvents memoir with so much ELEGANCE it's like, how can you write about horror with such ELEGANCE? Oh, that's right, you're a goddess, that's how. Trinie Dalton's writing is the shit because there's really not much out there that is weirder but in a super accessible way. Nikki Darling's poetry is too much and her poems are women. Imagine being able to create a gender through verse. Nikki can. In terms of artists who are making nonword things, I'm constantly thinking about Ana Mendieta and Francesca Woodman. They feel contemporary even though they're dead. Jenny Holzer, because she makes you pay attention to words in a way that transforms their wordiness. Molly Soda for how the internet becomes her, I hate to say it, but, playground. Kate Durbin for her shameless interest in the princesstual. Grace Miceli. Allyson Mitchell. Miriam Klein Stahl. Big fat yes to Erin Markey as a performance artist and national treasure. I'M HELL OF INTO THE ART HOE MOVEMENT, WHICH ENCOURAGES TEENS OF COLOR TO INSERT THEMSELVES INTO KEITH HARING PAINTINGS.

GA: What does your day-to-day life schedule look like, and where/how do you make time for artmaking?

MG: I'm a teacher, I teach of all things PSYCHOLOGY, and I'm not full-time right now so in the afternoons I have a small cave, it really is cave-like, that I use as a studio/office, and I go in there and do what I gotta do. I've also started doing this thing where I drive to the Mojave Desert, rent a cheap-ass motel room, forget my humanity, become one with the desolation, and write. I go jogging every other day. I eat irregularly. I have no pets or children to prevent me from manifesting my wildest dreams. I used to have pets. They're dead.

GA: Your chapbook *Richard* is forthcoming from Birds of Lace (insert
self-tooting horn). If you were making an abstract painting to
express the text, which colors/shapes would you use and why?

MG: The painting would actually come on a canvas known as an XL
sweatshirt. Lana Del Rey's face would be in the middle, blue smoke
curling out from between her fake, sausage lips. Marijuana leaves
would dapple the fabric. Looking at this sweatshirt would make
people happy, sad, and high. Dope.

ALL THE FEMINIST POETS:
Melissa Broder

Marisa Crawford, December 2014

ALL THE FEMINIST POETS was an interview series on Weird Sister *featuring a single poem and an interview from a feminist poet that we love.*

THOUSANDS
He is told to send a lock of hair
but instead sends a dossier
of charts. There are bullets,
vectors, single choice answers.
No questions. On every page
appears a yellowish husband.
The husband is a sick man.
I want the diagram-sender
sicker. I want every man
fainting in a reservoir
of contaminated water.
I have black chrysanthemums
in each hole and a gypsy smell.
My climax shakes the basin.
I hold out one hand for every man
but I'm looking at my snake.

Marisa Crawford: Can you talk a bit about the poem you chose and why you consider it feminist?

Melissa Broder: Okay, so how do I decide if one of my poems is feminist? Like, I feel that I am inherently a feminist and act and speak and live in that way, except for I am a terrible feminist in my treatment of myself in terms of what I have done to myself to try to fit certain standards of beauty. Like maybe I am a good feminist when it comes to other women but a bad feminist when it comes to me?

I grew up going to all-girls school for thirteen years, and it wasn't religious school. It was feminist school. Girls did everything. We were class president, editors of the newspaper, the jocks. We played all of the characters in the play (men and women). When we played the men, we were told to walk like we had something between our legs, and then we tortured that male drama teacher. I believe he later tried to sue the school for sexual harassment.

So I feel like I got a very skewed perception of the world, because in my early learning and conception of myself creatively and intellectually, boys weren't even in the picture. I think I have continued to just live from that place and, like, not see (or pretend not to see) any sexism that might appear in my path career-wise. Just trample that shit. At the same time, on a social and sexual level, I starved myself in high school and just wanted to be "beautiful" and "okay," and some of those related attitudes and behaviors have never gone away.

Actually, that's not all entirely true. Sometimes, while I am blindly trampling sexism, I let things affect me for just a sec. Like, recently I had some poems in *Poetry* magazine. This one poem, "Lunar Shatters" (which reimagines my body as having been born with a cock, which I then broke off, in relation to the myth of Pegasus as well as other myths—classic and personal) got posted on the magazine's Facebook page. Some bruh posts a comment that says, "Which of *Poetry*'s editors did this chick sleep with? So not good."

So I stopped and thought about this for a sec. I was like, wait. Did I sleep with any of *Poetry*'s editors? I didn't. But should I be sleeping with editors? Am I missing out? Maybe I should be fucking men in power? (Power, of course, being relative, since we are, after all, talking about poetry.) But now I'm thinking that maybe it could be really good for my career to change my tastes. Like, I haven't been published in the *Paris Review* yet. Is there anyone hot on the editorial board of the *Paris Review*? Maybe I should fuck him.

In terms of my poetry, though, the work itself, I like to think of it outside the constraints of time and space, let alone -ist labels. Like, I wanna get the fuck off of earth. It hurts my heart to put an -ist on my poetry. Any -ist. How do I know what is feminist? Is the poem where I eat boys feminist? Is the poem where I love every woman feminist? Is the poem where I suck a cosmic titty feminist? Is the poem where I have a cock feminist?

I think I see myself as a witch more than any kind of -ist. I have a tendency to shrink from -ists. It might be because I am an isolator and have social anxiety and don't like groups or labels. At the same time, there are some really good -ists who make me want to embrace my -istness. I recently reread both Shulamith Firestone's *The Dialectic of Sex: The Case for the Feminist Revolution* and Audre Lorde's *Sister Outsider* and am like *fuck yes, bitches*. My first exposure to feminism was through Audre Lorde, and the first time feminism clicked for me was reading her essay "Uses of the Erotic" while I was going through puberty.

One thing I hate seeing is when feminism is used as clickbait. Like think pieces about the feminism or lack of feminism in this particular TV show or that particular TV show. It kind of makes me want to puke or die. This is not a condemnation of the contemporary feminist movement (or movements) at all, but a revulsion to clickbait. To engage in-depth with the ephemeral that is pop culture just makes my inner witch nauseous. I feel like if I read the article I am being poisoned. Like, I am a vampire and clickbait is my garlic, and to turn feminism into clickbait is just a giant fucking puke— and not the sexy kind.

My deep desire, I think, is to just burn right through memes and clickbait and much of pop culture. Please keep that shit far away from my poetry. I don't like things that are time-sensitive. I don't even like time. I'd rather alchemize trash into something more evergreen. Like, I prefer to digest my own critiques of pop culture privately and then shit out universal magick that doesn't even fucking acknowledge the initial subject or give it any more power. In my desire to alchemize or transcend, I would say that I feel most aligned with witchcraft. And I would say that feminism is absolutely implicit in my witchery.

Yet, as I said before, I am a crappy feminist when it comes to my body and so am thus a crappy witch. Like, what the fuck kind of witch eats Lean Cuisine mac and cheese and not Kraft full-fat macaroni and cheese, or regular, homemade mac and cheese (or vegan mac and cheese, if she is a steward of the earth and all of god's creation, which seems to me would be implicit in being the best witch one could be and best feminist/humanist/person one could be) (I am not currently vegan). Like, if I were the CEO of a coven I would be like, "Yo, this Lean Cuisine–eating witch is unacceptable."

Though if I were truly the ultimate witch, I would accept me where I am and embrace me, so maybe in that way if I were the ultimate feminist I would do the same—not just for others but for myself. I feel that I do embrace others' humanity in this way. But for me there is still no embrace. I just cannot seem to give myself that fucking hug of the divine mother that is like *baby baby baby it's okay.*

Having said aaaaaaaalllll that, I went with the poem "Thousands" from *SCARECRONE*. This poem takes the feeling of rejection that can arise from reaching out to another human and then not receiving a response (or the desired response), and empowering oneself with that rejection. The speaker is a she. She wants a lock of hair from some bruh. He is told to send one, but instead he sends a logical, linear, totally unromantic dossier of charts and vectors (and also bullets, which may be read as actual bullets or like bullet points). This dossier explains—implicitly and, in my mind, literally—why they can't be together. One of the reasons is because she already has a husband. Oops. But this bruh clearly lacks imagination. Like, just because a woman has a husband doesn't mean she is monogamous. Lame. Hasn't he ever read *Madame Bovary*? I mean really. Also, it appears the husband is sick. This could be seen as mentally sick or socially poisoned (as in all men are sick), but when I wrote it I meant it literally. Ailing, physical ailment. The speaker is retaliating. She is pissed. She wants all the men sick. She wants to fuck them up with her sexual power. She wants a harem of them in a cosmic bathtub that is hers. She wants her orgasm to be an earthquake.

Also she wants to help them, too, not just kill them. Like, kill them and help them. Like, she is going to reach out her hand to them as she is killing them and maybe not kill them. She is a humanist. At the same time, though, there is treachery. She is looking at her snake—a snake being a symbol of the original sin, or whatevs, of Eve's fuckup. We also can infer (lol) that the snake is a phallic symbol. She is a woman and she has a cock. She has a mystic cock and mythic cock.

But here's the thing. Yes, this poem might appear feminist because the female speaker is reframing an experience of male rejection (and, frankly, male linear boringness) into personal power. But, like, is it? She isn't looking at her grapefruit. She isn't looking at her pomegranate or peach. Why does it have to be a snake? Why does she need a stand-in cock for power? Well, I hate to say

ALL THE FEMINIST POETS

it, but I wish I had a cock. Like, I'm sorry but I do. Also, we probably shouldn't kill all the men or poison them (as much as that would be really fun).

MC: Your poems feel so rich with feminist commentary to me—like, even if it is coming through subconsciously, it's totally there. It's one thing that I love about your work. For example, I read a lot of the poems in *Meat Heart* as related to ambivalence re: marriage and the female "wife" role, and in *SCARECRONE* I see a lot of connections to aging and what that means for women in particular. How does an overarching question, connection, or theme play into how you put together a manuscript of poems, if at all?

MB: I just write my obsessions, and usually I'm obsessed with the same thing(s) for an extended period of time. So all of the poems from that time (a year, let's say, which is about how long it took me to write *Meat Heart* and *SCARECRONE* each) have some sort of cohesion. And they become the manuscript. But I usually don't know what the cohesion is until the end of that period of time. It usually happens when I have around 120 poems. And then I work with my editor to make cuts.

MC: The female body is very present in your work, often in ways that are awesomely, stunningly gross, crass, and absurd—just flipping randomly through the pages of *SCARECRONE*, I see phrases including: "let me cream the cord / right to my heart," "humping god's knee," "I hold my legs / like two chicken drumsticks," "My climax shakes the basin," "I am the worst body," and "I want to lick a cosmic titty / because god built me / with these holes." What are your thoughts about the role of female embodiment and the grotesque in your work?

MB: I have struggled so much with living in a body and that body happens to be a female body, so that is the one I grapple with. I tend to also think that some of my struggles with living in a body are because it is a female body. Like, things I learned that I should do to it and what it should look like have caused me great pain, though maybe that would be true in other ways if I had a male body. I tend to think that if I had a male body all of my problems would be solved, but that's probably false. If I had a cock I'd probably never get it up. But as I said, I really do want a cock. It's not that I don't love my vagina. I love my vagina. But ideally I would have both.

MC: Favorite feminist poet(s), living or dead?

MB: Sappho.

MC: Last awesome feminist poetry book you read?

MB: Who am I to say what is or isn't feminist? Fine. *ROME* by Dorothea Lasky.

MC: Favorite girl band, "chick flick," or reality TV show (or all of the above)?

MB: Grimes and PJ Harvey. And Lil' Kim's *Hard Core* is still one of my fave albums of all time.

Tender Points: An Interview with Amy Berkowitz

Geraldine Kim, June 2015

THE FOLLOWING IS an interview between Amy Berkowitz and me about her book *Tender Points* (Timeless, Infinite Light, 2015; Nightboat Books, 2019). A narrative fractured by trauma and named after the diagnostic criteria for fibromyalgia, this book-length lyric essay explores sexual violence, gendered illness, chronic pain, and patriarchy through the lenses of lived experience and pop culture.

> My body is washing dishes and it's in pain. My body is on hold with California Blue Cross Blue Shield and it's in pain. My body is dancing and it's in pain. My body is Skyping Beth and it's in pain. My body is taking a shower and it's in pain. My body is riding BART and it's in pain. My body is politely saying no and it's in pain. My body is reading a book and it's in pain. My body is at work and it's in pain. My body is writing this and it's in pain. My body is walking to meet you and it's in pain.[1]

Geraldine Kim: So . . . are you experiencing pain this very moment?

Amy Berkowitz: [*Nods*] It's not excruciating. The best way I can explain it is that it feels like I had a hard workout yesterday . . . but I didn't. Which is why it's a problem. A lot of people with fibromyalgia and other chronic pain syndromes have pain that's much more unbearable than I usually experience.

GK: Why do you think women suffer from fibromyalgia more than men?

AB: I'm not sure. One thing to consider is that there's a connection between fibromyalgia and sexual abuse that hasn't been fully explored yet. In *Tender Points*, I quote fibromyalgia specialist Dr. Ginevra Liptan, who writes about studies estimating that more than half of women with fibromyalgia have experienced childhood sexual abuse. And in general, more women than men have experienced childhood sexual abuse, so this may be a factor, but I'm sure it's not the only factor.

GK: How do you feel about call-out culture?

AB: I'm mostly familiar with it in the context of survivors calling out their rapists, so I think it's important and useful. At the same time, I have seen cases when it's not done responsibly—for example, cases when folks called out a rapist without making sure they had the survivor's permission to call him out first. Because when you write a rapist's name on the internet, you're essentially writing the survivor's name on the internet. So yeah, let's call people out, but the survivor is the only person who can lead that process.

GK: Totally . . . So, since I just learned from you that *Tender Points* is nonfiction, have you ever thought about calling out the doctor [who raped you]?

AB: No, I haven't. Repressed memories are so complicated. I would have absolutely no case. I didn't remember it until twelve or thirteen years after it happened. But I do have a distinct memory of it in my head, which makes me think of this quote from the book:

> My memory of that day is in miniature. Although it's very clear, it's about two-and-a-half inches tall and stuck inside my head. I can't show it to anybody. I can't locate a corresponding full-size memory out in the world. And I can't even tell you what day *that day* was.[2]

I know that it happened, but I don't have the certainty around it to feel like it would feel good to say "This happened!" The memory of it just doesn't connect with the world enough for it to function as a useful piece of information in the world in any other way than I am using it by including it in the book.

It's a shame that I can't help out with the situation. He's still practicing. I just hope that he's not doing this to anyone else, although statistically, if he did, then he is.

> I have a wolf in my story. But he will not interrupt my walk through the forest. Which is to say he's already interrupted it: He's the reason I'm here, sorting out the aftermath. Which is to say the wolf is eternally interrupting my walk through the forest: emerging from behind the same tree again and again to block my path. Imagine it repeating like a GIF.[3]

GK: I want to say . . . After reading your book, I wanted to call out someone that did something similar to me, and I was like, "Why didn't I do it when it happened?" I got kind of mad at myself for not acting on it. It had to take me reading your book and really thinking deeply

about it. I have to say, as I read your book, I thought it was going to
lead to some ... "and that was the guy!" ... and that it didn't make
it feel like that experience is still lingering. That presence of that
absence is kind of haunting. Part of me wanted you to ...

AB: ... say the name?

GK: Yeah.

AB: I think I just wouldn't feel safe doing it. Which is why I made the
decision not to.

GK: Yeah, of course! Totally understandable—

AB: I understand that as a reader, you wanted that. Maybe I'm leading
by example with the first rule of call-out culture, which is to respect
the wishes of the survivor. So even though I may be a big propo-
nent of call-out culture, I also made the decision of not naming my
rapist. That's what's right for me. There's also this from the book:

> There was a professor in our department
> Who thought he was Ernest Hemingway
> He famously touched students' breasts
> He had these signature moves
> Like these tried and true tricks
> For how to surreptitiously touch his students' tits[4]

GK: We had one [at my graduate school] too ... He would invite
students to his room to ostensibly workshop poems or whatever
and just, like, grab their breasts ... Thankfully he's no longer working there, but still ... but the fact that he's out there (e.g., prominent
in the community), and no one said anything about that ... but I'm
not the survivor—I've heard firsthand accounts of this, but it's not
my job ...

AB: Exactly! I'm in the same position with this guy, which is why I
did what I did in the book. This is as close to the situation as I feel
comfortable getting.

Stephanie Young, who really likes naming names, not necessarily in regards to sexual assault but generally using specific person/
place names as part of her politics of writing, helped me with edit-
ing *Tender Points*. And I remember her asking me, "Why don't you
name the professor?" But again, it's not my fight, it's someone
else's fight. And also it's not hard to figure out. It's fucking folk-
lore around the university.

GK: Who influenced your writing of *Tender Points* alongside Stephanie Young?

AB: There was something about the book, with the way that I wrote it piece by piece and assembled it as a patchwork, where for the two years or so that I was writing it, I felt entirely porous and interested in taking in new information. So I was doing a lot of research and also really engaged in communicating with other writers. I quote a letter from Yosefa Raz, a poet who has written wonderful material on pain: "Chronic pain is always on a side slash main note."[5]

Also Maggie Nelson's writing was a big source of inspiration at the beginning. When I started writing *Tender Points*, I knew I wanted to write about my experiences and that I wanted to write them in fragments because my story is about trauma, and trauma is essentially nonlinear and fragmented. And I had read Nelson's *Bluets* a while before, and that felt like a kind of road map, a kind of suggestion that my parts could also amount to a coherent whole.

GK: Was it hard to finish the manuscript?

AB: It was hard to feel like it was in order. Stephanie and I spent an evening literally cutting it into pieces and spreading it out on my couch and floor. And once that was done, it felt like it was a book. I was a writer-in-residence at Alley Cat Books in San Francisco at the time, and that was also hugely helpful. I sat there for two days straight agonizing over the fact that I didn't know how to end it ... but I did. Now I'm sad that it's ended.

GK: Why?

AB: Did you see *The Punk Singer*, the Kathleen Hanna documentary? There's this part at the end where she's talking about abuse she's experienced, and she says, "I wouldn't want to tell anybody the whole entire story because it sounded crazy ... Like, who would believe me?" And she's swinging her arms in a big circle when she says "entire story"—and that's like what I feel like I did. I feel like I've just succeeded in telling my whole entire "crazy" story with all of its uncanny, unsettling details in a way that makes sense, and in a way that people can actually connect to and maybe find support in.

And that's why I'm sad. I'm glad that I did it. But I'm sad that I'm no longer working on a project that feels so essential to me.

GK: I felt like *Tender Points* did a really good job in that it was thoughtful and conceptual, but it was also really emotional/hard. I felt engaged with the content, but the form was also really interesting—it felt almost like a philosophical treatise that was leading up to something ...

AB: Did you feel like it led up to something?

GK: I felt it did. There was an accelerative feeling to it ... The quotes felt like philosophical evidence for a point. And I could see how one point led to another. It all felt seamless. Even though it "looks" fragmented, it didn't feel that way.

AB: Good! To some extent—I didn't think of this at the time, because I generally like the style of mixing quotes with personal narrative—the book is a little bit preoccupied with, "Hey, I'm going to tell you this in a way that you're going to believe me." The "male drag," or what I call "écriture féminine en homme." Undermining male authority by adopting a male voice.

> That's why I so firmly want prose here. Sentences. Periods. Male certainty. These are facts. No female vocal fry. No uptalk. No question about what I tell you. No metaphor. Go ahead. Fact check. "Did I stutter." Fuck off.[6]

GK: What are you working on now?

AB: I'm thinking about writing fiction focused on some of the same issues I touch on in the book: rape culture and disability.

GK: Why fiction?

AB: I feel terrible doing this to poetry, but I feel really frustrated with what I perceive as poetry's limitation to reach people who don't already read poetry. [*Laughs*] You're making a face.

GK: Yup.

AB: Tell me about that face?

GK: I agree! But at the same time, I don't really connect to most writing/fiction that's not aware of its artifice somehow.

AB: Have you tried reading fiction by women? I have a dedicated female fiction section on my bookshelf with books by Amy Hempel and Lorrie Moore.

> I just find it so much more compelling. I generally care more about how women experience the world. I find it more relatable and less ego driven.

GK: I feel really bad that you're in constant pain. That sucks.

AB: It does. I think at some point I'll probably try more things to relieve the pain. I'm just taking my time with it because of my own trauma around medicine. I think I needed to write the book first; as soon as I finished the book, I started getting acupuncture, which is the first thing I've done for the pain.

GK: Has acupuncture helped?

AB: Yes, it has. And I think one reason I was open to it is that it's not Western medicine.

GK: Aren't you angry?

AB: Sure, of course I'm angry. I fantasize about shooting him sometimes. But it's mostly a more diffuse anger: I mean, it's an anger at rape culture. It's an anger at the patriarchy of Western medicine and how it is informed by and informs rape culture.

GK: I have so much respect for you.

AB: [*Laughs*] That I haven't shot my doctor?

GK: That you've found some level of peace with it.

AB: What else can I do, right? It's less about him as one idiot who took advantage of somebody, and it's more about the societal structures that let people like that exist. So yes, I've had fantasies of killing him, but it's mostly more productive anger geared toward fighting the societal structures that permit this kind of violence. That's why I wrote the book.

Voice, Form, and Politics: Talking with Mecca Jamilah Sullivan about June Jordan

Marisa Crawford, March 2016

LATER THIS MONTH, Professor Mecca Jamilah Sullivan and her colleagues at the University of Massachusetts, Amherst's Women, Gender, Sexuality Studies and Afro-American Studies departments will present "Feminist Poetics: Legacies of June Jordan," a symposium "celebrating the work of feminist poet, scholar, and activist June Jordan, and her legacies in contemporary feminist poetics." The conference will feature panels on Writing Feminist Activism, The Combahee River Collective and Black Feminist Foundations, Feminist Poetics as Theory and Praxis, and more. Speakers, moderators, and performers include renowned feminist thinkers Sonia Sanchez, Evie Shockley, Alexis Pauline Gumbs, Cheryl Clarke, and many others.

For me, UMass Amherst is an extra-special place: I went to college there, and the Women, Gender, and Sexuality Studies department is where I learned about the intersections of art and activism and came into my own as both a writer and a feminist. When I learned about the Feminist Poetics symposium, I knew I had to reach out to Mecca Jamilah Sullivan to ask her about how it all came together, why June Jordan's legacy matters right now, and—because Mecca is an incredible fiction writer herself—how Jordan's poetics influence her own work as a writer.

Marisa Crawford: Can you talk a bit about the process and rationale behind planning this symposium? What made you and your colleagues at UMass decide to plan a conference focused on feminist poetics?

Mecca Jamilah Sullivan: The brainstorming for the conference began in 2013, when the Women, Gender, Sexuality Studies (WGSS) department at UMass hosted a conference titled Critical Feminist Thought in the African Diaspora. I was on a postdoctoral fellowship at the time and was preparing to come to UMass the following year. At that conference, I had a string of great conversations with Afro-American Studies chair John Bracey and WGSS professor emerita Arlene Avakian about June Jordan and how important her work is—and how striking it is that her work has not been celebrated more fully and more consistently than it has. Given all that was going on in social and political spheres at the time—and all that is going on now—we thought this would be the time to invoke her work and bring it to the fore in a broad and public context. This was especially exciting for me as a scholar and creative writer invested in black feminist theoretical work and creative praxis. For me, June Jordan is a model of politically engaged scholarly and creative work, and I was thrilled to learn that there would be support among my new colleagues for staging this kind of event.

MC: What was your role in organizing the conference?

MJS: I met with Dr. Bracey to brainstorm and conceptualize the symposium. Our earlier conversations about the possibility of a celebration of Jordan's work had stuck with me, and I was excited to move forward in bringing the idea to fruition. During the fall semester of 2015, Tricia Loveland, also of the Afro-American Studies department, and my fantastic colleagues in WGSS—chair Dr. Laura Briggs, Dr. Kirsten Leng, Dr. Abbie Boggs, and our wonderful graduate student program committee member Martha Balaguera and office manager Linda Hillenbrand—came onboard to help plan and organize the event. It's been great to have the support of such a committed team in bringing this vision to life.

MC: Why did you choose to focus on the poetics of June Jordan? How do you see Jordan's poetics as exemplary of a feminist poetics project?

MJS: As someone who studies the politics of black women's creative writing and poetics, Jordan has always been an extremely important figure for me. For me, June Jordan stands as one of many black feminist thinkers whose resistance of institutional, genre, and disciplinary boundaries has been inspiring and instructive. Jordan wrote over twenty-five book-length works of poetry, fiction, memoir, and critical prose, each engaging crucial questions of race, sexuality, class, imperialism, and power. As a scholar, I find it important to acknowledge this multidisciplinarity and genre-crossing as key aspects of black feminist literary and theoretical traditions. And as a creative writer, I think Jordan's work can offer us lessons in how important it is to bring our creative selves to all areas of our intellectual lives.

MC: Can you talk a bit about Jordan's legacy and why it's so important?

MJS: Absolutely. Jordan has been a major influence for so many writers and scholars. She's a well-known figure in the pantheon of queer, black, feminist, and anti-imperialist thinkers of the last third of the twentieth century. And yet, despite how incredibly prolific she was and the staggering scope of her work, in talking with friends and colleagues interested in these questions, there's a general sense that some of our students and colleagues are not as familiar with her work as they should be. Jordan's work was both right on time and ahead of its time. The poems and essays she wrote about state-sanctioned violence, US imperialism, violence against women, the complexity of gender and sexuality, intersections of race, class, and gender, and black women's invisibility—to name only a few topics—those pieces she wrote in the seventies, eighties, and nineties are every inch as meaningful and resonant today. I think of her poem "Apologies to All the People in Lebanon," or "Poem about My Rights," on race, sexual identity, and sexual violence, or her essay "A New Politics of Sexuality." These are all works that we need to be reading now, right this minute.

MC: In addition to your work as a scholar, you're also a fiction writer. Do you see the poetic legacies of June Jordan at work as an influence in your own writing?

MJS: Yes, for sure. My approach to scholarship is very much informed by my fiction, and vice versa. In both mediums, I'm interested in voice and how it can illuminate aspects of identity, power, and social/political experience. Jordan's poems exemplify this kind of connection between voice, form, and politics. Her essays often read as stories and include wonderfully interior, poetic prose. I think of her essay "Report from the Bahamas," which was the first piece of writing of hers I ever encountered. The essay narrates Jordan's developing awareness of national and class privilege in an encounter with a black woman domestic worker while on vacation in the Bahamas. She uses a striking narrative frame to make this critique, inviting her reader into her process of self-positioning and self-interrogation—the same process which, by the end of the piece, she asks us to take up. She brings in song lyrics, dialogue, and other forms of text to bring us along in this experience. As readers, we're both welcomed and implicated. It's our responsibility to recon what she's saying, not at a distance, but up close—in the tight space between the experience she's describing and our own experience reading the text.

In my scholarship, I write about how black women's artistic practices develop these kinds of strategies, using form and voice to engage their readers in new kinds of interpretive practices that emphasize intersectionality and difference. I feel strongly about this because, as a fiction writer, this is why I write—not only to show *what happens* in black lives, queer lives, and lives marked by difference, but to give readers a sense of what it is to experience multiple differences and multiple relationships to power from the inside. Highlighting black girl characters' voices through fiction makes that possible. For some readers that occurs as labor and disruption, and for others it brings the joy of recognition. Either way, this is the work that art can do. And I think it's extremely important.

Notes

Introduction

1. Andi Zeisler, *We Were Feminists Once: From Riot Grrrl to CoverGirl®, the Buying and Selling of a Political Movement* (New York: Public-Affairs, 2016).
2. Samhita Mukhopadhyay, quoted in Courtney E. Martin and Vanessa Valenti, *#FemFuture: Online Revolution*, New Feminist Solutions, vol. 8 (New York: Barnard Center for Research on Women, 2013), 28, https://bcrw.barnard.edu/wp-content/nfs/reports/NFS8-FemFuture-Online-Revolution-Report.pdf.

White Space, Banana Ketchup, and Karaoke: A Review of Kimberly Alidio's *after projects the resound*

1. Kimberly Alidio, "All the Pinays are straight, all the queers are Pinoy, but some of us," in *after projects the resound* (Black Radish Books, 2016), 66.
2. Kimberly Alidio, "Our lady of the banana ketchup," in *after projects the resound* (Black Radish Books, 2016), 16.
3. Kimberly Alidio, "I wanna be your dog," in *after projects the resound* (Black Radish Books, 2016), 56.

Writing the Wound: A Letter to Hélène Cixous

1. Hélène Cixous, *Three Steps on the Ladder of Writing*, trans. Sarah Cornell and Susan Sellers (New York: Columbia University Press, 1993).
2. Hélène Cixous, "The Laugh of the Medusa," trans. Keith Cohen and Paula Cohen, *Signs* 1 no. 4 (Summer 1976): 875–93, www.jstor.org/stable/3173239.
3. Juliet Jacques, "Écriture trans-féminine?," *Mal Journal*, no. 1 (November 2018), maljournal.com/1/that-obscure-object/juliet-jacques/ecriture-trans-feminine/.

4. Jules Gill-Peterson, *Histories of the Transgender Child* (Minneapolis: University of Minnesota Press, 2018), viii–ix.
5. Hélène Cixous, *Philippines*, trans. Laurent Milesi (Malden, MA: Polity, 2011).
6. Svetlana Boym, "Nostalgia," *Atlas of Transformation*, tranzit, 2011, monumenttotransformation.org/atlas-of-transformation/html/n/nostalgia/nostalgia-svetlana-boym.html.

The Honesty of Jean Rhys

1. Jean Rhys, *After Leaving Mr. Mackenzie* (New York: W. W. Norton & Company, 1997), 36.
2. Jean Rhys, *Good Morning, Midnight* (New York: W. W. Norton & Company, 1999), 42.
3. Rhys, *Good Morning, Midnight*, 106.
4. Rhys, *After Leaving Mr. Mackenzie*, 14.
5. Rhys, *Good Morning, Midnight*, 63.
6. Rhys, *Good Morning, Midnight*, 70.
7. Rhys, *Good Morning, Midnight*, 62.
8. Rhys, *Good Morning, Midnight*, 162.
9. Rhys, *Good Morning, Midnight*, 162.
10. Rhys, *Good Morning, Midnight*, 173.

The Many Names of Barbara Grier: On Naiad Press, Lesbian Publishing, and Pseudonyms

1. Quoted in Joanne Passet, *Indomitable: The Life of Barbara Grier* (Tallahassee, FL: Bella Books, 2016).
2. "Letter from G.D.," *The Ladder* 1, no. 11 (August 1957), 24–25.
3. Gene Damon, "Lesbiana," *The Ladder* 6, no. 3 (December 1961).
4. Stephanie Andrea Allen, Cheryl Clarke, Katherine V. Forrest, Joan Nestle, Barbara Smith, and Julie R. Enszer, "It's a Lot Like Falling in Love: Lesbian Publishing in the '70s, '80s, '90s, and Beyond," virtual roundtable streamed live on October 13, 2022, Lesbian Herstory Archives and the Program in Women's, Gender, and Sexuality Studies at Florida State University, YouTube video, 1:18:11, https://www.youtube.com/watch?v=asYvzynNM04.
5. Ginny Farrell, "Living Propaganda," *The Ladder* 8, no. 3, (December 1963), 15–16.

A Pre Narrative Manifesto: kari edwards's Trans Poetics

1. An earlier version of this piece was originally published as "Time, Identity, and the Persistence of the Salad Bar in kari edwards's Writing" in *From Our Hearts to Yours: New Narrative as Contemporary Practice*, eds. Rob Halpern and Robin Tremblay-McGaw (Oakland, CA: ON Contemporary Practice, 2017).
2. kari edwards, "life is a salad bar," in *POST / (PINK)* (Boulder, CO: Scarlet Press, 2000), 12.
3. edwards, "life is a salad bar," 13.
4. "Program #385," *GenderTalk*, WMBR Cambridge, November 11, 2002, http://www.gendertalk.com/radio/programs/350/gt385.shtml.
5. "Program #385," *GenderTalk*.
6. Robert Glück, "Long Note on New Narrative," in *Biting the Error: Writers Explore Narrative*, eds. Mary Burger, Robert Glück, Camille Roy, and Gail Scott (Toronto: Coach House Books, 2004), 27.
7. kari edwards, *a day in the life of p.* (New York: subpress collective, 2002).
8. kari edwards, *succubus in my pocket* (Brooklyn: EOAGH Books, 2015).
9. kari edwards, *obedience* (New York: Factory School, 2005).

The Tell-Tale Sign of Living: Blackness and Sensuality in Ntozake Shange's *nappy edges*

1. In the epigraph of *nappy edges*, Ntozake Shange defines nappy edges as "the tell-tale sign of living." All Shange quotes reprinted by the permission of Salky Literary Management as agent for the author. Copyright © 1972, 2000 by Ntozake Shange.
2. Ntozake Shange Papers, 1913–2022, box 9, folder 2, Barnard Archives and Special Collections, Barnard College, New York.
3. E. Patrick Johnson, "Black Performance Studies: Genealogies, Politics, Futures," in *The SAGE Handbook of Performance Studies*, eds. D. Soyini Madison and Judith Hamera (Thousand Oaks, CA: Sage, 2005), 459.
4. Patricia Hill Collins, Alice Walker, Audre Lorde, bell hooks, Combahee River Collective, June Jordan, Pearl Cleage, Barbara Smith, and many more.
5. Ntozake Shange, *nappy edges* (New York: St Martin's Press, 1978), 90.
6. Hortense Spillers, "Close to the Bone," minute 15:00.
7. Ntozake Shange, "hands & holding," *nappy edges* (New York: St Martin's Press, 1978), 43.

8. Angela Davis, *Blues Legacies and Black Feminisms* (New York: Pantheon Books, 1998), 33.
9. Davis, *Blues Legacies and Black Feminisms*, 24.
10. Saidiya Hartman, *Wayward Lives, Beautiful Experiments: Intimate Histories of Social Upheaval*, (New York: Norton, 2019), 46.
11. Ntozake Shange, "hands & holding," in *nappy edges* (New York: St Martin's Press, 1978), 43.
12. Derrick Gilbert, *Catch the Fire!!!* (New York: Riverhead, 1998), 96.
13. Ntozake Shange, "where the mississippi meets the amazon," in *nappy edges* (New York: St Martin's Press, 1978), 28.
14. Shange, "where the mississippi meets the amazon," 29.
15. Shange, "where the mississippi meets the amazon," 29.
16. Hortense Spillers, *Black, White, and in Color: Essays on American Literature and Culture* (Chicago: The University of Chicago Press, 2003), 153.

Sex Permeates Everything: The Poetry of Lola Ridge

1. "Pig Cupid his rosy snout / rooting erotic garbage."
2. Cyril Kay Scott, *Sinbad: A Romance* (New York: Thomas Seltzer, 1923), 55.
3. Alfred Kreymborg, *Troubadour: An Autobiography* (New York: Liveright, 1925), 160.
4. Lola Ridge, *Verses*, unpublished manuscript, 1905, TS item 1, CY reel 2694, frames 144–237, A.G. Stephens Papers, 1855–1933, Mitchell Library, State Library of New South Wales, Sydney, Australia.
5. Paul Avrich, *The Modern School Movement: Anarchism and Education in the United States* (Oakland, CA: AK Press, 2005), 167.
6. Avrich, *The Modern School Movement*, 167.
7. Christine Stansell, *American Moderns: Bohemian New York and the Creation of a New Century* (Princeton, NJ: Princeton University Press, 2009), 274.
8. Lola Ridge, *The Ghetto and Other Poems* (New York: B. W. Huebsch, 1918), 26–27.
9. Ridge, *The Ghetto*, 70.
10. Lola Ridge, *Sun-Up and Other Poems* (New York: B. W. Huebsch, 1920), 36.
11. Ridge, *Sun-Up*, 64.
12. Ridge, *Sun-Up*, 62.
13. Ridge, *Sun-Up*, 41.
14. Ridge, *Sun-Up*, 51.

15. Ridge, *Sun-Up*, 52.
16. Ridge, *Sun-Up*, 54.
17. Ridge, *Sun-Up*, 84.
18. Evelyn Scott to Lola Ridge, 1920, Lola Ridge Papers, Sophia Smith Collection, Smith College, Northampton, MA.
19. Margaret Widdemer, *A Tree with a Bird in it: A Symposium of Contemporary American Poets on Being Shown a Pear-Tree on Which Sat a Grackle* (New York: Harcourt Brace, 1922), 42.
20. Lola Ridge, *Red Flag* (New York: Payson & Clark, 1927), 52.
21. Ridge, *Red Flag*, 41.
22. Ridge, *Red Flag*, 79.
23. Lola Ridge, *Firehead* (New York: Payson & Clark, 1929), 34.
24. Julia Lisella, "Lola Ridge's *Firehead*," *HOW2* 1, no. 8 (Fall 2002).
25. Ridge, *Firehead*, 95.
26. Ridge, *Firehead*, 98.
27. Lola Ridge to Louise Adams Floyd, August 12, 1932, Lola Ridge Papers, Sophia Smith Collection, Smith College, Northampton, MA.
28. Letters to Lenore Marshall, n.d., Lenore Marshall Papers, Columbia University Archives, Special Collections, New York, NY.

Bad or Boring: Doing Without Ethics in Poetry

1. "The Tortoise and the Hare: Dale Smith and Kenneth Goldsmith Parse Slow and Fast Poetries," *Jacket* no. 38 (2009), http://jacket-magazine.com/38/iv-smith-goldsmith.shtml.
2. Cathy Park Hong, "Delusions of Whiteness in the Avant-Garde," *Lana Turner: A Journal of Poetry & Opinion* 7 (2014).
3. Ron Silliman, "I have been using this blog somewhat differently . . .," *Silliman's blog*, March 23, 2015, https://ronsilliman.blogspot.com/2015/03/i-have-been-using-this-blog-somewhat.html.

Tender Points: An Interview with Amy Berkowitz

1. Amy Berkowitz, *Tender Points* (New York: Nightboat Books, 2019), 127. Originally published in 2015 by Timeless, Infinite Light. All quotes reprinted with permission of Nightboat Books.
2. Berkowitz, *Tender Points*, 44.
3. Berkowitz, *Tender Points*, 15.
4. Berkowitz, *Tender Points*, 108.
5. Berkowitz, *Tender Points*, 42.
6. Berkowitz, *Tender Points*, 24.

About the Contributors

Gina Abelkop is the author of the poetry collections *I Eat Cannibals* (2014) and *Darling Beastlettes* (2012).

Hossannah Asuncion is a Filipino poet and the author of *Object Permanence* (Magic Helicopter Press, 2016), winner of the Ted Hawkins Innovative Poetry Prize. The recipient of prizes and fellowships from Kundiman, the Laundromat Project, and the Poetry Society of America, she lives in Brooklyn with her wife and child.

Neelanjana Banerjee's writing has appeared widely in places like *The Rumpus, Prairie Schooner, Teen Vogue, Virginia Quarterly Review, Los Angeles Review of Books*, and many other places. She is the managing editor of Kaya Press and teaches writing and Asian American literature at UCLA and Loyola Marymount University.

Amy Berkowitz is the author of *Gravitas* (2023) and *Tender Points* (2019). Her writing and conversations have appeared in places like *Bitch, The Believer, BOMB*, and *Jewish Currents*. She lives in San Francisco where she's writing a novel.

Emily Brandt is the author of the poetry collection *Falsehood*, as well as three chapbooks. She's a cofounding editor of *No, Dear*, curator of the LINEAGE reading series at Wendy's Subway, and member of the video art collective Temp.Files. She's of Sicilian, Polish, and Ukrainian descent, and lives in Brooklyn.

Melissa Broder is the author of three novels: *Death Valley, Milk Fed*, and *The Pisces*, the essay collection *So Sad Today*, and five books of poems including *Superdoom: Selected Poems*. She lives in Los Angeles.

Olivia Campbell is author of the *New York Times* bestseller *Women in White Coats: How the First Women Doctors Changed the World of Medicine*. Her work has appeared in *The Atlantic, New York Magazine, HISTORY, The Guardian*, the *Washington Post, Smithsonian Magazine*, and Literary Hub, among others.

Flannery Cashill is an artist and writer living in Kansas City, Missouri. Her website is flanland.com.

Sam Cohen is the author of *Sarahland*. Her stories and essays appear in *BOMB, Fence, O Magazine*, Electric Literature, Literary Hub, and others. She currently teaches at Oberlin College.

Amanda K. Davidson is thankful to be in this book, because sometimes you're howling alone in the wilderness, except the wilderness is social media and your howls are cartoons, and someone (Marisa Crawford) pops out of the bushes in this friendly, get-shit-done way and says, "Come howl over here, with us." For more howling, visit amandakdavidson.com.

Cathy de la Cruz (she/they) is a Brooklyn-based writer and filmmaker originally from San Antonio, Texas. She is a graduate of both the University of Arizona's Creative Writing MFA program and UC San Diego's Visual Arts MFA program. She was a member of Sister Spit's twentieth-anniversary tour.

Rios de la Luz is the author of the novella *Itzá* (Broken River Books, 2017) and the short story collections *The Pulse between Dimensions and the Desert* (Ladybox Books, 2015) and *An Altar of Stories to Liminal Saints* (Broken River Books, 2023). She lives in Oklahoma with her son and partner.

Julián Delgado Lopera is the author of the *New York Times*–acclaimed novel *Fiebre Tropical* (Feminist Press, 2020), the winner of the 2021 Ferro-Grumley Award and a 2021 Lambda Literary Award and a finalist for the 2020 Kirkus Prize in Fiction and the 2021 Aspen Literary Prize. They are the former executive director of RADAR Productions and one of the founders of Drag Queen Story Hour.

Naomi Extra is a poet, writer, scholar, and cartoonist. In both her creative and scholarly work, she explores the themes of agency and pleasure in the lives of black women and girls. You can find her work in places like the *Boston Review*, Zora, the *New Yorker*, *The Lily*, and elsewhere. Currently, she teaches at Rutgers University, Newark.

Emily Gaynor is an artist and writer based in the Hudson Valley.

Myriam Gurba is the author of several books, including *Creep* (Avid Reader Press, 2023). Her writing has appeared in publications such as the *New York Times*, the *Los Angeles Times*, and *The Believer*.

Forsyth Harmon is the author and illustrator of *Justine* (Tin House, 2021), a finalist for the Connecticut Book Award. She is also the illustrator of Melissa Febos's National Book Award winner *Girlhood* (Bloomsbury, 2021) and Catherine Lacey's *The Art of the Affair* (Bloomsbury, 2017), the artwork from which was celebrated with a solo show at Julie Saul Gallery. Her work has been featured in *Granta*, *BOMB*, Refinery29, *The Believer*, and more. She received both a BA and an MFA from Columbia University and currently lives in New York.

Soleil Ho is an opinion columnist and cultural critic at the *San Francisco Chronicle*.

Geraldine Kim is the author of *Povel* and *Things I'd Let You Do to Me*. She has also contributed to the anthologies *Starting Today* and *Gurlesque*. Her play *Donning Cheadle* was performed with a real cast and crew and everything. She is currently trying to sell a genre-bending screenplay.

Becca Klaver is the author of the poetry collections *LA Liminal*, *Empire Wasted*, and *Ready for the World*. Recent publications include *Midwinter Constellation*, a collaborative book in homage to Bernadette Mayer's *Midwinter Day*, and *Greetings from Bowling Green*, a chapbook of postcard poems. She's the (weird) third of four sisters.

Grace Kredell is the associate director of Golden Dome School, a community dedicated to mysticism and the arts. She recently completed an MA in womxn's history at Sarah Lawrence College, where she wrote about female occult workers during the time of Spiritualism. In her private practice, she works with clients drawn to mystic tools and perspectives.

Aja Leilam Love, FKA Carrie Leilam Love, makes poems, fiction, film photographs, and, recently, humans. Her words and photos have been published in a place or two. Every piece of art she makes is a Black Feminist spell for getting free. This includes her two perfect kids, whom she lives with in Oakland.

Caolan Madden's poems and essays can be found in various journals and anthologies, including *We Are the Baby-Sitters Club*, *Buffy to Batgirl: Women and Gender in Science Fiction and Fantasy*, and the collaborative poem *Midwinter Constellation*. She is the author of the poetry chapbook *VAST NECROHOL* (Hyacinth Girl Press, 2018).

Megan Milks is the author of *Margaret and the Mystery of the Missing Body*, named a Lambda Literary Award finalist, and *Slug and Other Stories*, both published by Feminist Press, as well as *Tori Amos Bootleg Webring*, published in Instar Books' Remember the Internet series. With Marisa Crawford, they coedited *We Are the Baby-Sitters Club: Essays and Artwork from Grown-Up Readers*.

Eileen Myles (they/them) is a poet, novelist, and art journalist whose practice of vernacular first-person writing has become a touchstone for our identity-fluid internet age. *Pathetic Literature*, the anthology of 106 writers that Eileen edited, has just arrived in the world. They live in New York and Marfa, Texas.

Christina Olivares is the author of the books *Future Botanic* (2023); *No Map of the Earth Includes Stars* (2015), winner of the 2014 Marsh Hawk Press Book Prize; and *Interrupt* (Belladonna* Collaborative, 2015).

Morgan Parker is the author of *Who Put This Song On?*, a young adult novel, as well as the poetry collections *Other People's Comfort Keeps Me Up At Night*, *There Are More Beautiful Things Than Beyoncé*, and *Magical Negro*, which won the 2019 National Book Critics Circle Award.

Li Patron is a poet and essayist who lives and writes in San Jose, California. You can find Li's writing in self-published zines and online at www.romancingthevoid.com and elsewhere.

Trace Peterson is a poet, editor, and literary scholar. Author of the poetry book *Since I Moved In (new & revised)* (Chax Press, 2019), she also coedited the groundbreaking anthology *Troubling the Line: Trans and Genderqueer Poetry and Poetics* (Nightboat Books, 2013) and *Arrive on Wave: Collected Poems of Gil Ott* (Chax Press, 2016). Peterson is founding editor of the literary journal and small press EOAGH, which has won two Lambda Literary Awards and a National Jewish Book Award. She is currently a visiting assistant professor of English at UConn, Storrs.

Kristin Sanders is the author of *CUNTRY*, a finalist for the National Poetry Series, and two poetry chapbooks. Her work has recently been included in *Prose Poetry: An Introduction* (Princeton University Press, 2020) and published in *Columbia Journal,* Longreads, Literary Hub, and the *Los Angeles Review of Books*. She is based in Paris.

Christopher Soto is a poet based in Los Angeles. Their debut poetry collection, *Diaries of a Terrorist*, was published by Copper Canyon Press in 2022. This collection demands the abolition of policing and human caging.

Mecca Jamilah Sullivan, PhD, is the author of *Big Girl*, a *New York Times* Editors' Choice and winner of the Balcones Fiction Prize and the Next Generation Indie Book Award for First Novel; *Blue Talk and Love*, winner of the Judith A. Markowitz Award from Lambda Literary; and *The Poetics of Difference: Queer Feminist Forms in the African Diaspora*, winner of the William Sanders Scarborough Prize from the MLA. Originally from Harlem, NY, she is an associate professor of English at Georgetown University and lives in Washington, DC.

Terese Svoboda, author of the biography *Anything That Burns You: A Portrait of Lola Ridge, Radical Poet*, celebrates Lola Ridge's one hundredth birthday this year. Author of twenty-one books of poetry, fiction, memoir, biography, and translations from the Nuer, Svoboda has received a Guggenheim, Bobst Prize in fiction, Iowa Poetry Prize, National Endowment for the Humanities translation grant, Graywolf Press Nonfiction Prize, Jerome Foundation and National Endowment for the Arts media grants, O. Henry Award, Pushcart Prize, Money for Women/Barbara Deming Memorial Fund grant, three New York Foundation Artist Fellowships, and a Juniper Prize. *Theatrix: Poetry Plays* was named one of the best poetry books of 2020. *Roxy and Coco*, her ninth book of fiction, and *The Long Swim*, her third story collection, will be published in 2024.

Mariahadessa Ekere Tallie is author of the award-winning children's book *Layla's Happiness*, the poetry collections *Strut* and *Karma's Footsteps*, and *Dear Continuum: Letters to a Poet Crafting Liberation*. She is a PhD candidate in the Theatre Arts and Performance Studies program at Brown University and the mother of three galaxies who look like daughters.

Jennif(f)er Tamayo is a poet, performer, and essayist whose works reimagine the narratives about and politics of undocumented figures in the contemporary US. They are the author of the books *[Red Missed Aches, Read Mistakes]*, *YOU DA ONE*, and most recently, *Bruise/Bruise/Break*.

Virgie Tovar is an author, lecturer, and leading expert on weight-based discrimination and body positivity. She lives in San Francisco. Find her at www.virgietovar.com.

Zoe Tuck was born in Texas, became a person in California, and now lives in Massachusetts. She is the author of *Bedroom Vowel* (Bunny, 2023), *Terror Matrix* (Timeless, Infinite Light, 2014), and the chapbooks *Vape Cloud of Unknowing* (Belladonna*) and *The Book of Bella* (DoubleCross Press). She loves to weave people together and make spaces for writers.

MT Vallarta is a poet and assistant professor of ethnic studies at California Polytechnic State University, San Luis Obispo. They are the author of the poetry collection *What You Refuse to Remember* (Small Harbor, 2023). They received their PhD in ethnic studies from the University of California, Riverside.

Camille Wanliss is a New York–based writer and the founder of Galleyway, an online platform that spotlights opportunities for BIPOC writers. She is a 2023 MacDowell Fellow and a 2022 Periplus Fellow. She was selected for AWP's Writer-to-Writer Mentorship Program (2021) and the NYFA/DCLA City Artist Corps Grant (2021), and was among the winners of the 2020 Pigeon Pages Essay Contest.

Eleanor C. Whitney is a writer and community builder living in Brooklyn and the Mojave Desert. She is the author of *Riot Woman*, *Promote Your Book*, and *Quit Your Day Job*, and holds an MFA in creative nonfiction from CUNY Queens College.

Vanessa Willoughby is an editor and a pop culture writer whose bylines include the *New York Times*, Bitch Media, *Allure*, *Teen Vogue*, and BookPage. She is based in Brooklyn.

Acknowledgments

THANK YOU TO everyone who made this book, and *Weird Sister*, possible. Special thanks to all of the writers and artists who have contributed to the *Weird Sister* blog and community, those who are included in this book and those who we didn't have space for in these limited pages; I wish I could have included every piece on the blog in this collection.

So much gratitude and admiration to Becca Klaver, Naomi Extra, Cathy de la Cruz, Caolan Madden, Geraldine Kim, C. A. Kaufman, and Gina Abelkop for their amazing work and vision as editors and collaborators on the *Weird Sister* blog, events, and beyond. Thank you again to Becca Klaver, Jennif(f)er Tamayo, Caolan Madden, Hanna Andrews, and Lily Ladewig for encouraging me to start *Weird Sister* in the first place, and for their help in getting the blog off the ground. Thank you to all the spaces, curators, and organizers who have hosted and collaborated on *Weird Sister* events and helped support and grow this community.

Thank you to Lauren Hook, Nadine Santoro, and Feminist Press for giving this work a home, for supporting and collaborating with me in the vision of turning this blog into a book, and for carrying the torch of over fifty years of feminist publishing; what an incredible inspiration. Thank you to Michelle Tea for her gorgeous foreword, for championing this project, and for being a total feminist literary superhero.

Thank you to my amazing writer friends and community for all their support and inspiration on this project. Thank you to Eleanor C. Whitney, MC Hyland, Megan Milks, Julián Delgado Lopera, Seth Landman, Beth Pickens, Hossannah Asuncion, Emily Brandt, Vanessa Willoughby, Amy Berkowitz, Michael Braithwaite, and Morgan Parker. Thank you to all the writers, editors, and publishers who made the feminist and literary blogs, magazines, and projects that inspired this one; there are too many to name, but where would we be without them?

Thank you to Mary Anne Carter for this book's gorgeous cover, to Molly Prentiss for creating the original *Weird Sister* website art that inspired it, and to Matt L. Roar for designing the *Weird Sister* logo and for his creative energy and encouragement every step of the way. Thank you to my friends. Thank you to my parents. Thank you to my sisters.

MARISA CRAWFORD is the author of the poetry collections *Diary, Reversible,* and *The Haunted House,* and coeditor, with Megan Milks, of *We Are the Baby-Sitters Club: Essays and Artwork from Grown-Up Readers.* Marisa's writing has appeared in *The Nation, Harper's Bazaar,* Hyperallergic, *BUST,* and elsewhere. Marisa is the creator and editor-in-chief of *Weird Sister,* a website and organization that explores the intersections of feminism, literature, and pop culture, and cohost of the nineties rock podcast *All Our Pretty Songs.* She lives in New York.

The Feminist Press publishes books that
ignite movements and social transformation.
Celebrating our legacy, we lift up insurgent
and marginalized voices from around the
world to build a more just future.

See our complete list of books at
feministpress.org

THE FEMINIST PRESS
AT THE CITY UNIVERSITY OF NEW YORK
FEMINISTPRESS.ORG